BEST of the BEST
from
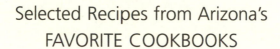
ARIZONA
COOKBOOK

Selected Recipes from Arizona's
FAVORITE COOKBOOKS

Located entirely in northern Arizona, Grand Canyon National Park encompasses 277 miles of the Colorado River and adjacent uplands. A World Heritage Site, the canyon is visited by over five million people each year.

BEST of the BEST from
ARIZONA
COOKBOOK

Selected Recipes from Arizona's FAVORITE COOKBOOKS

EDITED BY

Gwen McKee

AND

Barbara Moseley

Illustrated by Tupper England

QUAIL RIDGE PRESS
Preserving America's Food Heritage

Library of Congress Cataloging-in-Publication Data

Best of the best from Arizona : selected recipes from Arizona's favorite cookbooks / edited by Gwen McKee and Barbara Moseley ; illustrated by Tupper England.
   p. cm.
   ISBN 1-893062-16-3
   1. Cookery, American 2. Cookery—Arizona. I. McKee, Gwen. II. Moseley, Barbara.

TX715.B4856362 2000
641.59791—dc21   00-030454
                                                          CIP

QUAIL RIDGE PRESS
P. O. Box 123 • Brandon, MS 39043 • 1-800-343-1583
e-mail: info@quailridge.com • www.quailridge.com

CONTENTS

The young pads of the prickly pear cactus (shown in bloom here) are called nopalitos and are fat free, low in calories and high in vitamins and minerals.

PREFACE

People outside Arizona probably picture arid deserts and cactus when they envision this beautiful state, but we found out quickly that the state is fertile ground for cultivating great cooks and a rich cooking tradition. Throughout our work in the BEST OF THE BEST STATE COOKBOOK SERIES, we have found that one of the best ways to understand a state's personality is to explore its culinary tradition. We were anxious to know what Arizonans like to cook, serve, and eat.

From a culinary standpoint, we of course expected to find a strong southwestern flavor in Arizona, but well beyond that, we found a treasure of other culinary wonders. Truly there is a surprising bounty of food sources among the cactus and sand dunes. Ranch lands produce an abundance of beef and dairy products. And also the irrigation from rivers and lakes encourage the land to offer a variety of fruits and vegetables. Not only is Arizona known for chiles, corn, and tomatoes, but also peaches, pears, citrus fruits, and nuts and berries.

And while we discovered Arizona cookbooks, we also came away with a deep appreciation for the people of Arizona, for its history, its stunning natural beauty, and its rich and diverse culture. We found that the heritage of Native Americans and Arizonans of Mexican and Spanish descent is certainly evident in its cuisine. You'll find within these pages delightful dishes from restaurants, chefs, and home cooks who take pride in the preparation of their meals. Consider the recipes themselves: one may not be surprised to find Bronc Rider Beef Strips, Sonoran Chicken Chili, and Tortilla Apple Strudel, but the book also contains such delights as Painted Cookies, Shrimp Quesadillas, and Chocolate Tacos Filled with Hazelnut-Chocolate Mousse! It seems the Grand Canyon state's cooks are capable of conjuring up everything from Dutch oven cooking to elegant dinner party fare. And they do! But further, if you want to know how to make Prickly Pear Jelly, Rattlesnake Chili, and Coyote Caviar, then you have come to the right place.

Sixty-five of the leading cookbooks from throughout the state have shared some of their most popular recipes to make up this

outstanding collection. Each recipe is a proven favorite and is deserving of special praise. We invite you to order any of the contributing cookbooks directly from the publisher (see Catalog of Contributing Cookbooks section that begins on page 259). And please forgive us if we inadvertently left out any cookbook that might have been included.

We could not have accomplished the enormous amount of work required to compile this book without the assistance of wonderfully talented people. Annette Goode, Sheila Williams, Cyndi Clark, and Carol Mead each made significant contributions in helping us bring the book together. We thank Tupper England for her winsome illustrations, and Keith Odom, who traveled the state to bring us his alluring photographs; they enable us to capture the splendor of Arizona visually as well as tastefully. We further thank the kind people of the Arizona tourist bureaus, the many food editors at newspapers and magazines, bookstore owners, gourmet shop personnel, home cooks, authors, committee chairpersons, and many other Arizonans who love cooking and cookbooks as much as we do.

In our continuing effort to Preserve America's Food Heritage, we hope this outstanding cookbook delivers to you recipes as beguiling as the state's landscape, as colorful as its deserts, as grand as its canyons . . . recipes truly deserving of being the *Best of the Best from Arizona.*

Gwen McKee and Barbara Moseley

CONTRIBUTING COOKBOOKS

The Arizona Celebrity Cookbook
Arizona Chefs: Cooking at Home with 36 Arizona Chefs
Arizona Chefs: Dine-In Dine-Out Cookbook
Arizona Cook Book
Arizona Heart Institute Foundation Cookbook
Arizona Highways Heritage Cookbook
Arizona Small Game and Fish Cookbook
Arizona State Fair Blue Ribbon Recipes
Arizona Territory Cookbook
Arizona's Historic Restaurants and their Recipes
Bon Appetit: Healthy Recipes
By Request
Chips, Dips & Salsas
Christmas in Arizona Cook Book
Chuck Wagon Cookin'
Cooking with Cops
Corazón Contento
Coronado's Favorite Trail Mix
Cowboy Cookin
Dishes from the Deep
The Dog Gone Delicious Cookbook
Dutch Oven and Campfire Cookbook
The Fat Free Living Family Cookbook
Favorite Recipes from the Foothills of Carefree, Arizona
Favorites for All Seasons
First Baptist Favorites...Can I Have That Recipe?
Flavors of the Southwest
Fruits of the Desert
The Garden Patch
Gourmet Gringo
Heard in the Kitchen
Heavenly Delights
Hopi Cookery
Hospice Hospitality

CONTRIBUTING COOKBOOKS

Janos: Recipes and Tales from a Southwest Restaurant
Kids in the Kitchen
Kingman Welcome Wagon Club Cookbook
Kosher Kettle
License to Cook Arizona Style
Lion's Club of Globe, Arizona Cookbook
Mountain Mornings
The National Firefighters Recipe Book
Outdoor Cooking: From Backyard to Backpack
Padre Kino's Favorite Meatloaf
Par Excellence
Pioneer Family Recipes
Pleasures from the Good Earth
Portal's Best Little Cookbook
Purple Sage and Other Pleasures
Recipes for Fat Free Living Cookbook 2
Recipes from Arizona with Love
Recipes from Our Mothers' Kitchens
Red, White & Blue Favorites
Reflections Under the Sun
Savor the Southwest
Savory Southwest
Sedona Cookbook
St. Francis in the Foothills 30th Anniversary Cookbook
Taste of Tombstone: A Hearty Helping of History
That Hungarian's in My Kitchen!
Tostitos Fiesta Bowl Cookbook
Tucson Cooks!
Tucson Treasures
Vegetarian Southwest
Vistoso Vittles II
What's Cooking Inn Arizona
Wild Thyme and Other Temptations

Beverages & Appetizers

Havasu Falls is the most popular and most photographed waterfall in Havasu Canyon, located on the Havasupai Reservation. Havasupai translates to "people of the sparkling blue-green waters."

Super Nachos

½ pound lean ground beef
½ pound chorizo sausage, casing removed
1 large onion, chopped
Salt and pepper to taste
Liquid hot pepper seasoning
1 or 2 cans (about 1 pound) refried beans
1 (4-ounce) can whole California green chiles (for mildest flavor, remove seeds and pith), chopped

2–3 cups shredded Jack or mild Cheddar cheese
¾ cup prepared taco sauce (green or red)
Garnishes (suggestions follow)
8 cups crisp-fried tortilla pieces or corn-flavored chips

Crumble ground beef and sausage in a frying pan. Add onion and cook on high heat, stirring, until meat is lightly browned. Discard fat; season with salt, pepper, and liquid hot pepper seasoning to taste.

Spread beans in a shallow 10x15-inch oval or rectangular pan or oven-proof dish (or one of equivalent area). Top evenly with meat. Sprinkle chiles over bean and meat layer, cover evenly with cheese, and drizzle with taco sauce. Cover and chill if made ahead. Bake, uncovered, in a 400° oven for 20–25 minutes or until very hot throughout.

Remove from oven and quickly garnish with some or all of the following: about ¼ cup chopped green onion (including some tops) and about 1 can pitted ripe olives; in the center, mound 1 can (about 8 ounces) thawed avocado dip (or 1 medium-sized ripe avocado, peeled, pitted, and coarsely mashed, and top with 1 cup sour cream. Add a mild, red pickled pepper and fresh coriander (cilantro) or parsley sprigs. Quickly tuck about 8 cups fried tortilla pieces or corn flavored chips just around edges of bean mixture (making a petaled flower effect) and serve at once.

Scoop bean mixture with tortilla pieces; if desired, keep platter hot on an electric warming tray while serving. Makes 10–12 appetizer servings.

I have used refried beans with chiles, cutting down on the amount of canned chiles. Do not omit the chorizo sausage because it has such a good flavor and texture. You may cut down or add seasonings depending on whether you're a "hot" or "mild" person.

Note: If not using chorizo, use 1 pound of ground beef.

Vistoso Vittles II

Loaded Nachos

Tortilla chips
1 (15-ounce) can black beans
1 (4-ounce) can chopped green
  chiles or 2 tablespoons chopped
  jalapeños

1 small tomato, chopped
½ pound pepper jack or Sonoma
  Jack cheese, shredded
1 cup sour cream (optional)

Preheat broiler.

   Layer chips onto two 10x15-inch jellyroll pans. Sprinkle with beans, chiles, and tomato. Cover evenly with cheese. Place under broiler for 3–5 minutes. Remove from oven and serve immediately, with a dab of sour cream on top of each loaded chip, if desired. Makes 3 or 4 dinner-size servings, or several more servings as a snack.

Chips, Dips, & Salsas

Sonoran Strata

1 (15-ounce) can black beans,
  drained but not rinsed
½–1 chipotle pepper, dried and
  rehydrated, or chipotle in adobo
  sauce
Garlic powder to taste
2 ripe avocados

Juice of one lime
Salt to taste
1 large, ripe tomato, chopped, or 1
  cup fresh tomato salsa
1 cup crumbled Mexican cotija
  cheese or farmer's cheese

In a food processor or blender, pureé beans, chipotle, and garlic powder. Spread in a clear serving bowl or onto a serving platter and level the top with spatula.

   Mash avocados with lime juice, garlic powder, and salt. Spread carefully on top of the bean layer. Spread tomatoes or salsa on top of avocado. Sprinkle evenly with cheese.

   Serve with sturdy tortilla chips. Provide a knife to encourage dipping down through all the layers. Makes about 3 cups.

Chips, Dips, & Salsas

Cilantro Pesto Tortas

PESTO:

**2 cups trimmed and washed
  cilantro leaves**
2 garlic cloves
2 tablespoons pine nuts, roasted
¾ cup grated Parmesan cheese

2 tablespoons fresh lime juice
2 teaspoons kosher salt
**1 teaspoon fresh ground black
  pepper**
5 tablespoons olive oil

In a food processor, combine cilantro, garlic, pine nuts, Parmesan, lime juice, salt and pepper. With motor running, slowly add olive oil until sauce is emulsified.

TORTAS:

2 cups corn oil
4 flour tortillas, cut into quarters

2 cups white Cheddar cheese, grated
Guacamole

In a large skillet, fry tortillas in oil over medium heat. Fry until crisp and drain on paper towels. Spread each tortilla with pesto and top with cheese. Bake at 400° until cheese melts. Top with guacamole and serve on cocktail tray.

Favorite Recipes from the Foothills of Carefree, Arizona

Jalapeño Cheese Squares

4 eggs
**2 cups shredded sharp Cheddar
  cheese**
**1 (4-ounce) jar sliced pimentos,
  drained**

**1 (4-ounce) jar sliced jalapeños,
  drained (or diced green chiles)**

Preheat oven to 400°. Coat an 8x8-inch baking pan with cooking spray or oil. Set aside. Beat eggs with fork in medium bowl. Add remaining ingredients and blend thoroughly, mixing by hand. Pour into prepared pan and bake approximately 20 minutes or until set. Let cool slightly and cut into squares. Serve hot or cold. Makes 8 servings.

Vistoso Vittles II

Festive Florentine Crescents

1 (10-ounce) package frozen
   chopped spinach, thawed, well
   drained
8 ounces Velveeta cheese, cubed

¼ cup dry bread crumbs
3 slices bacon, crisp-fried, crumbled
2 (8-ounce) cans crescent rolls
1 egg, beaten

Combine spinach, cheese, bread crumbs and bacon in 1½-quart saucepan. Cook over low heat until cheese melts, stirring occasionally. Separate roll dough into 16 triangles; cut each triangle into halves lengthwise to form 32 triangles. Spread with spinach mixture; roll up from wide end to enclose filling. Place on greased baking sheet. Brush with egg. Bake at 375° for 11–13 minutes or until golden brown. Yields 32 servings.

Heard in the Kitchen

Caliente Cheese Fritters

3 eggs, separated
2 cups corn, canned or fresh
½ teaspoon salt
¼ teaspoon black pepper
1 teaspoon baking powder
¾ cup flour
1 cup finely shredded Cheddar
   cheese

½ cup canned green chiles,
   chopped
¼ cup chopped red bell pepper
¼ cup finely chopped onion
Oil for frying
Salsa and sour cream for garnish
   (optional)

Beat egg whites until almost stiff. Pour corn into a separate mixing bowl. Add to corn the beaten yolks, salt, pepper, baking powder, flour, cheese, chiles, red pepper and onion. Mix well with a wooden spoon or spatula. Gently fold in beaten egg whites.

   Heat about 1 inch of oil in skillet. When the oil gets hot, drop fritters by spoonfuls. Brown on both sides. Drain on paper towels. Serve with salsa and a dollop of sour cream on the side, if desired. Makes 8–10 appetizer servings.

Savory Southwest

The Battle of Picacho Pass on April 15, 1862 was the only Civil War battle in Arizona.

Chile Rounds

2 eggs
½ cup milk
4 ounces Cheddar or Monterey
Jack cheese, shredded

1 (4-ounce) can chopped green
chiles
1 (10-ounce) can flaky biscuits

Combine eggs, milk, cheese and green chiles in bowl; mix well. Separate each biscuit into 3 layers; press into miniature muffin cups. Fill with chile mixture. Bake at 375° for 20 minutes. Yields 30 servings.

Heard in the Kitchen

Stuffed Jalapeño "Mice"

These darling appetizers look meek, but roar in your mouth. The cheese counteracts most of the heat, but there's still a nice bite to the finish.

½ cup crumbled feta cheese
1 tablespoon extra virgin olive oil
1 teaspoon finely chopped garlic
1 teaspoon coarsely chopped fresh
oregano
¼ teaspoon freshly ground black
pepper

7 kalamata olives, pitted and
coarsely chopped
16 jalapeño chiles, roasted and
peeled
Salt to taste

In a small bowl, with a fork mix together feta, olive oil, garlic, oregano, pepper and 6 of the chopped olives until well blended. Cover and refrigerate while preparing the chiles.

With the tip of a small, sharp knife, slice each chile open lengthwise from the base of its stem to the tip, leaving the stem attached. Open it up flat and remove the seeds and ribs. Lightly salt the inside of each chile.

With a teaspoon, neatly mound the filling in the center of each chile, distributing it evenly. Close the sides of each chile around the filling.

Place the chiles, seam-side-down, on a small serving platter, all pointing in the same direction like scurrying mice. With the pieces of reserved chopped olive, give each mouse two little black eyes, pressing them gently into each chile near its narrow tip, opposite the stem (tail) end. Serve immediately.

Note: These can be stuffed a day ahead, covered, and refrigerated.

Recipe by Chef John Rivera Sedlar / **Savor the Southwest**

Mexican Egg Rolls with Fresh Salsa

SALSA:

½ pound tomatillos, husked and washed

1 large tomato

½ medium onion

1 teaspoon fresh cilantro

1 can (3½ or 4 ounces) chopped green chiles

1 tablespoon white wine vinegar

Salt to taste (if desired)

Finely chop tomatillos, tomato, onion, and cilantro. Whirl green chilies in food processor until smooth. Mix together tomatillos, tomato, onion, cilantro, green chiles, and white wine vinegar. Add salt to taste if desired. Cover and refrigerate 6 hours or overnight.

EGG ROLLS:

½ pound mild chorizo

½ medium onion, finely chopped

1 cup refried beans

1 cup shredded Monterey Jack cheese

¼ teaspoon ground cumin

⅛ teaspoon cayenne pepper

24 won-ton skins

Oil for deep frying

Sour cream for topping

Fry chorizo and onion in medium skillet until chorizo is crumbly. Drain well. Add beans, cheese, cumin, and cayenne pepper (use more pepper if you like it hotter). Stir until cheese is melted. Let cool to room temperature.

Place 1 teaspoon of filling close to one corner of won-ton wrapper. Fold corner over filling to cover. Fold over left and right corners, then brush sides and top of triangle with water. Roll, sealing corner. Place on a baking sheet and cover while rest of skins are filled.

In a deep pan, pour vegetable oil to depth of 1 inch and heat to 360°; fry 7 or 8 filled rolls at a time until golden brown, 2–3 minutes. Remove and drain on paper towels. Keep warm in 200° oven until all are done. Serve warm with salsa and sour cream. Makes 24 eggs rolls.

Savory Southwest

Crab Meat Biscuits

1 package flaky biscuits
1 (7½-ounce) can crab meat,
   drained
1 tablespoon scallions, chopped
1 cup grated Swiss or sharp
   cheese

½ cup mayonnaise
1 teaspoon lemon juice
¼ teaspoon curry powder
1 can water chestnuts, sliced thin

Separate biscuits. Cut each biscuit into thirds and press flat. Combine the crab, scallions, cheese, mayonnaise, lemon juice and curry. Stir. Spread mixture on each biscuit and top with water chestnuts. Bake at 400° for 10–12 minutes. Yields 30 appetizers.

Favorites for All Seasons

Crab Appetizers – Crabbies

1 can crab meat
1½ tablespoons mayonnaise
¼ teaspoon garlic salt
1 jar Old English sharp Cheddar
   cheese

¼ cup butter or margarine
6 English muffins

Place crab meat in bowl and break up into small pieces. Add mayonnaise, garlic salt, cheese, and butter. Mix well. Spread mixture on muffins and freeze slightly by placing muffins on cookie sheet. Take out of freezer and cut each muffin half into half, then quarters, then eighths. Either bake 10 minutes at 350° or freeze in plastic bags for later use. Makes 96 pieces.

Tostitos Fiesta Bowl Cookbook

Cranberry Chicken Spread

¾ cup cubed and shredded
   chicken (or 6 ounces canned
   chicken)
¼ cup cashew pieces

2 tablespoons chopped celery
½ cup mayonnaise
¼ cup sweetened dried
   cranberries

Combine all ingredients in a medium bowl, mix, and chill well. Use as a dip, a spread, or a sandwich filling. Makes 1¼ cups.

Chips, Dips, & Salsas

Debbie's Chile Con Queso

¼ cup butter or margarine
½ cup finely chopped onion
1 (1-pound) can tomatoes,
   undrained
1½ or 2 (4-ounce) cans green
   chiles, drained and chopped
   (more, if you like it hotter)

Salt to taste
1 pound Monterey Jack cheese,
   cubed
½ cup heavy cream

Heat butter in medium skillet; sauté onion until tender. Add tomatoes, chiles, and salt. Mash tomatoes with a fork. Simmer, stirring occasionally, for 15 minutes. Add cheese cubes, stirring until cheese is melted. Stir in cream. Cook, stirring constantly for 2 minutes. Remove from heat and let stand for 15 minutes. Serve warm in casserole over candle warmer as dip with veggies and corn chips. Makes 10–12 servings.

Pleasures from the Good Earth

Brenna's Chile Con Queso Dunk

Dunk works just as well on a houseboat, or in the RV circle—in short, anywhere there is an electrical outlet.

1 can Cheddar cheese soup
1 can stewed tomatoes with juice
1 (4-ounce) can chopped green
   chiles

1 small onion, chopped
1 bunch green onions, diced
   with tops

Mix all ingredients in the crockpot and stir. Heat about 1 hour. Serve with baskets of fresh corn chips for dunking. Serves 20. It may be made hotter with a larger can of chiles.

Outdoor Cooking

Traveling Taco Dip

1 (16-ounce) can refried beans
2 cups sour cream
8 ounces frozen guacamole,
   thawed
1 (7-ounce) can diced green
   chiles

1 (7-ounce) can black olives,
   drained and diced
2 plum tomatoes, diced
4 ounces shredded Cheddar
   cheese

Spread the refried beans over the bottom of a 10-inch pie plate. Top with layers of sour cream, guacamole, green chiles, black olives, tomatoes, and cheese. Refrigerate, covered, until chilled. Serve with tortilla chips. Serves 8–10.

Tucson Treasures

Seven Layer Fiesta Dip

24 ounces refried beans
6 ripe avocados
2 tablespoons lemon juice
1 cup sour cream
4 tablespoons mayonnaise
1 package taco seasoning mix

1 bunch green onions
3 medium tomatoes
1 small can sliced black olives
1 (8-ounce) package shredded
   Cheddar cheese

In a large dish, spread beans. Layer mashed avocados over the beans and sprinkle with lemon juice. Mix sour cream, mayonnaise, and taco seasoning mix, then spread over avocados. Chop green onions and tomatoes for the fourth and fifth layers. Spread olives on top; sprinkle with Cheddar cheese. Chill. Serve with tortilla chips.

Red, White & Blue Favorites

Hot Cheese, Mushroom, and Chorizo Dip

1 cup chorizo, cooked and well
   drained
2 green onions, chopped, or ¼ cup
   finely chopped white onion

6 ounces mushrooms, sliced
12 ounces Mexican asadero or
   Monterey Jack cheese, cut into
   chunks

Combine all ingredients in a 2-quart microwavable bowl. Heat at 70 percent power in microwave for 3 minutes.

Remove and stir well. Heat again at 70 percent power for 2 minutes. Stir and check to determine if cheese is melted. If not, continue heating at one-minute intervals, stirring after each minute. When all the cheese is melted, the mixture will have a uniform color. Serve immediately with tortilla chips. Makes about 3 cups.

Note: For a buffet, keep warm over heat or in a slow cooker. Or serve half and keep the rest, covered, in a 250° oven until ready to serve. If needed, thin with a couple of tablespoons of sour cream.

Chips, Dips, & Salsas

Nacho Dip

1 pound ground beef, cooked
   and seasoned
2 cans fiesta nacho cheese soup
1 jar chunky salsa (to your taste)

1 small can chopped green chiles
   (or if you want it hotter, chopped
   jalapeños)

Combine all ingredients in crockpot and heat thoroughly. Spoon over corn chips. Increase or decrease soup according to size of party.

Lion's Club of Globe Cookbook

The ancient village of Oraibi, located on the Third Mesa of the Hopi Indian Reservation, is the oldest continuously inhabited community in the country; the community began around 1100 AD. Mesas are the flat-topped mountains found in the desert.

Baked Artichoke Dip

1 (15-ounce) can unmarinated
   artichoke hearts
1 cup mayonnaise
1 cup Parmesan cheese

1 (2¼-ounce) can chopped green
   chiles
1 cup shredded mozzarella cheese

Drain and cut artichoke hearts into smaller pieces. Mix together artichoke hearts, mayonnaise, Parmesan cheese, and chiles. Spread in an 8x8-inch baking dish. Top with shredded cheese and bake at 350° for 15–20 minutes.

License to Cook Arizona Style

Eggplant Dip

1 onion, minced
2 cloves garlic, minced
2 green peppers, chopped fine
¼ cup olive oil
3 eggplants, peeled and diced
1½ (10-ounce) cans Ro-Tel
   tomatoes

1 tablespoon sugar
¼ cup ketchup
1 tablespoon Worcestershire sauce
1 teaspoon salt
3 tablespoons white wine
1 (2¼-ounce) bottle small capers,
   drained

Sauté onion, garlic, and peppers in oil until limp (12 minutes). Add eggplant to onion mixture and simmer 20 minutes, stirring. Add tomatoes, sugar, ketchup, sauce, salt, and wine. Cook on low 30–40 minutes. Cook and add capers. Refrigerate. Makes 70 (1-tablespoon) servings. Serve warm (in chafing dish) or at room temperature on toasted rye rounds.

Bon Appétit

Hot Bean Dip

1 (16-ounce) can refried beans
1 cup canned tomatoes, drained
½ (4-ounce) can diced green
  chiles
½ pound grated cheese, Cheddar
  or Jack

¼ teaspoon onion powder
¼ teaspoon salt
¼ teaspoon garlic powder,
  optional

Mix together well in a skillet and heat until cheese melts, stirring occasionally. Serve warm as a dip with crisp corn tortillas.

Arizona Cook Book

Guacamole Dip

1 tablespoon instant minced
  onion, soaked 5 minutes in
  1 tablespoon water
1 large avocado, peeled and
  seeded
1 tablespoon lemon juice

¼ cup sour cream
2 (3-ounce) packages cream
  cheese
½ teaspoon dill weed
¾ teaspoon salt
Dash of Tabasco

Blend for 30 seconds or until smooth. Makes 2 cups.

Vistoso Vittles II

Pretty Platter Dip

1 can bean dip
1 large can refried beans
3 or 4 ripe avocados, mashed
2 teaspoons lemon juice
Salt
1 cup sour cream

1 package taco seasoning mix
4 tomatoes, diced
2 cans sliced black olives
2 bunches green onions, diced
1½ cups finely grated Cheddar
  cheese

Mix bean dip and refried beans; spread on round serving platter. Mix avocados, lemon juice and salt and spread on bean layer. Combine sour cream and taco seasoning and spread on avocado layer. Place diced tomatoes around outer edge; black olives next circle; green onions next circle and cheese as center. Serve with dipping chips.

The Garden Patch

Smoked Oyster Dip

1 (8-ounce) package cream cheese, softened
1 (4-ounce) can chopped black olives, drained
1 (3¾-ounce) can smoked oysters, drained, chopped
½ cup sour cream
½ cup mayonnaise
5 dashes hot pepper sauce
1 tablespoon fresh lemon juice

Combine cream cheese, olives, oysters, sour cream, mayonnaise, pepper sauce and lemon juice in bowl; mix well. Chill until serving time. Serve with crackers. Yields 2 cups.

Heard in the Kitchen

Smoked Salmon Dip

8 ounces cream cheese (soft and whipped)
¼ cup plain yogurt or sour cream
1 tablespoon lemon juice
¼ cup chopped green onions
2 tablespoons dill weed
¼–½ pound smoked salmon
2 tablespoons chopped capers, drained

Combine all ingredients. Chill. Serve on crackers with capers. Serves 8.

Kingman Welcome Wagon Club Cookbook

Mushrooms Stuffed with Sun-Dried Tomatoes

5 dry-pack sun-dried tomatoes	¼ cup minced fresh parsley
18 mushrooms	½ teaspoon dried basil,
2 tablespoons olive oil	crumbled
¼ cup finely chopped shallots	Salt to taste
⅓ cup fine dry bread crumbs	2 tablespoons grated Parmesan
1 large egg yolk, lightly beaten	cheese

Soak sun-dried tomatoes in hot water to cover in small bowl for 5 minutes; drain, reserving 1 tablespoon liquid. Remove stems from mushrooms and chop fine; reserve caps.

Heat olive oil in small skillet over medium heat until hot but not smoking. Add chopped mushroom stems and shallots and sauté until the shallots are tender.

Combine sautéed vegetables, sun-dried tomatoes, bread crumbs, egg yolk, parsley, basil, salt and reserved soaking liquid in a bowl and mix well. Mound into reserved mushroom caps.

Arrange in a lightly greased shallow baking pan. Sprinkle with cheese. Bake at 400° on the center oven rack for 15 minutes. Serves 18.

Wild Thyme and Other Temptations

Broccoli and Lemon Sauce

6 bunches broccoli, cut into florets	1 tablespoon grated lemon peel
with 3-inch stems	⅓ cup lemon juice
1 cup reduced-fat mayonnaise	2 teaspoons white horseradish
3 cups plain nonfat yogurt	2 teaspoons hot Chinese mustard

Steam broccoli over boiling water (or microwave) until crisp-tender. Immediately plunge broccoli into ice water to stop the cooking and keep its color bright green. Drain well and chill.

To make Lemon Sauce, combine remaining ingredients and chill. Serve broccoli on platter with bowls of Lemon Sauce for dipping. Makes appetizers for 25.

Calories 69; %Fat 38; Fat 3g; Sat Fat 0.5g; Cholesterol 3mg; Sodium 105mg; Carbohydrate 8g; Protein 4g; Fiber 3g. Exchanges: Vegetable 1½, Fat ½

Arizona Heart Institute Foundation Cookbook

Coyote Caviar

A very Southwestern appetizer. Sure to be a hit.

1 (15-ounce) can black beans, drained, rinsed
1 (4-ounce) can chopped black olives, drained
¼ cup chopped onion
1 (4-ounce) can chopped green chiles
1 clove of garlic, chopped
¼ cup chopped cilantro
2 tablespoons vegetable oil
2 tablespoons freshly squeezed lime juice
2 teaspoons chili powder
¼ teaspoon salt
¼ teaspoon crushed red pepper flakes
¼ teaspoon cumin
1 teaspoon black pepper
8 ounces cream cheese, softened
2 hard-cooked eggs, peeled, chopped
Salsa to taste
1 green onion, sliced

Combine the black beans, black olives, onion, green chiles, garlic, cilantro, oil, lime juice, chili powder, salt, red pepper flakes, cumin and black pepper in a bowl; mix well. Chill, covered, for 2 hours. Spread the cream cheese on a round serving plate. Cover with black bean mixture. Arrange the eggs and salsa around the edge of the black bean mixture. Sprinkle with the green onion. Serve with tortilla chips. Serves 12.

Reflections Under the Sun

Delicious Mexican Salsa

1 (28-ounce) can crushed tomatoes
1 (6-ounce) can tomato sauce
1 teaspoon salt
¼ teaspoon pepper
¼ teaspoon garlic salt
1 teaspoon crushed red pepper
3 small green onions, chopped
Cilantro to taste

Mix ingredients in order. Refrigerate for ½ hour before serving.

Cooking with Cops

Cocktail Meatballs

2 pounds ground beef
1 cup bread crumbs
1 envelope onion soup mix
3 eggs
1 (16-ounce) can sauerkraut, drained

1 (16-ounce) can whole berry cranberry sauce
1 (12-ounce) bottle chili sauce
1½ cups water
1 cup packed brown sugar

Combine the ground beef, bread crumbs, onion soup mix, and eggs in a bowl, and mix well. Shape into 1-inch meatballs. Place the meatballs in a 3-quart baking dish.

Combine the sauerkraut, cranberry sauce, chili sauce, water, and brown sugar in a bowl and mix well. Spoon over the meatballs.

Bake, covered, at 350° for 1½ hours, stirring occasionally. Uncover the baking dish. Bake for 30 minutes longer or until the meatballs are cooked through. Serves 8.

Tucson Treasures

Pico de Gallo

A great salsa to use for fajitas, a dip, or as an accompaniment to meat or fish.

2 large tomatoes, seeded and diced
1 medium white onion, diced
2 cloves garlic, minced
⅔ cup cucumber, peeled and diced

5 radishes, diced
⅓ cup fresh cilantro leaves, chopped
3–4 fresh serrano chiles, seeded, very finely chopped

In a medium bowl, mix together all of the ingredients, adding salt to taste. Refrigerate covered at least one hour before serving. Makes 3 cups.

License to Cook Arizona Style

The Gila River provides irrigation for more than 15,000 crop acres that form the Gila River Farms. The farms are diversified, growing cotton, grains, alfalfa hay, olives, citrus, pistachios, vegetables, onions, and fish.

Fresh Avocado Salsa

6 green onions, chopped
2 medium tomatoes, chopped
1 small can green chiles
⅓ cup fresh cilantro, chopped

2 large or 3 medium avocados, cubed
1 tablespoon fresh lemon juice
1 teaspoon garlic salt

Combine all ingredients; let set at least 1 hour for juices to combine. Serve as sauce for tacos, tostadas, steak, or use as a dip with tortilla chips.

Pleasures from the Good Earth

Fiesta Salsa

A mild salsa that can be used on tacos and enchiladas. Especially good heated and poured over thinly sliced strips of steak or roast beef. For spicier taste, use more green chiles.

4 fresh tomatoes, chopped
2 fresh green chiles, finely chopped, or 1 (4-ounce) can chopped green chiles
1 large Bermuda onion, chopped
1 green bell pepper, chopped
1 tablespoon sugar

1 tablespoon red wine vinegar
1 teaspoon olive oil
Salt and pepper to taste
2 tablespoons chopped fresh cilantro
¼ teaspoon oregano

Mix all ingredients and refrigerate. Yields 2 cups.

Purple Sage and Other Pleasures

Salsa de Chile Colorado

12 dried red chiles
2 quarts water, boiling
3 tablespoons oil

¼ cup garlic purée
3 tablespoons flour
½ teaspoon salt, or to taste

Rinse chiles in cold water and remove stems. Cook in boiling water until tender, about 15 minutes. Remove chiles and reserve cooking liquid. Place a few chiles into blender or food processor with ½ cup reserved liquid, and blend to a paste. Remove to a bowl. Repeat with remaining chiles.

Heat oil in large skillet. Add garlic purée and flour, stirring until flour browns. Add chile paste, stirring constantly until it boils and thickens. Season with salt. Thin slightly with reserved liquid. Yields approximately 2 quarts.

Recipe from El Charro Restaurant / ***Tucson Cooks!***

Roasted Rainbow Salsa

3 large green chiles, such as
   Anaheims or poblanos
2 large firm tomatoes
1 yellow onion
1 red onion
1 head garlic
1 red bell pepper

1 yellow bell pepper
1 green bell pepper
½ cup chopped cilantro
Juice of ½ lemon
1 clove fresh garlic, minced
Salt and pepper to taste

Spray grill with cooking spray to prevent sticking and preheat to high.

Place whole vegetables directly on the grill and roast the chiles, tomatoes, onions, garlic, and peppers, turning frequently, until the skins are charred all over.

Remove the vegetables from the grill and place in a brown paper bag or a large bowl. Fold the bag over or cover the bowl and let sit at least 15 minutes, until vegetables are cool enough to handle. The charred skins should easily slip off the chiles, tomatoes, and peppers, using a paring knife to help remove the outer layers of the onions and garlic.

Cut vegetables into large chunks and place in a food processor or blender. Gently pulse to the desired consistency (do not over-process). Place in a large bowl and add cilantro, lemon juice, fresh garlic, salt, and pepper. Chill at least 4 hours, preferably overnight. Makes about 4 cups.

Chips, Dips, & Salsas

Spicy Red Pecans

¼ cup butter or margarine
2 teaspoons ground red chile

¾–1 teaspoon garlic salt
3 cups pecan halves

In large skillet, melt butter over medium heat. Stir in red chile, garlic salt, and pecans. Cook and stir pecans 4–5 minutes, until browned and well coated with chile.

Recipes from Arizona with Love

Strawberry Plop Sangría

Sangría is a red wine punch of Spanish origin. In Mexico, it is basically red wine, a sliced orange, lime or lemon, sparkling water, or/and a heavy helping of sugar. It is one letter away from Sangrita, but a totally different beverage. No chile, no tequila follow-up in Sangría. But we have added strawberries.

1 quart large, stemmed,
  sun-ripened strawberries
1 cup sugar
1 bottle (fifth) chilled rosé or
  red wine
1 unpeeled seedless orange, sliced

1 unpeeled lemon, sliced and
  seeded
6 ounces club soda
Clear ice cubes
Fresh mint leaves

Marinate strawberries in sugar until heavy syrup develops (refrigerated overnight works best). To serve, pour into large glass pitcher, reserving a few perfect berries to plop into deep wine or champagne glasses. Add wine and citrus slices to pitcher and stir. Pour soda over fruit and stir again. Fill glasses with ice, then Sangría. Garnish with mint.

Outdoor Cooking

Historically, Arizona's strongest economic support came from the Four C's: cotton, copper, cattle, and citrus. In recent years a fifth—climate—has been added.

Sangría

1 apple, sliced and cored	½ cup triple sec
1 orange, sliced	7-Up
½ cup brandy	Orange juice
1 bottle Burgundy wine	Sugar, optional

Soak fruit in brandy overnight. Fill large water pitcher with ice. Pour wine in pitcher, filling to half. Add triple sec, 7-Up to fizz preference, and orange juice to color preference. Add fruit and brandy. Sugar can be added for sweetness.

Favorite Recipes from the Foothills of Carefree, Arizona

Christmas Glug

1 box raisins	2 teaspoons fennel
24–30 whole cloves	4 sticks cinnamon
2 oranges (juice and peel), reserve juice	1½ quarts water
24 cardamon seeds, broken open	4 cups sugar
½ pound sliced or crushed almonds	½ gallon (1.75 liters) 100-proof vodka
2 teaspoons anise	1 gallon port wine
	½ gallon claret or sherry wine

Use a 16- to 20-quart pot to cook in. Use a wooden spoon to stir, not a metal spoon. In a large piece of cheesecloth, put raisins, cloves, orange peel, cardamon seeds, almonds, anise, fennel and cinnamon. Close tightly so as not to let anything fall out. Boil in water for 30–45 minutes. Remove bag carefully and put in strainer over pot. Press all liquid out of bag and discard bag. To liquid, add sugar. Stir to dissolve. Add vodka, port wine, claret and juice from oranges. Stir well.

Red, White & Blue Favorites

Suvipsi "Lemonade"

Squaw bushes grow readily on the mesas, in crevices and other shady, rocky areas. The berries ripen in summer and are small, somewhat flat in shape, and deep red in color. The berries are extremely sour, even when ripe, but make a refreshing hot or cold drink.

Gather ripe berries from the suvipsi, or squaw bush, plant. Add water to berries, bring to a boil, and allow mixture to steep. Mash berries slightly, if desired. Pour water off berries and add sugar or honey and ice cubes. Discard berries.

Hopi Cookery

Strawberry Margarita Slush

**1½ cups frozen sliced
  strawberries with sugar, thawed**
¼ cup tequila
¼ cup triple sec
¾ cup sweet and sour bar mix

**1½ cups frozen limeade
  concentrate**
1 cup water
**2–3 tablespoons simple syrup
  (optional, to taste)**

Mix all ingredients together and place in plastic container to freeze overnight (or at least 8 hours). Remove from freezer and buzz briefly in a blender or set out a few minutes to thaw slightly before serving. Makes 5 cups.

Gourmet Gringo

Goldfield, one of several ghost towns throughout the state, was once a booming mine town. The gold discovered in 1892 was one of the richest strikes at that time, yielding more than three million dollars worth of gold.

Indian Fry Bread

4 tablespoons honey
3 tablespoons oil
1 tablespoon salt
2 cups hot water
1 tablespoon (1 package) active
   dry yeast

3 cups unbleached white flour
2 teaspoons baking powder
2–4 cups additional flour

Start the dough mixture about 2–2½ hours before serving.

Mix together the honey, oil, and salt. Stir in the hot water. Mix well. Sprinkle yeast on top of mixture. Cover with a cloth and allow to stand about 10 minutes or until yeast bubbles. Add flour and baking powder. Stir well. Add more flour until mixture is firm and cleans the hands. Use from 2–4 cups flour for this step.

Place dough in greased bowl. Turn dough over to grease top. Cover and allow to rise until double (about an hour). Punch down and divide first in half, then each half into 8 parts. Form each piece into a ball and permit to rise until ready to cook.

Heat deep fat to frying temperature. Take ball of dough and flatten with hands, using stretching action. When dough is very thin and about 6–8 inches in diameter, drop into hot fat and cook until golden (about 1½ minutes each side). Drain on paper towels and serve hot with honey or powdered sugar.

Arizona Cook Book

Mexican Spoon Bread

A Southwestern classic.

1 (16-ounce) can cream-style corn
¾ cup milk
⅓ cup vegetable oil
2 eggs
1 cup yellow cornmeal
½ teaspoon baking soda

1 teaspoon salt
1 (4-ounce) can chopped green
   chiles
2 cups shredded longhorn cheese
   or Cheddar cheese

Combine the corn, milk, oil, eggs, cornmeal, baking soda and salt in a mixer bowl. Beat until well mixed. Pour ½ of the mixture into a buttered 1½-quart casserole. Sprinkle green chiles and 1 cup of the cheese over the corn mixture. Spoon the remaining corn mixture over the cheese. Top with remaining cheese. Bake at 400° for 45 minutes or until puffed and golden. Serves 4.

Reflections Under the Sun

Hopi Hush Puppies

Hush puppies are served with stews or beans instead of bread. Although made of corn, they are corn in a different form and add variety to meals. Yellow cornmeal can be substituted for blue, but does not have as delicate a flavor.

2 cups blue cornmeal
1 teaspoon salt
2 teaspoons baking powder
1¼ cups milk

2 beaten eggs
1 small onion, chopped fine
Shortening

Combine cornmeal, salt and baking powder into a mixing bowl. Stir milk into beaten eggs and gradually add to cornmeal mixture. Add chopped onions to cornmeal and mix well. Drop by teaspoonfuls into 1½ inches of very hot shortening. Fry hush puppies until golden brown, turning to brown all sides. Serves 6.

Hopi Cookery

Green Chile Cornbread

1 medium-size can creamed corn
1 beaten egg
½ cup cornmeal
½ teaspoon garlic salt
¼ cup salad oil

¼ teaspoon baking powder
1 (4-ounce) can diced green
chiles
⅓ pound grated longhorn cheese,
divided

Mix all ingredients together, except for two handfuls of cheese. Pour into greased casserole dish (the flatter the better). Sprinkle remaining cheese on top. Bake at 350° for 40 minutes or so. Recipe can easily be doubled, tripled, etc. But, if using a deep dish, allow extra baking time. Serves 4.

Padre Kino's Favorite Meatloaf

Bonanza Bread

A powerhouse loaf that improves with age.

1 cup flour, all-purpose
1 cup whole wheat flour
½ teaspoon each, salt and baking
soda
2 teaspoons baking powder
⅔ cup nonfat dry milk powder
½ cup wheat germ or oat germ
½ cup brown sugar, packed
½ cup dry-roast, unsalted peanuts,
chopped

¼ cup chopped pecans
½ cup raisins
3 eggs
½ cup canola or corn oil
½ cup molasses
¾ cup orange juice
2 ripe, mashed bananas
⅓ cup chopped, dried apricots

In a large bowl, mix first 7 ingredients. Add peanuts, pecans and raisins, mixing each in turn. In the blender, mix together the eggs, oil, molasses, orange juice and bananas. When blended, add apricots just long enough to chop coarsely. Pour liquid mixture into bowl and stir just until all flour is moistened. Pour into 2 greased loaf pans. Bake 1 hour at 325°. Cool slightly on rack, then remove from pan and cool completely. Wrap tightly when cold.

Outdoor Cooking

Arizona is divided into 7 distinct areas: Grand Canyon Country, Indian Country, Central Territory, Arizona's West Coast, Valley of the Sun, High Country and Old West Country.

Quick Potato Bread

1 package yeast	¾ cup milk
4–4½ cups flour, divided	¼ cup butter or margarine,
¼ cup sugar	melted
2 teaspoons salt	2 eggs
Instant mashed potatoes (amount	
for 2 servings)	

In large bowl, stir together yeast, 1½ cups flour, sugar, and salt. In a pan, prepare 2 servings of potatoes according to package directions, using the amounts of water, milk, butter, and salt called for on the package. Then stir in milk, melted butter, and eggs until well blended.

Add potato mixture to flour/yeast mixture and beat for 2 minutes at medium speed, scraping bowl occasionally. Add 1 more cup of flour and beat 2 minutes longer. With a spoon, stir in 1 more cup of flour to form a semi-stiff dough. Turn into a floured bowl and knead 5–10 minutes until smooth and satiny.

Turn dough over in a greased bowl; cover and let rise until double (1½ to 2 hours). Punch dough down, knead briefly and shape into 2 loaves. Place each into well greased pans or baking sheet. Cover and let rise until almost double (45 minutes). Bake in 350° oven for 35 minutes or until well browned and "hollow" when tapped. Cool on rack.

Portal's Best Little Cookbook

Orange Marmalade Bread

½ cup margarine, softened	2 teaspoons baking powder
½ cup brown sugar, packed	1 teaspoon salt
2 eggs	½ teaspoon baking soda
1 (10-ounce) jar orange	½ cup orange juice,
marmalade	unsweetened
2¾ cups flour	½ cup nuts, chopped

Cream margarine and sugar until light and fluffy. Add eggs, one at a time, mixing well. Blend in marmalade. Add combined dry ingredients alternately with orange juice. Stir in nuts. Pour into greased and floured loaf pan. Bake at 350° for approximately 1 hour. Test with toothpick before removing from oven. Cool 15 minutes before removing from pan. Makes one loaf.

The Dog-Gone Delicious Cookbook

Holiday Treasure Loaf

1 cup flour, sifted
1 cup sugar
½ teaspoon salt
½ teaspoon baking powder
3 cups pitted dates, whole

1 (8-ounce) jar Maraschino
  cherries, whole
1 pound walnut meats, whole
4 eggs
1 teaspoon vanilla

Sift dry ingredients into a large bowl. Add dates, cherries and nuts to flour and coat well. Beat eggs well and add vanilla and pour into first mixture. Mix thoroughly with hands.

Line greased pan (5½x9½x2¾-inch) with heavy brown paper and grease paper well. Bake at 325° for 1¾–2 hours, or until "pick" clean. Remove from pan and wrap in a brandy-moistened cloth, then foil. Let stand a day or two. Fruit juice may be used instead of brandy. Serves 10.

The Dog-Gone Delicious Cookbook

Mile-High Biscuits

3 cups flour
¼ cup sugar
4 teaspoons baking powder
½ teaspoon cream of tartar

¾ teaspoon salt
½ cup shortening
1 egg
1½ cups milk

Combine dry ingredients. Cut in shortening. Add egg and milk. Mix well. Knead 10–12 times. Roll and cut. Place on baking sheet and freeze. When frozen, may be stored in plastic bag until needed. To bake, place on greased cookie sheet. Bake at 475° for 12–15 minutes. Makes 1 dozen.

The Garden Patch

Grandmother Stewart's Raisin Biscuits

4 cups sifted flour
8 teaspoons baking powder
1 teaspoon salt
1 cup sugar

1 cup butter, softened
2 cups raisins
¾ cup milk
1 cup cream

Sift the first four ingredients into a bowl. With hands, mix in butter. Add raisins, milk and cream. When dough forms a ball and leaves sides of bowl, pat out lightly on floured board to about ⅓-inch thickness. Cut with lightly floured 2-inch biscuit cutter. If you like crustier biscuits, roll out thinner. Bake 10–15 minutes on ungreased baking sheet in 425° oven. Recipe makes 3 dozen rich, flaky, tender biscuits.

Arizona Highways Heritage Cookbook

Quick Bubble Rolls

¾ cup packed brown sugar
¼ cup sugar
1 (3½-ounce) package
   butterscotch pudding mix (not
   instant)

1 teaspoon cinnamon
¾ cup chopped walnuts
½ (48-ounce) package frozen
   dinner rolls
½ cup melted butter

In small bowl, mix together brown sugar, sugar, dry pudding mix, cinnamon and nuts. Coat an angel food pan (not two-piece variety) with nonstick cooking spray. Place frozen rolls tightly in bottom of pan in one layer. Sprinkle with pudding mixture. Drizzle melted butter over top. Cover loosely with aluminum foil sprayed with nonstick cooking spray. Place in cold oven overnight. Next day bake in preheated 350° oven for 20 minutes uncovered. Place aluminum foil tent over pan for 10 more minutes of baking time. Take out of oven and invert pan onto platter. Serve immediately. Makes 8–12 servings.

What's Cooking Inn Arizona

Val's Famous Firehouse Cinnamon/Orange Rolls

DOUGH:

4 cups milk
1 cup white sugar
1 cup shortening
4 cups flour

2 tablespoons instant yeast
2 teaspoons salt
4 eggs

Scald or scold milk (I stand over it and call it bad names). Add sugar and shortening and continue heating until shortening is melted. Cool slightly. In a large bowl, mix flour, instant yeast and salt. Pour hot milk mixture in with dry ingredients. Mix well. Add 4 eggs, one at a time, mixing well after each.* Allow dough to rise to double. Punch down. Let rise again. On floured counter top, roll dough to oblong strip approximately 12–14 inches wide, 3 feet long, and ½-inch thick.

CINNAMON FILLING:

1 stick butter or margarine
2 cups brown sugar
1 tablespoon cinnamon
Nuts and raisins (optional)

ORANGE FILLING:

1 stick butter or margarine
2 cups white sugar
Grated rind of one orange
Nuts and raisins (optional)

Melt butter or margarine. Pour evenly over dough. Mix dry ingredients of preferred filling together. Sprinkle over buttered dough. Roll dough and slice to 1-inch-thick slabs. Place on baking pan and let rise until double in size. Bake 350° for 20–30 minutes depending on the elevation, humidity, and how hungry the guys are!

VANILLA FROSTING:

4 cups powdered sugar
4 tablespoons soft butter
1 teaspoon vanilla
Milk for smooth consistency

ORANGE FROSTING:

4 cups powdered sugar
4 tablespoons soft butter
1 teaspoon grated orange rind
Milk for smooth consistency

Blend sugar, butter, and vanilla or orange rind together. Add enough milk to give a smooth consistency. Spread mixture over hot rolls. I stick my CLEAN hand into the frosting and spread it evenly over the rolls while still hot from the oven. Makes 4–5 dozen rolls.

*If needed, add additional flour, 1 cup at a time, until dough is "sticky"—NOT dry or stiff—4–6 cups will be sufficient. Be careful not to add too much flour (10 cups is too much).

The National Firefighters Recipe Book

Loucoumades
(Honey Puffs)

2 ounces yeast
½ pint warm water, divided
1 cup (8 ounces) flour, divided

½ teaspoon salt
Oil for frying
Powdered cinnamon

Dissolve yeast in a large bowl with some water (¼ cup). Add 2 tablespoons flour and let rise in a warm place for ½ hour. When yeast has worked, add the rest of the flour, salt, and enough water to make a thick batter of dropping consistency. Cover the bowl with a cloth and let stand for 2–3 hours, until bubbles appear on the top. The batter is then ready for frying.

Put at least 1 pint of oil into deep pan, and when very hot, drop batter from a spoon, dipping the spoon into cold water each time before dipping into batter, so that batter does not stick to spoon. Cook until golden. Drain on paper towels and pile on a warm plate for serving. Dust with cinnamon and pour on warm Honey Syrup. Serve at once.

HONEY SYRUP:
1 cup honey
½ cup water

Juice of 1 lemon

Mix ingredients together and heat in small pan.

Recipes from Our Mothers' Kitchens

Sticky Buns, Breakfast Sweets

This is a sure winner for all ages.

⅔ cup brown sugar
⅛ cup water
1 cup chopped pecans or walnuts
5 tablespoons melted butter or
   margarine

2 packages buttermilk biscuits
   (tear apart in quarters)
1 teaspoon cinnamon mixed with
   ¼ cup sugar

Mix brown sugar, water, pecans, and butter together. Spread in 9x13-inch pan. Place quartered biscuits on top of this mixture. Sprinkle cinnamon-sugar on top. Bake at 375° for 20 minutes. Turn upside down on a serving dish immediately.

Favorite Recipes from the Foothills of Carefree, Arizona

Pop's Famous Caramel Rolls

DOUGH:

1 package active dry yeast
1 cup lukewarm water
4 tablespoons sugar, divided
6 cups flour, divided

2 teaspoons salt
1 cup milk
4 tablespoons shortening

Dissolve yeast in lukewarm water, add 1 tablespoon sugar, let stand 20 minutes. Mix 5 cups flour, remaining sugar and salt together. Warm milk and shortening to lukewarm in microwave; have ready. Add dissolved yeast mixture to flour mixture, mix well. Add warmed milk and shortening to flour and yeast mixture. Mix well and knead, adding remaining cup of flour as needed to make a smooth but not sticky dough. Cover bowl with cloth and place in a warm spot and let rise till double in size.

CARAMEL-PECAN TOPPING:

2 cups brown sugar
1/8 cup water

1 stick butter
3/4 cup pecans

ROLL FILLING:

1 cup sugar
1 teaspoon cinnamon

1 stick butter, melted
Raisins (optional)

Line a 12x15x2-inch pan with aluminum foil. In saucepan make a syrup of brown sugar, water and 1 stick butter. Bring to a boil, then pour the syrup into foil-lined pan. Arrange pecans on top of syrup. Have ready a small bowl containing sugar and cinnamon, mixed, and a small bowl of melted butter. When dough has doubled, flour an area and roll out dough to an 18x12-inch rectangle. Spread melted butter evenly over entire area of dough, sprinkle with sugar mixture and sprinkle with raisins, if desired.

Starting at the long side of the dough, roll dough in a medium-tight roll. Mark roll into 16 equal rolls. Cut through, making 16 rolls, carefully placing each as it is cut, flat-side-down onto the syrup and pecan mixture. You will have 3 rows of 5, squeezing in the last roll. Cover and let rise in a warm place until double. Bake at 350° until brown and bubbly, about 25-30 minutes. (For high altitude 30-35 minutes.)

Using hot pads, place another large cookie sheet over baked rolls and carefully turn roll pan upside down onto cookie sheet, allowing syrup to run down over rolls. Gently peel off aluminum. Enjoy.

First Baptist Favorites

Oven Baked French Toast

¼ cup butter, melted
2 tablespoons sugar
½ teaspoon cinnamon
3 eggs

¾ cup orange juice
8 slices sourdough bread, ¾-inch
    thick and cut on an angle, or
    Texas toast

Pour melted butter into large pan, large enough for all 8 slices. Swirl the butter to coat the pan. Mix sugar and cinnamon together, sprinkle over butter. Beat eggs with orange juice and dip each slice of bread for 15 seconds on each side. Lay in pan. Bake at 425° for 10–15 minutes.

Par Excellence

Orange Stuffed French Toast

1 (16-inch) long loaf of French
    bread (about 1 pound), unsliced
10 teaspoons orange marmalade
10 teaspoons light cream cheese
4 large eggs
½ cup skim milk

1 drop orange oil or ½ teaspoon
    orange zest
Powdered sugar
Orange slices, twisted for
    garnish

Preheat electric griddle to 350°.

Slice French bread into 10 slices, 1½ inches wide. Discard end pieces or save for another use. Use a small knife to slit a ½-inch "pocket" along the top of each slice.

Use a teaspoon to fill each pocket with 1 teaspoon orange marmalade, followed by 1 teaspoon cream cheese. The cream cheese will seal the slit.

Just before cooking, use a paper towel to wipe griddle with a thin film of canola oil. (Wipe in between cooking each batch, too.) Beat eggs, milk, and orange oil or zest together. Dip each stuffed slice of French bread into the batter, then fry on heated, greased griddle until golden brown, flipping once. Make sure slices are on the griddle long enough to warm the marmalade and slightly melt the cream cheese.

Place 1 piece on a plate. Sprinkle with powdered sugar and garnish with a twist of orange. Makes 10 servings.

Mountain Mornings

Bobbi's Apple Pancakes

"I use it for recruits," says Bobbi Olson, wife of Lute Olson, UA basketball coach. *"They love it, and want their mothers to have the recipe."*

CINNAMON SYRUP:

2 cups light corn syrup
4 cups sugar
1 cup water

1 tablespoon cinnamon
2 cups evaporated milk

Combine all ingredients except the milk and bring to a full boil in a medium-size pot. Cook for 2 minutes, stirring constantly. Let cool a full 5 minutes. Add milk, and serve warm.

BATTER:

2 medium-size green apples,
   (Jonathan or Granny Smith),
   peeled, cored, and chopped
2 eggs
2 tablespoons sugar

2 tablespoons butter, softened
2 cups evaporated milk
2 cups Bisquick All-Purpose
   Baking Mix

While waiting for the syrup to cool, mix all the batter ingredients in a large bowl. Spoon onto a greased pancake grill or frying pan and cook over medium-high heat. Serves 4.

The Arizona Celebrity Cookbook

Prune Butter

2 pounds prunes
2 cups sugar
1 cup white or cider vinegar
1 teaspoon cinnamon

1 teaspoon allspice
½ teaspoon nutmeg
½ teaspoon cloves

Wash prunes, cover with water, and simmer for one hour. Cool and drain, remove pits. Mash, add remaining ingredients, and boil 10 minutes. Put in hot sterilized jars and seal.

Chuck Wagon Cookin'

Glen Canyon Dam and power plant, at the southern edge of Lake Powell, contain over five million cubic yards of concrete—that is equal to building a four-lane highway stretching from Phoenix, Arizona to Chicago, Illinois.

Joyce's Buttermilk Syrup

1 cup sugar
½ cup margarine
½ cup buttermilk

1 teaspoon white Karo syrup
½ teaspoon baking soda
½ teaspoon vanilla

Mix all ingredients except vanilla, and bring to a boil. Boil for 5 minutes over low heat. Remove from heat and let cool. Add vanilla. Keep refrigerated.

The Garden Patch

Grand Betty's Doughnuts

The charming part of this recipe is the teamwork and involvement...and the resulting funny shapes. To roll out the dough and cut them with a form would ruin the event. (The trick is to make the holes quite large, because the doughnuts expand.) While an adult is needed to do (or supervise) frying, young children can shape their own doughnuts and shake the sack.

2 eggs, beaten
1 cup sugar
1 cup milk
1 teaspoon baking powder

1 teaspoon shortening
1 teaspoon nutmeg
Flour (approximately 4 cups)

Mix all ingredients and add flour last (enough to work the soft dough), to roll between your hands and mold into circles. Fry in hot grease, turning when brown. Drain doughnuts on paper towels. Then, shake in paper sack with powdered sugar.

Padre Kino's Favorite Meatloaf

Potato Doughnuts

2 medium potatoes
2 tablespoons lard or good clean
    drippings
2 well-beaten eggs

1½ cups sugar
1 gill (½ cup) milk
3 teaspoons baking powder
5 cups flour

Boil and mash potatoes. Stir in lard while potatoes are still hot. Then add eggs, sugar, milk, and the flour that has been sifted with the baking powder. Knead more flour in on board if necessary. Cut and fry in deep fat. Makes a bunch.

Arizona Territory Cook Book

Pan Fried Apples, 1919

These make a great camp meal anywhere, even at the backyard barbecue.

**3 or 4 large, tart apples, cored and
  sliced**
**2 tablespoons bacon drippings or
  butter**

**⅓ cup wild honey or brown
  sugar**
Salt and cinnamon

Heat apple slices in hot bacon drippings in skillet until they soften, stirring
to turn over. Add honey or brown sugar and a little salt and cinnamon, if
available. If not, honey or sugar will glaze the slices if allowed to remain on
the fire, covered, 5–10 minutes, depending on heat.

Arizona Highways Heritage Cookbook

Apple Cinnamon Jelly

2¾ cups apple juice
5¾ cups sugar
**4–6 large cinnamon sticks
  (broken into pieces)**

1 box fruit pectin
**½ teaspoon margarine or
  butter**

Pour apple juice into 6 or 8-quart pot. Place sugar in a separate bowl; set
aside. Into apple juice stir cinnamon sticks, fruit pectin, and margarine (to
prevent foaming during cooking). Bring mixture to full rolling boil over high
heat, stirring constantly. Quickly add sugar to juice and return to full rolling
boil for 1 minute, stirring constantly. Remove from heat. Skim off any foam
and remove cinnamon sticks. Pour into hot sterilized jars to within ⅛ inch
of top. Add sterilized lids and process in boiling water bath for 10 minutes.
Yields 4–5 (½-pint) jars.

Arizona State Fair Blue Ribbon Recipes

Lake Mead National Recreation Area exhibits a startling contrast of desert and water,
mountains and canyons, primitive backcountry and modern technology. Lake Mead and
Lake Mohave (man-made reservoirs created by the contruction of Hoover Dam and Davis
Dam, respectively) and their shorelines form the recreation area, located on the Arizona/Nevada
border.

Pepper Jelly

1–2 cups ground bell peppers
  (4 or 5 medium)
¼–½ cup ground hot peppers
  (12 or more)

6½ cups sugar
1½ cups white vinegar
1 bottle Certo®

Mix all ingredients together except Certo. (Add hot peppers to taste.) Boil mixture 5 minutes, remove from heat, let stand 20 minutes. Add Certo and bring to a boil. Let boil 2 minutes. Pour into hot sterilized jars to ⅛ inch of top and add sterilized lids. Process in boiling water bath for 10 minutes. Yields 2–3 pints of jelly.

Arizona State Fair Blue Ribbon Recipes

Prickly Pear Jelly

6½ cups prickly pear juice
2 packages Sure-Jell

½ cup lemon juice
9 cups sugar

Do not peel prickly pears. Wear gloves and rub spines off with gunny sack. Wash them well; it's not necessary for all spines to be removed. It's amazing how they disappear when cooked.

Put fully ripe fruit in kettle with a small amount of water, not more than 3 cups for an 8-quart kettle. Bring fruit to a boil, and mash with potato masher. Do not overcook. If pears are fully ripe, they will be fairly juicy. Drain through cloth.

Measure juice into large kettle and bring to boil. Add 2 packages of Sure-Jell. Boil hard 1 minute, a full rolling boil that cannot be stirred down. Add lemon juice and sugar. Bring to a hard boil, and let boil 1 full minute.

Be sure you measure exactly. If a more firm jelly is desired, omit ¼ cup of juice and add ½ cup sugar. Jelly will be a beautiful claret red and firm.

Chuck Wagon Cookin'

Breakfast Burritos

1 pound pork sausage	Salt and pepper to taste
1 small sweet onion, chopped	1 (16-ounce) can refried beans
1 clove garlic, diced	1 package (10-inch) flour tortillas
12 eggs	¼ pound Cheddar cheese, shredded
3 tablespoons milk	Salsa
Tabasco sauce to taste	Garnishes*

Preheat 12-inch Dutch oven.** Fry sausage, onion and garlic. Beat eggs and milk. Add Tabasco and salt and pepper to taste. Add to sausage mixture and cook, stirring often. Use 12–14 coals underneath the uncovered Dutch oven. Heat refried beans in separate saucepan.

To heat the tortillas, use your Dutch oven lid, inverted, over about 20 briquets or in your camp stove. Spread refried beans on tortilla and add a generous helping of egg mixture, burrito style. Add cheese and salsa. Roll tortilla and fold the ends in. You don't want to lose any of the goodies inside.

*Garnish with sour cream, guacamole, chopped green onions, chopped olives, chopped peppers and chopped tomatoes, if desired.

Dutch Oven Cooking and Heat Control: The first step to Dutch oven cooking is to start hot coals or briquets to cook with. After you ignite them, it will take about 15–20 minutes for the coals to be ready. When the coals are ready, place the oven on a level spot. A sheet of foil, shiny-side-up, works well to keep the oven hot. Next, place coals under the oven in a circular pattern and on the lid in a checker board pattern. To avoid uneven cooking, do not bunch the coals.

Heat control is the hardest step of Dutch oven cooking. The following temperature chart will help you determine how many coals to use to reach the desired temperature.

When cooking with a Dutch oven, remember to preheat the oven, unless the recipe states otherwise. Preheating is very easy. Simply start the fire and let it heat to required temperature. Remember it is best to have too few coals rather than too many. You can always cook a dish longer, but you can't undo an overdone dish.

The chart below shows the number of briquets to be used on the bottom (first number) and top (second number) of oven.

Temperature	10-inch oven	12-inch oven	14-inch oven	16-inch oven
325°	13/6	16/7	20/10	22/12
350°	14/7	17/8	21/11	24/12
375°	16/7	18/9	22/12	25/13
400°	17/8	19/10	24/12	27/13
425°	18/9	21/10	25/13	28/14
450°	19/10	22/11	26/14	30/14

Dutch Oven and Campfire Cookbook

Breakfast Chimichangas

2⅔ cups ricotta cheese
3 (8-ounce) packages cream
   cheese, softened
2 egg yolks
¾ cup sugar
2 teaspoons grated lemon rind

1 teaspoon cinnamon
1 tablespoon vanilla
16 (8-inch) flour tortillas
Melted butter
Fresh strawberries, blueberries, or
   peaches for topping

Combine cheeses, egg yolks, sugar, rind, cinnamon, and vanilla. Mix well. Soften tortillas and place ¹⁄₁₆ amount of filling on each tortilla. Fold 2 sides in and over to enclose filling. Brush top with melted butter. Bake on cookie sheet at 350° for about 20 minutes until light brown. Serve topped with fresh fruit. These can be prepared ahead and frozen. Makes 16 servings.

What's Cooking Inn Arizona

Brunch Enchiladas

2 cups ground ham, fully cooked
½ cup sliced green onions
½ cup chopped green bell
   pepper
2½ cups shredded Cheddar
   cheese
8 (7-inch) flour tortillas
4 eggs, beaten

2 cups light cream or milk
1 tablespoon flour
¼ teaspoon salt
¼ teaspoon garlic powder
Few drops Tabasco sauce
Avocado slices
Salsa
Sour cream

In a bowl combine ground ham, onion and green pepper. Place ⅓ cup of mixture and 3 tablespoons cheese at one end of a tortilla and roll up. Repeat with remaining tortillas. Arrange tortillas, seam-side-down, in a greased 7x12x2-inch oven-proof casserole. Combine eggs, cream or milk, flour, spices and hot sauce. Pour over tortillas, cover and refrigerate several hours or overnight. Remove from refrigerator 45 minutes before baking. Preheat oven to 350° and bake 45–60 minutes or until set. Sprinkle with remaining cheese and bake an additional 3 minutes. Let stand 10 minutes before serving. Garnish with avocado slices, salsa and sour cream. Serves 8.

Hospice Hospitality

South of the Border Wrap

Wraps are sandwiches with a twist—fillings wrapped in tortillas or other flat breads.

½ cup drained canned black beans
2 tablespoons salsa
1 tablespoon chopped green onions
1 tablespoon chopped fresh cilantro

1 large tomato, chopped
1 cup shredded Monterey Jack cheese
4 (8-inch) flour tortillas
Butter as needed

Mash beans slightly with a fork and combine with salsa, green onions, and cilantro. Divide mixture between the tortillas, then top each with chopped tomato and cheese. Roll up tortilla. Melt butter in a large skillet and grill the wraps, seam side down, over medium heat for 5 minutes, turning to brown on all sides. Makes 4 wraps.

License to Cook Arizona Style

Prosciutto & Green Chile Frittata

This makes an excellent start to a festive Christmas morning or use it as one of your dishes for a Christmas Eve buffet.

8 eggs or equivalent egg substitute
1 tablespoon tequila
2 tablespoons olive oil
½ medium-size yellow onion, chopped
½ cup chopped green bell pepper
⅓ cup shredded prosciutto or ham

1 tablespoon chopped parsley
½ teaspoon ground black pepper
2 tablespoons butter
½ cup chopped ripe tomato
¼ cup diced green chiles
½ cup crumbled feta cheese
1 tablespoon grated Romano cheese
Sour cream
Chopped black olives

Beat eggs with a wire whisk. Add tequila and beat again. Heat olive oil in large, heavy non-stick frying pan. Cook onion and green pepper until just soft, stir in prosciutto, parsley and black pepper and warm through. Add butter to pan and pour in eggs. Sprinkle tomato, chile, and cheeses over eggs, cover pan and cook over very low heat for 20 minutes or until eggs are nicely set. Cut into quarters and serve garnished with a dollop of sour cream, and sprinkle with chopped black olives. Serves 4.

Christmas in Arizona Cook Book

Red Pepper Bruschetta with Feta Cheese

1 (7-ounce) jar roasted red
   peppers, drained and chopped
1 clove garlic, minced
Olive oil
1 teaspoon lemon juice

¼ cup chopped green onions
4 ounces feta cheese, chopped
1 loaf French bread sliced into
   ½-inch slices

Mix peppers, garlic, 1 tablespoon olive oil, lemon juice, onions, and feta cheese. Set aside. Brush bread lightly with olive oil; place on cookie sheet. Broil on each side until lightly toasted. Top each slice with about 1 tablespoon of pepper mixture.

Kids in the Kitchen

Oak Creek Eggs

Vegetable oil
2 (6-inch) flour tortillas
2 ounces chorizo
2 eggs

2 black olives
2 ounces (¼ cup) Cilantro
   Hollandaise

Heat oil in deep heavy pot to 350°. Drop in flour tortilla and push down with a 2-ounce ladle and cook until golden brown and holds the shape of a cup. Repeat with second tortilla. Cook chorizo and poach the eggs. Spoon half of the chorizo in each tortilla cup and place egg over chorizo. Ladle 1 ounce of Cilantro Hollandaise over each egg. Garnish each with a black olive and serve with home fries or hash browns.

CILANTRO HOLLANDAISE:

2 egg yolks
1 teaspoon water
4 ounces (½ cup) clarified
   butter
¼ cup lemon juice

Dash Tabasco
Dash Worcestershire sauce
¼ bunch cilantro, chopped
1 teaspoon white wine
Pinch of garlic

Beat egg yolks with water in a double boiler over low heat until eggs become fluffy (do not let eggs stick to the bowl). Slowly drizzle in butter while beating rapidly. Stir in lemon, Tabasco, Worcestershire, cilantro, wine and garlic. Serves 2.

Sedona Cook Book

Potato Egg Bake

½ cup margarine
1 (16-ounce) package frozen hash
　browns
1 cup Cheddar cheese, shredded
2 cups Swiss cheese, shredded

2 cups diced ham
4–5 eggs
1 cup milk
Chopped onions, to taste
　(about 1 cup)

Melt margarine in 9x13-inch pan. Add hash browns. Bake at 425° for 30 minutes. Mix balance of ingredients together and pour over browned hash browns. Bake at 350° for 30 minutes. This can be made the day before and baked for 30 minutes before serving. Let stand 5 minutes before cutting into pieces.

Red, White & Blue Favorites

Southwestern Egg Bake

8 corn tortillas
¾ pound grated Co-Jack cheese
　or combination of Cheddar and
　Monterey Jack cheeses
8 ounces diced green chiles
Sliced black olives
4 eggs

2 cups milk
¾ teaspoon chili powder
¾ teaspoon black pepper
½ teaspoon salt
Crushed corn chips
Sour cream and cilantro (for
　garnish, optional)

Break tortillas into greased 9x13-inch pan. Mix together grated cheese, chiles, olives, eggs, milk, and seasonings. Pour over tortillas and top with crushed corn chips. Bake at 350° for one hour. Top with sour cream and cilantro, if desired. Makes 8–10 servings.

What's Cooking Inn Arizona

Egg Casserole Supreme

Serve with fresh fruit and muffins for a perfect brunch!

6 eggs
3 cups milk
2 tablespoons minced onion
½ teaspoon salt
¼ teaspoon pepper
2 (10-ounce) packages frozen
   broccoli in cheese sauce

12 slices white bread, crusts
   removed, divided
2 cups diced ham
2½ cups grated Cheddar cheese,
   divided

Beat eggs with milk, onion, salt, and pepper. Cook broccoli per directions. Spray a 9x13-inch (or larger) dish with Pam. Line with 6 slices bread (or more to fill dish). Layer as follows: broccoli, ham, and 1 cup cheese. Top with 6 slices of bread (or more to fill dish). Pour egg mixture over bread. Cover with foil and refrigerate overnight. In the morning add remaining 1½ cups cheese and bake at 325° for 1 hour. Let stand 10 minutes before serving. Serves 8–10.

Tostitos Fiesta Bowl Cookbook

Southwest Breakfast Omelet

8 slices white bread, buttered
2 cups grated Cheddar or longhorn
   cheese (retain ¼ cup to
   sprinkle on top before baking)
1 onion, diced
1 pound mushrooms, sliced
1 (7-ounce) can chopped green
   chiles

4 eggs
1½ teaspoons salt
¼ teaspoon pepper
½ teaspoon table mustard
3 cups milk

Put 4 slices of bread in bottom of casserole dish. Sprinkle with half the cheese and half of onion, mushrooms and chiles. Add another layer of bread and remainder of cheese, onion, mushrooms and chiles. Beat eggs with seasonings, adding milk. Pour over bread and sprinkle some of cheese over top. Bake for 1 hour at 350°. Cover with foil for the first 40 minutes. Let stand about 10 minutes before serving. (Can be made the night before, covered with foil, and put in the refrigerator.) Serves 8.

Padre Kino's Favorite Meatloaf

Pineda's Wake-up Huevos Rancheros

Oil for sautéing and frying
1 (7-ounce) can green chiles,
   drained
2 cloves garlic, minced
1 small onion, chopped

2 medium fresh tomatoes
2 cups water
½ cup grated longhorn cheese
8 corn tortillas
8 eggs

Sauté chopped chiles, garlic, and onion in a little oil until clear. Chop tomatoes and add, stirring a few minutes. Add water and simmer to sauce consistency. (I add a shake of salt.) Stir in cheese and set aside. Fry corn tortillas in very hot oil quickly, only until soft. Drain on paper bag or towel. Place 2 on each of 4 hot serving plates. Fry eggs over easy. Place on each tortilla. Pour warm chile sauce over eggs. Serve immediately to four.

Outdoor Cooking

Soups, Chilis & Stews

Mule rides into the Grand Canyon have been popular since Bright Angel Trail opened in 1891. The trips can be grueling and last from 1-3 days. Average summer temperatures inside the canyon can exceed 100°.

Chilled Peach Soup

Peach soup, a family favorite, adapts to any dining situation—poolside, picnic, with bread or muffins as a main course, or as a dessert, with pound cake and fresh blueberries or raspberries.

**2 (1-pound) bags frozen peaches,
    or 10 medium-size fresh peaches,
    peeled and pitted
1½ cups softened vanilla ice
    cream**

**½ cup half-and-half
¼ cup white wine
¼ teaspoon freshly ground
    nutmeg
½ cup sugar (approximately)**

Pureé the peaches in food processor or blender. Add ice cream, half-and-half, wine, and nutmeg; blend until smooth. Add sugar to taste, and chill at least 2 hours before serving.

Outdoor Cooking

Gazpacho

**5 small cans Snap-E-Tom tomato
    juice cocktail, divided
½ medium cucumber, coarsely
    chopped
1 tablespoon sugar
¼ cup fresh lemon juice
¼ cup olive oil**

**1 medium-sized tomato, chopped
4 or 5 crushed cloves of garlic
1 teaspoon salt
3 tablespoons chopped Bermuda
    onion
⅛ teaspoon white pepper
Tabasco sauce, to taste**

Put 2 cans of the juice and the other ingredients in blender or food processor and liquefy. Add remaining juice and blend. Refrigerate 24 hours. Prepare garnishes of diced tomato (squeeze out pulp), Bermuda onion, green pepper, cucumber, and croutons to pass. Makes 12 first-course portions (about 64 ounces).

Coronado's Favorite Trail Mix

Blender Gazpacho

1 (48-ounce) can tomato juice,
  divided
1 medium onion, quartered
1 small clove garlic
1 teaspoon salt
¼ teaspoon pepper
1 medium green pepper, unpeeled

1 large or 2 small cucumbers,
  unpeeled
3 tablespoons salad oil (preferably
  olive oil)
3 tablespoons wine or wine
  vinegar

TO MAKE IN BLENDER:

Pour ⅓ tomato juice into blender container. Add onion, garlic, salt and pepper. Blend until vegetables are grated.

Pour mixture into large (3-quart) bowl. Next blend ⅓ tomato juice and green pepper and until grated. Add this to mixture in bowl. Pour remaining ⅓ tomato juice into blender container. Add cucumber, oil, and vinegar. Repeat the process. Pour into bowl. Stir mixture to blend. If a finer gazpacho is desired, return some of the mixture to blender and repeat process until the desired texture is reached.

TO MAKE IN A FOOD PROCESSOR:

Place onion, garlic and green pepper in processor bowl and pulse in short bursts until vegetables are grated. Remove to separate bowl large enough to hold all the soup. Quarter cucumber and pulse processor about 2 seconds, or chop by hand. Add to other vegetables, then stir in the tomato juice, salt, pepper, oil and wine or white vinegar.

Gazpacho should be made 24 hours ahead of time and refrigerated so flavors blend and develop. Serves 8–10.

Savory Southwest

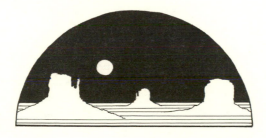

Caldo de Queso
(Potato-Cheese Soup)

6 large potatoes, peeled and
   cubed
1 medium to large onion, chopped
1 large clove garlic, chopped
1 tablespoon olive oil
½ quart chicken broth and
   ½ quart milk, or ½ quart of
   milk, ½ quart of water, and
   2 chicken bouillon cubes

3–4 fresh green chiles, peeled,
   seeded, and chopped (enough
   for ¾ cup) or 1 (6-ounce) can
   chopped chiles
½ pound shredded Cheddar
   cheese
Cilantro for garnish, optional

Sauté potatoes, onion, and garlic in oil in a large soup pot. Cover ingredients with liquid, and simmer until tender, about 30 minutes. Toward end of the cooking time, add chiles. When serving, add a handful of cheese (to taste) to each bowl.

Note: Cheese can be added to the soup before serving; let it melt in the soup, if desired.

Corazón Contento

Low-Calorie Potato Soup

1 tablespoon margarine
1 cup chopped onions
1 garlic clove, chopped
4 pareve chicken soup cubes
5 cups hot water
3 medium potatoes, peeled and cut
   in wedges
2 medium carrots, peeled and
   sliced
1 zucchini, sliced

2 celery ribs with leaves, chopped
1 tablespoon fresh or ½ teaspoon
   dry dill
2–3 sprigs fresh parsley or 1
   teaspoon dry
1 teaspoon salt
½ teaspoon pepper
1 tablespoon cornstarch or potato
   starch
3 tablespoons water

Melt margarine in a soup pot. Sauté onions and garlic until translucent. Dissolve chicken soup cubes in hot water. Add to pot. Add potatoes, carrots, zucchini, and celery, but save celery leaves. Bring to a boil, reduce heat and simmer 15–20 minutes. Add celery leaves, dill, parsley, salt, and pepper. Dissolve cornstarch or potato starch in 3 tablespoons water and add to soup. Simmer until slightly thick. Yields 6 servings.

Kosher Kettle

Sopa De Elote
(Corn Soup)

1 cup sliced green onion
1 cup chopped red bell pepper
2 tablespoons butter or
  margarine
2½ cups cooked corn kernels

5 cups chicken broth, divided
Salt
Freshly ground pepper
1 cup half-and-half

In 2-quart saucepan, sauté onion and red pepper in butter until vegetables are tender. Place corn in blender or food processor with 1 cup broth; purée. In saucepan, stir corn purée and remainder of broth together. Season to taste with salt and pepper. Simmer mixture over low heat for 15 minutes. Stir in cream and bring to a boil. Remove from heat and serve immediately. Garnish with chopped red pepper and sliced green onion, if desired. Makes 6 servings.

Recipes from Arizona with Love

Chicken Lemon Soup
(Avgolemono)

5½ cups water
5½ teaspoons chicken soup
  powder
4 teaspoons cornstarch

3 egg yolks
2 cups rice, cooked
Juice of 1 lemon
Salt to taste

Place chicken soup powder and water in a soup pot. Bring to a boil. Reduce heat. Add cornstarch and yolks and blend. Add rice, lemon juice and salt. Simmer until very hot. Yields 4–6 servings.

Kosher Kettle

Church Square in the historic district of Douglas is listed in the Guinness Book of World Records as the only city block in the U.S. containing four different churches. When the new city of Douglas was planned in 1903, this block was designated and deeded only for church use. The Southern Baptist, Presbyterian, Lutheran and Methodist churches were built shortly after.

Baja Bouillabaisse

ROUILLE:

1 large red bell pepper, coarsely
  chopped
4 tablespoons bread crumbs
2 tablespoons chopped garlic

Salt and freshly ground pepper to
  taste
3 tablespoons olive oil

Purée red pepper, bread crumbs, garlic, salt and pepper in a food processor.
Slowly add olive oil to form a thick paste. Set aside.

BROTH:

4 cups fish stock
1 large pinch saffron
1 cup dry white wine

2 tablespoons brandy
2 tomatoes, peeled, seeded, and
  roughly chopped

SEAFOOD:

12 littleneck clams, mulched
12 mussels, mulched
8 large Guaymas shrimp, peeled
  and deveined
12 large sea scallops, cleaned
4 pieces cabrilla (3 ounces each) or
  other firm fish of your liking

½ cup olive oil
1 tablespoon chopped garlic
Salt and pepper to taste
4 stone crab claws, cooked and
  cracked

Add clams and mussels to broth mixture; cover, and simmer until they open,
about 3 minutes. Meanwhile, brush shrimp, scallops and cabrilla with mixture of oil, garlic, salt and pepper, and grill. Scallops will take about 1
minute per side, shrimp 2½ minutes per side, and cabrilla 3–4 minutes per
side depending on thickness.

GARNISH:

16 Anaheim chiles, peeled, seeded,
  and cut into ½x4-inch strips
1 zucchini squash, finely diced
1 yellow squash, finely diced

1 red bell pepper, finely diced
8 ounces unshelled English peas
  (you will need 1 cup shelled)

Warm chile strips in broth, then place them decoratively in the bottoms of
4 large individual serving bowls. Warm crab claws in broth. Pour ¼ cup
broth into each bowl and attractively compose equal portions of seafood in
each. Add diced vegetables and peas to remaining broth to cook them
slightly, then ladle them with broth into each bowl. With each portion serve
a dish of Rouille and garlic toast. Serves 4.

Note: Mulch clams and mussels by setting them in a tub of water with ½ cup cornmeal and refrigerating overnight.

Janos: Recipes and Tales from a Southwest Restaurant

Cream of Zucchini Soup

4 cups zucchini, thickly sliced
  (seeded, if large)
1 medium onion, quartered
1 can chicken broth
1 teaspoon salt
¼ teaspoon pepper
½ teaspoon dried basil
1½ cups milk
½ cup cream

Combine zucchini, onion, chicken broth, salt, pepper and basil in pan. Cover and simmer about 20 minutes or until tender. Cool slightly and pour into blender. Cover and purée at high speed. May be frozen. When ready to serve, add milk and cream and heat. Serves 6.

Favorites for All Seasons

Gulf Oyster and Wild Mushroom Chowder

¼ pound bacon, finely diced
¼ pound butter, divided
2 dozen raw oysters, shucked
1 pound assorted wild
  mushrooms, diced
1 tablespoon fresh minced garlic
2 onions, diced
2 celery stalks, diced
4½ cups diced potatoes
2 bay leaves
1 teaspoon fresh thyme
4 cups fish stock
1 cup white wine
Salt and pepper
Worcestershire sauce
Tabasco sauce
1 cup heavy cream

Brown bacon in heavy pan and drain. Add ½ the butter. When butter is melted, add oysters and cook until lips curl. Remove and reserve. Add mushrooms and sauté. Remove and reserve. Add remaining butter, garlic, onions, celery, potatoes, bay leaves and thyme. Cook until onions are translucent and potatoes are soft. Add stock and wine; simmer 10 minutes or until it reaches desired thickness.

Stir in oysters and mushrooms. Season with salt and pepper, Worcestershire and Tabasco. Finish with cream. Reduce if necessary. Serves 4–6.

Recipe from Kingfisher Bar & Grill / ***Tucson Cooks!***

Chile-Corn Chowder

Thick and creamy, this hearty chowder will satisfy the hungriest appetite, especially when accompanied by hot muffins. You can freeze it, but it will not be as creamy when reheated.

4 cups vegetable stock
1 onion, chopped
2 tomatoes, chopped
2 potatoes, chopped
1 carrot, diced
1 stalk celery, minced
2–3 cloves garlic, minced
1 cup frozen or fresh corn, cut
 from the cob
¼ cup chopped mild chiles
½ cup arrowroot or cornstarch,
 dissolved in ½ cup soymilk or
 rice milk

½ teaspoon cumin powder
½ teaspoon chili powder
Cayenne or hot sauce, to taste
1 cup soymilk or rice milk
1 cup grated soy Cheddar or
 jalapeño Jack cheese (optional)
¼ cup minced fresh cilantro for
 garnish

In a large pot or soup kettle, combine all the ingredients except the soymilk or rice milk, cheese and cilantro. Cook uncovered about 30 minutes, or until all of the vegetables are tender. Add the milk and cheese, and cook another 10 minutes, or until it begins to thicken. Yields 6 servings.

Variations: You can add bell peppers, mushrooms, zucchini or any other squash, and a half a cup of black or red beans.

Per serving: Calories 139; Protein 3g; Fat 1g; Carbohydrates 30g

Flavors of the Southwest

The most common type of chile used in the U.S. is the Anaheim. They are available fresh, canned or frozen, are mild to hot in flavor and their large size makes them ideal for stuffing.

Black Bean and Corn Soup

1 onion, chopped
1 shallot, chopped
8 cloves garlic, chopped
¼ pound (1 stick) butter
2 pounds black beans
2 gallons vegetable stock (nineteen
   13¾-ounce cans)
2 cups apple cider vinegar
2 teaspoons celery salt
1 teaspoon pepper
Corn Mixture

In a large stock pot, cook onion, shallot, and garlic in butter until tender. Add beans and mix well so that each bean is coated with butter. Add remaining ingredients except Corn Mixture. Cover and simmer for 3 hours or until beans are soft. Stir in Corn Mixture and simmer an additional 20 minutes. Serves 8–10.

CORN MIXTURE:
6 ears corn, husked and grilled
2 tablespoons chopped, roasted
   green chiles
2 tablespoons ground cumin
1 tablespoon chopped cilantro
1 red bell pepper

Cut corn from cobs. In a bowl, combine corn kernels with chiles, cumin, cilantro and red pepper. Yields 2 cups.

Note: If corn is not in season, roast frozen corn under a broiler.

Eddie's Grill, Phoenix / ***Vegetarian Southwest***

Bean with Bacon Soup

1½ cups dried navy beans, rinsed
2 cups cold water
6 slices bacon, cooked and drained
1 carrot, sliced
1 rib celery, chopped
1 onion, chopped
1 small turnip, cut in 1-inch pieces
1 teaspoon dried Italian seasoning
⅛ teaspoon black pepper
1 (46-ounce) can chicken broth
1 cup 1% milk
12 strips pimento, garnish

Soak beans overnight in cold water. Crumble bacon and place in slow cooker. Combine carrot, celery, onion, turnip, seasoning and beans with bacon in slow cooker, mixing slightly. Pour broth over top. Cover and cook on low 7½–9 hours or until beans are crisp tender. Ladle 2 cups soup into food processor and purée, then return to slow cooker. Add milk; cover and heat on high 10 minutes or until heated through. Serves 6.

Bon Appétit

Southwest Black Bean Soup

This is my favorite version of black bean soup. The orange juice and pulp really add a nice touch. As with any bean soup, a crockpot can really make it a simple operation. This soup freezes wonderfully.

2 cups dry black beans (turtle beans)
1 tablespoon extra-virgin olive oil (optional)
1 onion, chopped
2 stalks celery, minced
1 carrot, diced
3–4 cloves fresh garlic, minced
1 fresh green chile, roasted, peeled, and minced

1 tablespoon chili powder
1 tablespoon cumin powder
1 tablespoon fresh minced cilantro
Salt-free vegetable seasoning, to taste
1 teaspoon tamari
Juice of 2 limes or 1 lemon
Juice of 1 orange with just a little of the orange pulp

Pick through the the dry beans, discarding any rocks, field corn, shrivelled beans, etc. Soak the beans in plenty of water overnight (preferably at least eight hours). Pour off the soaking water and cover the beans with fresh water about 1/2 inch above the beans. Add the vegetables, chili powder, cumin, cilantro and salt-free vegetable seasoning. Cook for 1–1 1/2 hours over medium heat or until the beans are very tender. If using a crockpot, let cook all day.

Add the tamari, lime or lemon juice, and orange juice and pulp. Cook uncovered about 30 minutes more. Garnish with a dollop of non-fat yogurt and a fresh cilantro leaf. Yields 6 servings. Enjoy!

Note: Although it's not absolutely necessary to soak beans before cooking them, it does help. First, it cuts down on cooking time by quite a bit. Second, it makes them more digestible. All beans except lentils and split peas should be soaked.

Per serving: Calories 225; Protein 12g; Fat 0g; Carbohydrates 43g

Flavors of the Southwest

Colossal Cave is one of the largest dry caverns in the world; explorers have yet to find its end.

Southwest Taco Soup

1½ pounds lean ground beef
1 (23-ounce) can ranch-style beans
1 (15-ounce) can pinto beans
1 (15-ounce) can kidney beans
1 (15-ounce) can corn, drained
1 (14-ounce) can Mexican-style
  tomatoes
1 large onion, chopped
3 ribs celery, chopped
2 (1-ounce) envelopes taco
  seasoning mix
1 (1-ounce) envelope ranch salad
  dressing mix

Brown the ground beef in a skillet, stirring until crumbly; drain.

Combine the browned beef, undrained ranch-style beans, undrained pinto beans, undrained kidney beans, corn, undrained tomatoes, onion and celery in a slow cooker and mix well. Stir in the taco seasoning mix and salad dressing mix. Cook, covered, on low for 8 hours. Serves 10.

Tucson Treasures

Dinah's Tortilla Soup

2 tablespoons butter
1 small onion, chopped
1 clove garlic, diced
1 cup water
1 can cream of chicken soup
1 can Swanson's chicken broth
1 can Swanson's beef broth
1 teaspoon chili powder
1 teaspoon cumin
2 tablespoons Worcestershire
  sauce
½ small can mild green chiles
1–2 cups cooked, diced chicken
2 cups (16 ounces) Velveeta cheese
  (do not use generic)
6 corn tortillas, cut into ½x2-inch
  strips

Sauté onion and garlic in butter. Add next 9 ingredients. Blend together and simmer 1 hour. Stir in cheese and tortilla strips. Cook 10 minutes longer. Makes 6 servings.

Vistoso Vittles II

Tortilla Soup with Chicken and Lime

4 (5 to 6-inch) corn tortillas
2 teaspoons olive oil
2 (14½-ounce) cans low-salt chicken broth
2 cups water
¾ cup canned Mexican-style stewed tomatoes with juices
1 bay leaf
1 garlic clove, minced
¼ teaspoon ground cumin
⅛ teaspoon dried crushed red pepper
12 ounces precooked shredded chicken
2 green onions, sliced
¼ cup chopped fresh cilantro
2 tablespoons fresh lime juice
Salt and pepper

Preheat oven to 350°. Brush 1 side of tortillas with oil, cut in half. Stack halves and cut crosswise into ⅓-inch wide strips. Spread strips on nonstick baking sheet. Bake until light golden, about 15 minutes. Cool on baking sheet. Combine broth, water, tomatoes, bay leaf, garlic, cumin and red pepper in saucepan, bring to boil. Reduce heat, simmer 5 minutes. Add chicken, simmer 5 minutes. Stir in green onions, cilantro and lime juice. Season with salt and pepper. Ladle soup into bowls. Sprinkle with tortillas and serve. Makes 4 servings.

Favorite Recipes from the Foothills of Carefree, Arizona

Hamburger Soup

This is very low calorie. Enjoy!

2 pounds lean ground chuck or turkey
2 (46-ounce) cans tomato juice
1 can stewed tomatoes
2 cups (2 stalks) chopped celery
1 cup (5–6 medium) carrots, grated
2 cups green beans (frozen or canned, drained)
2 cups (½ head) sliced cabbage
2 bay leaves
1 tablespoon garlic powder
2 teaspoons ground basil
2 teaspoons ground oregano
2 teaspoons onion flakes
1 tablespoon Worcestershire sauce
1 (8-ounce) can mushrooms, drained

Brown ground chuck or turkey; drain well and combine with remaining ingredients. Bring to boil, lower heat and simmer 2–4 hours.

Note: Entire pot has only 1724 calories made with beef and 824 calories with turkey.

Heavenly Delights

Albondigas Soup
(Mexican Meatball Soup)

MEATBALLS:

4 pounds ground beef
4 ripe tomatoes, smashed
½ cup cilantro, chopped
1 large onion, finely chopped
2 eggs
1½ teaspoons oregano

1½ teaspoons garlic salt
1 teaspoon onion salt
1 cup salsa
2 teaspoons salt
1 teaspoon pepper

Mix all ingredients together well and form into meatballs.

SOUP STOCK:

4–5 quarts beef broth
1 or 2 bouillon cubes
1 large onion, chopped
3 ripe tomatoes, chopped
1 tablespoon cumin
1 teaspoon oregano
1 teaspoon onion salt

1½ teaspoons garlic salt
1½ cups salsa
3 teaspoons salt
1 teaspoon pepper
½–1 cup rice
1 cup cilantro, chopped

Mix all ingredients together in a large soup kettle. Bring to a rolling boil.
Add meatballs. After soup returns to a boil, turn down to low heat.
Simmer for 2 hours.

Par Excellence

Rattlesnake Chili

No, there is no rattlesnake meat in this. It was named for the type of bean I used—rattlesnake beans—the first time I made this. Pintos, kidneys, black turtles, Anasazis, and teparies also work well.

3 cups cooked beans
1 onion, chopped
1 sweet red or green bell pepper, chopped
2 ears of corn, cut from the cob, or 1 (10-ounce) package frozen corn
3 tomatoes, chopped
1 (6-ounce) can tomato sauce
3–4 cloves garlic, minced
2 mild or hot chiles, roasted, peeled, and minced

2 tablespoons chili powder
1 tablespoon cumin powder
1 teaspoon epazote*
2 tablespoons minced fresh cilantro
Pinch of ground cloves
Salt or vegetable seasoning, to taste
1 bottle beer (optional)
Juice of 1 lime

Mix all the ingredients together in a large pot (or crockpot), and cook about an hour or longer—the longer the better. Serve with cornbread or tortillas, and perhaps a little grated low-fat dairy or soy cheese. Enjoy! Yields 8 servings.

Variations: Add chopped zucchini or yellow squash, chopped cooked potatoes, or mushrooms. For something deliciously different, try serving this over a baked potato.

*Epazote: An herb native to Mexico commonly used in long-simmering dishes.

Per serving: Calories 149; Protein 6g; Fat 0g; Carbohydrates 30g

Flavors of the Southwest

Bisbee is a colorful Victorian town, both in history and in hue. This Old West mining camp of the 1880s proved to be one of the richest mineral sites in the world. By 1900, Bisbee was the largest, most cultured city between St. Louis and San Francisco. The historic downtown has changed little since the early 1900s.

Yavapai Vegetarian Chili

2 large eggplants, peeled and
diced
1½ tablespoons kosher salt
¾ cup olive oil
1 large onion, diced
2 tablespoons minced garlic
2 large green bell peppers, seeded
and diced
2 pounds canned tomatoes,
including juice
1½ pounds fresh tomatoes, diced
2 tablespoons chili powder
1 tablespoon dried oregano

1 tablespoon dried basil
1 tablespoon freshly ground black
pepper
½ cup fennel seed
½ cup chopped fresh parsley
1 cup Anasazi beans (soaked
overnight)
1 cup garbanzo beans (if fresh,
soaked overnight; if canned,
drained)
¼ cup fresh dill (or 2 tablespoons
plus 2 teaspoons dried)
2 tablespoons lemon juice

Place diced eggplant in perforated pan and sprinkle with the kosher salt.
Let stand 1 hour and pat dry. Preheat olive oil in a large stock pot and
kettle. Add the eggplant, onion, garlic and green bell peppers. Sauté
until tender. Add remaining ingredients and cook over medium heat for
40 minutes. Stir occasionally while cooking. Beans should be tender.
Serves 8.

Enchantment Resort, Sedona, Arizona / ***Vegetarian Southwest***

Chief's Cabbage Chili

1 pound extra-lean ground beef
1 medium onion, sliced
1 cup shredded cabbage
½ cup diced celery
2 cups water

1 (16-ounce) can kidney beans
1 cup diced canned tomatoes
1 teaspoon salt
Dash of pepper
1 teaspoon chili powder

Brown ground beef, then add onions, cabbage and celery. Cook until vegetables are tender. Add water and simmer for 15 minutes. Add beans, tomatoes and spices. Continue cooking for 15–20 minutes. Serve with cornbread or fritters. Serves 4–6.

Cooking with Cops

Chandler Chili

Chili is the most popular stew served in the United States. This Arizona version has a true Southwestern flavor.

1 large onion, chopped
2 cloves garlic, minced
3 tablespoons olive oil
1 pound ground round
½ teaspoon ground oregano

½ teaspoon ground cumin
2 tablespoons red chili powder
2 cups crushed tomatoes
1 tablespoon chopped parsley
1 cup water

Sauté onion and garlic in olive oil in heavy pot or Dutch oven until onion is soft. Stir in ground meat and brown it. Add oregano, cumin, chili powder, crushed tomatoes, parsley and water and cook for 2 hours over low heat. Add more water, if necessary. Serves 4–6.

Variations: Use cubed beef instead of ground beef; add ½ teaspoon nutmeg; add ¼ cup red wine; add jalapeños or jalapeño juice; add drained, cooked pinto beans; and/or, add 1 wedge of Mexican Ibarra Chocolate.

Christmas in Arizona Cook Book

Marshall Trimble's Cowboy Chili

5 pounds javelina, elk, deer, goat meat, or beef, cut into ½-inch cubes
2 cups hot water
½ pound green chiles, peeled and diced

2 tablespoons red chili powder
2 cloves garlic, chopped
1 teaspoon oregano
1 tablespoon cayenne pepper
2 large onions, chopped
1 horseshoe, cleaned

Combine meat, water, chiles, chili powder, garlic, oregano, cayenne pepper and onion in large cooking pot and bring to boil. Lower heat and simmer for 1 hour. Drop in horseshoe. If horseshoe sinks, simmer for another hour or until horseshoe rises to the top. If using javelina, this is ready to eat when horseshoe is tender enough to cut (joke!) Skim off the grease, and serve. Serves 10.

Recipe by humorist/historian Marshall Trimble.
The Arizona Celebrity Cookbook

Chili Casserole

1 large bag corn chips
½ head iceberg lettuce
1 can chili with beans

1 can chili without beans
Longhorn cheese, grated
1 small can diced green chiles

Spread corn chips in the bottom of a 9x13-inch pan. Shred lettuce over corn chips. In a saucepan, heat the 2 cans of chili and pour over the corn chips and lettuce. Cover with grated cheese and chiles. Bake in oven at 400° until cheese melts. Serve hot.

Pioneer Family Recipes

Sonoran Chicken Chili

1 tablespoon olive oil
½ cup chopped shallots
3 cloves of garlic, minced
2 (14-ounce) cans chopped
tomatoes with garlic, oregano, and basil
1 (14-ounce) can whole tomatoes, chopped
1 (14-ounce) can no-salt-added chicken broth
1 (4-ounce) can chopped green chiles

½ teaspoon oregano
½ teaspoon coriander
¼ teaspoon cumin
4 cups chopped cooked chicken
1 or 2 (16-ounce) cans white beans, drained
3 tablespoons freshly squeezed lime juice
¼ teaspoon pepper

Heat the olive oil in a large saucepan over medium-high heat. Add the shallots and garlic. Sauté until the shallots are soft. Add the seasoned tomatoes, undrained chopped tomatoes, broth, green chiles, oregano, coriander and cumin. Bring to a boil. Reduce the heat. Simmer for 20 minutes. Add the chicken and beans; mix well. Cook until heated through. Add the lime juice and pepper; mix well. Garnish with shredded Cheddar cheese. Serves 8.

Reflections Under the Sun

White Chili

A Dutch oven delight. This can also be made in a large electric cooker and toted to picnics and ballgames.

1 onion, chopped
1 clove garlic, minced
1 teaspoon cumin
1 tablespoon corn oil
2 large whole chicken breasts, skinned and cooked
1 (15-ounce) can garbanzo beans, drained
1 (15-ounce) can white beans, drained

1 (12-ounce) can white corn, drained
2 (4-ounce) cans chopped green chiles
2 chicken bouillon cubes
1½ cups boiling water
1 cup shredded Monterey Jack cheese

In Dutch oven, medium hot, cook onion, garlic, and cumin in hot oil. Mince or chop chicken breasts, and when garlic and onion are tender, stir in chicken, then add beans, corn, and chiles. Stir to blend. Combine chicken bouillon with 1½ cups boiling water, and stir through chili. Cover and let chili cook over low coals or heat, or in ashes, until flavors blend—about 30 minutes. Stir with wooden spoon, as both beans and corn have tendency to scorch or stick if heat is too high. Just before serving, sprinkle cheese over top. Return cover for a few minutes. Serve with red or green salsa or sauce, but there goes the White Chili. Serves 6 with tortillas and salad.

Outdoor Cooking

Three Sisters Stew with Corn Dumplings

Traditionally, Native Americans grow corn, squash, and beans—the Three Sisters— together in mounds as garden companions. The beans and squash actually replace nutrients in the soil that the corn depletes, while the corn stalk acts as a natural trellis for the bean vine.

½ cup dried Anasazi beans or
   pinto beans
½ cup dried lima beans
½ cup dried white beans
½ cup dried black beans
1 tablespoon olive oil
1½ cups finely chopped yellow
   onion
1½ cups finely chopped green
   bell pepper
2 tablespoons finely chopped garlic
1 jalapeño chile, stemmed,
   seeded, and finely chopped

2 teaspoons cumin seed
⅛ teaspoon cayenne pepper
2 teaspoons chile powder
1 (28-ounce) can peeled tomatoes,
   with juice
3 quarts water
3 ears corn (about 3 cups corn
   kernels)
½ cup beer
2 cups diced zucchini, yellow
   squash, and/or other summer
   squash
Salt and pepper

Place the beans in a large saucepan or Dutch oven. Cover with water by 2 inches and soak 2 hours or overnight. Drain and set aside.

Heat olive oil in large saucepan or Dutch oven over medium-high heat; sauté the onion, bell pepper, garlic and jalapeño until soft, about 5 minutes. In a dry small skillet, toast the cumin seed until aromatic and lightly browned; grind in a mini food processor or coffee spice grinder, and add to the onion mixture. In the same skillet, toast cayenne and chile powder for just 1 or 2 minutes, being careful not to burn; add to the onion mixture. Add the tomatoes to the onion mixture and simmer for 15 minutes. Add water and drained beans to pan and bring to boil. Reduce heat and simmer until beans are tender, about 1½–2 hours. Cut corn kernels off cob. Add beer, corn kernels and squash and cook until squash is tender, about 10 minutes. Add salt and pepper to taste.

DUMPLINGS:
½ cup yellow cornmeal
½ cup all-purpose flour
2 teaspoons baking powder
½ teaspoon salt
½ teaspoon sugar
1 egg

⅓ cup milk
1 tablespoon unsalted butter,
   melted
½ cup cooked fresh, thawed
   frozen, or drained canned corn
   kernels

(continued)

(continued)

In a bowl, stir together cornmeal, flour, baking powder, salt and sugar. In another bowl or glass measuring cup, whisk together egg, milk and butter. Add the liquid mixture to the dry and mix just until incorporated; fold in the corn. Drop the batter by heaping tablespoons into slowly simmering stew (there should be about 16 dumplings). Cover and cook until a wooden toothpick inserted into centers of dumplings comes out clean, about 15 minutes.

Spoon the stew into bowls and top each serving with 2 dumplings. Serve immediately. Serves 8.

Note: You don't have to soak beans overnight. To quick-soak; pick and sort the beans, then cover with cold water. Bring to a boil, cover the pot, and remove it from the heat. Let sit 1 hour. Drain off soaking liquid and fill pot with fresh water. Cook as directed.

*Recipe by chef Loretta Barrett Oden / **Savor the Southwest***

Blue Corn Dumplings

1 cup blue corn flour
2 teaspoons baking powder
1 teaspoon salt

1 teaspoon bacon drippings, lard, or
  other shortening
⅓–½ cup milk

Mix (or sift) dry ingredients thoroughly in a mixing bowl. Cut in shortening and add enough milk to make a drop batter. Drop by spoonfuls on top of simmering stew. Cover kettle and steam dumplings for 15 minutes. Stew should be kept bubbling. Serves 4–6.

Hopi Cookery

Indians once used shaped stone bowls to grind corn. These bowls are called metate (ma-tah-tay) and can be seen in ruins all across the Southwest.

1890 State House Stew

2 pounds fresh beef stew meat,
  cut in chunks
Water
Salt and pepper
Oregano, sweet basil, and bay
  leaf

¼ cup flour
Paprika
Shortening or oil
6–8 carrots, peeled and cut
2 onions, quartered
6 potatoes, peeled and quartered

Bring beef to a boil in water to cover in heavy pot. Remove any resulting scum, then season to taste with salt, pepper, oregano, sweet basil and bay leaf. Cover and simmer until tender. Remove meat and bay leaf. Set beef aside. Season flour with salt, pepper and paprika to taste. Add vegetables to broth and cook. Roll drained meat in seasoned flour. Brown on all sides in small amount of hot shortening. This is the secret to State House Stew's popularity: browned, seasoned, tender meat with juicy vegetables. Strain broth through several layers of cheesecloth. Place meat on platter and vegetables in bowl with juice. Serve with hot biscuits, well coated with melted butter before baking to ensure golden crust firm enough to sop up juices without sogging. Secret number two: those butter-crunch biscuits.

Arizona Highways Heritage Cookbook

Chuckwagon Beef Stew

This is a hearty cross between soup and stew. Depending on accompaniments, it can be lunch or a light dinner.

10 cups water
1 chicken bouillon packet
1 beef bouillon packet
3 cups tomato sauce
1 pound top sirloin, cut into 1-inch
  cubes
1½ cups diced celery
1½ cups diced onion
1½ cups diced potatoes

1½ cups diced carrots
2 or 3 garlic cloves, minced
1½ cups diced tomatoes
1½ cups diced yellow squash
1½ cups diced green beans
1½ cups sliced mushrooms
1 tablespoon salt
1 teaspoon black pepper

In a large stockpot combine water, bouillon and tomato sauce. Add beef, celery, onions, potatoes, carrots and garlic. Bring to a boil, lower heat, and simmer 1 hour. Add tomatoes, squash, beans, mushrooms, salt and pepper, and simmer an additional 30 minutes.

Contributed by Rawhide Western Town and Steakhouse, Scottsdale
Arizona Chefs: Cooking at Home with 36 Arizona Chefs

Pueblo Stew

1 large onion, chopped
2 cloves garlic, minced
1½ tablespoons chili powder
2 teaspoons cumin seed
1 teaspoon dry oregano
2 tablespoons olive oil
1 each zucchini, pattypan, and
    crooked neck squash, cut into
    1-inch chunks
1 (12-ounce) container tofu,
    cubed
1 (14-ounce) can golden hominy,
    drained

1 pound tomatoes, chopped
¼ pound green beans, cut into
    1-inch lengths
2 cans or 2 pounds cooked pinto
    beans
4 bouillon cubes
2 cups water
1 tablespoon cilantro
Garnish: Monterey Jack cheese
    and sour cream

In a 4–5 quart pan, cook onion, garlic, and spices in oil until onion starts to brown. Add squash, tofu, hominy, and tomatoes and cook about 5 minutes. Add green and pinto beans, bouillon and water. Simmer uncovered about 30 minutes, until tender and until consistency is that of thick stew. Add minced cilantro and ladle into bowls. Garnish with cilantro, sour cream, and shredded Jack cheese. Serve with warm tortillas.

Portal's Best Little Cookbook

Pony Express Stew

3½ tablespoons all-purpose
  flour
3½ teaspoons chili powder, divided
1 tablespoon paprika
1 teaspoon salt
3 pounds beef, cubed
4 tablespoons cooking oil
2 onions, sliced

1 clove garlic, minced
2 (28-ounce) cans tomatoes
1 tablespoon cinnamon
1 tablespoon ground cloves
1 red pepper, sliced
2 cups potatoes, sliced
2 cups carrots, sliced

Mix flour, 1 teaspoon chili powder, paprika and salt. Coat beef in mixture. Brown beef in hot oil in Dutch oven. Add onions and garlic and cook until soft. Add tomatoes, remaining 2½ teaspoons chili powder, cinnamon, cloves and red pepper. Cover and simmer 2 hours. Add potatoes and carrots, and cook until done, about 45 minutes. Serves 6.

Cowboy Cookin'

Cazuela
(Stewed Jerky)

All Mexican housewives have two stones to pound the jerky. Usually these are selected from stream beds. Both must be smooth. One is round or oval and about fist size for pounding. The other is larger and heavier with a flat top on which to place the jerky to be pounded.

2 pounds beef jerky
2 medium potatoes
¼ cup chopped green onions
½ cup chopped green chiles
1 cup chopped fresh tomatoes
⅓ cup chopped cilantro

2 teaspoons lard
1 clove garlic, minced
1 teaspoon oregano
1 teaspoon flour
8 cups water
Salt to taste

Soak jerky in water for 15 minutes. Pound jerky to separate fiber and to fluff meat. Peel and dice potatoes in 1-inch cubes. Fry onions, chiles, tomatoes and cilantro slowly in lard. Add beef, garlic, oregano and flour. Add water and salt. Bring to a boil and simmer about 20 minutes. Serves 6–8.

Arizona Territory Cook Book

Salads

The Barringer Meteorite Crater is a gigantic hole in the middle of the arid sandstone of the Arizona desert. A rim rises 150 feet above the level of the surrounding plain. The crater itself is nearly a mile wide and 570 feet deep.

Tossed Fajita Salad

EACH SALAD:

3–4 ounces beef loin, thinly
  sliced
1 teaspoon vegetable oil
Salt and freshly ground pepper
¼ cup green bell pepper, cut in
  thin strips
¼ cup red bell pepper, cut in thin
  strips
¼ cup yellow bell pepper, cut in
  thin strips

1–2 green onions, sliced (with some
  green tops)
⅓ cup sliced and drained water
  chestnuts
Dressing
About a handful (maybe more)
  romaine lettuce
Salt and freshly ground pepper
Crisped tortilla strips

To prepare meat, remove fat from beef loin and cut it into narrow 2 to 2½-inch strips. Use a heavy skillet to heat oil and stir-fry meat strips 1 or 2 minutes, just long enough for redness to disappear. Season with salt and pepper to taste. Remove to covered storage container.

Add prepared bell peppers, onions and water chestnuts to meat strips. Toss with sufficient amount of Dressing to match individual taste and enough to slightly marinate salad ingredients. Chill at least 15 minutes but no longer than 30 minutes before serving. When ready to eat, break romaine into bite-size pieces and toss with other ingredients, including tortilla strips. Season to taste and present on chilled plate or in shallow bowl.

DRESSING:

½ cup light salad oil (such as
  imported sunflower)
2 teaspoons white wine

3 tablespoons Oriental seasoned
  (sweet) rice vinegar

Make dressing by mixing all ingredients with a whisk to thoroughly blend. (It will keep indefinitely when refrigerated.) Makes ¾ cup.

Gourmet Gringo

Taco Salad

1 pound ground round
½ envelope dry onion soup mix
⅓ (7-ounce) can green chile salsa
⅛ teaspoon garlic salt
¾ cup water
1 small head lettuce, finely cut

1 large tomato, cut into wedges
1 thinly sliced onion
½ cup thinly sliced green pepper
1 cup shredded sharp Cheddar
   cheese
1 (6-ounce) package tortilla chips

Brown ground meat. Sprinkle onion mix, chile salsa and garlic salt over meat and add water. Simmer 10 minutes and drain. Arrange lettuce in bowl or on platter. Place tomato wedges, onion rings and green pepper on lettuce. Spoon meat into center of lettuce. Sprinkle cheese over salad and top with tortilla chips. Serves 6.

Pioneer Family Recipes

African Tuna Salad

½ cup fresh squeezed lemon
   juice
2 tablespoons soy or canola oil
1 teaspoon granulated garlic
2 small cans albacore tuna, drained
   (leave chunky)

¼ cup sliced black olives
⅛ cup shredded coconut
4 green onions, thinly sliced
½ red bell pepper, diced

Combine liquid ingredients and garlic. Toss in remaining ingredients. Serves 2.

Recipe from Delectables Restaurant / ***Tucson Cooks!***

Old Tucson Studios is known as "Hollywood in the Desert." More than 200 movies, TV shows, commercials and documentaries have been filmed there since it was built as a set for the movie *Arizona* in 1939.

Southwestern Shrimp Caesar

Toasted olive bread is the ideal accompaniment to this hearty and flavorful salad.

SALAD:

20 (16/20-size) shrimp, peeled and deveined
Shrimp Marinade
2 tablespoons olive oil
Caesar Dressing
3 hearts of romaine lettuce, cores removed, washed in cold water and torn into 1½-inch pieces

1 cup fresh corn kernels
2 medium tomatoes, cut in ½-inch cubes
½ cup grated Parmesan cheese,

SHRIMP MARINADE:

¼ cup olive oil
2 tablespoons soy sauce
2 tablespoons fresh oregano, chopped

2 tablespoons basil, chopped
1 tablespoon garlic, chopped

CAESAR DRESSING:

1 cup mayonnaise
¼ cup lemon juice
3 tablespoons soy sauce
2 tablespoons Parmesan cheese, grated

2 teaspoons brown sugar
½ teaspoon cayenne pepper

In medium bowl, combine marinade ingredients with shrimp, tossing well. Cover and refrigerate ½ hour, mixing occasionally. Sauté shrimp in 2 table-spoons oil over medium heat until just pink and firm (do not overcook). Set aside. Mix Caesar Dressing ingredients together.

ASSEMBLY:

In deep bowl, toss romaine, corn, tomatoes, and dressing to taste. Divide between 4 chilled plates, topping each with 4 or 5 sautéed shrimp. Garnish with grated Parmesan.

Contributed by Squash Blossom, Scottsdale
Arizona Chefs: Dine-In Dine-Out Cookbook

Shrimp and Napa Cabbage Salad with Roasted Peanuts

DRESSING:

½ cup rice wine
⅓ cup peanut oil

2 tablespoons chile oil
2 tablespoons sugar

In mixing bowl, whisk together all ingredients.

SALAD:

1 head Napa cabbage, cleaned and sliced crosswise in thin ribbons
1 large carrot, peeled and thinly julienned
1 cup cilantro leaves
¼ pound pancetta (Italian bacon, available at Italian delis and specialty stores), fried crisp and crumbled

1 pound shrimp, peeled, deveined, and cooked
Dressing to taste
½ cup roasted peanuts

Toss cabbage, carrot, cilantro, bacon, shrimp and dressing together about 20 minutes before serving. Garnish with peanuts.

Contributed by Kingfisher, Tucson
Arizona Chefs: Cooking at Home with 36 Arizona Chefs

Margarita Shrimp Salad

Every amateur mixologist in the Southwest claims to know the secret to the perfect margarita, the region's popular cocktail made with tequila, triple sec, and lime juice. Test their margarita IQ with this spirited shrimp salad to see if they can identify the basics in the dressing. It's a dynamite first course or centerpiece of a summer dinner.

SHRIMP:

2 tablespoons chopped cilantro
2 cloves garlic, minced
1 serrano chile, stemmed, seeded, and finely diced
⅓ cup tequila
2 tablespoons triple sec or Grand Marnier
¼ cup freshly squeezed lime juice

1 teaspoon ground cumin
1 pound shrimp (16-20 per pound), peeled, deveined, and slit open along the backs
¼ cup olive oil
Salt and freshly ground black pepper to taste

Combine the cilantro, garlic, chile, tequila, triple sec, lime juice and cumin seed in a nonreactive bowl. Add the shrimp, turn to coat, and refrigerate for at least 1 hour. Drain the shrimp and reserve the marinade.

In a small saucepan over high heat, bring the reserved marinade to a boil. Reduce the heat to medium and simmer until reduced by half. Remove from the heat, transfer to a bowl, and let cool. Whisk in the olive oil and season with salt and pepper to taste. Set aside.

Prepare a barbecue grill or preheat a broiler. Grill or broil the shrimp until just pink, about 1 minute per side. Keep warm.

SALAD:

Vegetable oil for frying tortillas
4 corn tortillas, 6 inches in diameter, cut into julienne
1 teaspoon chili powder
1 tomato, cored, seeded, and diced

1 yellow bell pepper, cored, seeded, and diced
6 cups torn romaine lettuce leaves, washed and thoroughly dried

Fill a small skillet with oil to a depth of about 1 inch and place over medium heat. When oil is about 375°, fry the tortilla strips in batches until light brown and crisp. Drain on paper towels. Sprinkle with chili powder while still warm.

In a large bowl, mix together the tomato, bell pepper and lettuce. Toss with the marinade/oil dressing and divide among 4 large plates or shallow bowls. Top the salad with grilled shrimp and fried tortilla strips. Serve immediately. Serves 4.

Savor the Southwest

My Favorite Chicken Salad

6 large chicken breasts
1 large carrot, sliced
1 small onion, chopped
1 stalk celery, chopped
½ teaspoon dill
1 teaspoon salt
½ teaspoon pepper
½ teaspoon basil
1 cup blanched almonds
2 tablespoons butter

1 cup chopped celery
1 cup green grapes, seeded and halved
⅓ bottle capers
3 eggs, hard-boiled and chopped
12 olives, slivered
2 cups mayonnaise
2 tablespoons cream
Salt and pepper to taste

Boil chicken breasts with carrot, onion, celery, dill, salt, pepper and basil. Then allow to simmer until chicken is tender. Leave chicken in broth overnight. Brown almonds in butter. Debone and skin chicken; cut in generous size squares and add chopped celery, grapes, almonds, capers, eggs and olives. Blend mayonnaise with cream. Add salt and pepper to taste. Mix lightly with chicken mixture and serve on lettuce leaves.

Par Excellence

Margarita Chicken Pasta Salad

DRESSING:

¼ cup olive oil or vegetable oil
¼ cup sour cream
3 tablespoons fresh lime juice
1 (4.5-ounce) can green chiles,
  chopped

½ cup fresh orange juice
2 teaspoons sugar
1 teaspoon cumin
⅛ teaspoon salt
3 teaspoons tequila (if desired)

In blender container, combine dressing ingredients. Blend 30 seconds or until well blended.

4 cups uncooked rainbow rotini
  (spiral pasta)
1 pound skinned, boned chicken,
  cut in strips or pieces for frying
1 (1.25-ounce) package taco
  seasoning mix

1 tablespoon olive oil
1 (11-ounce) can Mexicorn,
  drained
1 (15-ounce) can black beans,
  drained and rinsed

Cook pasta as directed on package. Drain and rinse in cold water. In resealable food storage plastic bag, combine chicken and taco seasoning mix; shake to coat. In large nonstick skillet, heat 1 tablespoon oil over medium-hot heat. Add chicken; cook and stir 8–10 minutes or until golden brown and no longer pink. Remove from heat. In large serving bowl, combine cooked rotini, corn, beans and dressing. Toss to coat. Fold in cooked chicken. Serve warm or cold. Makes 8 servings.

Kingman Welcome Wagon Club Cookbook

How big is the Grand Canyon? Counted in river miles it is 277 miles long. The width is as much as 18 miles and the deepest point is 6000 vertical feet from rim to river. A trip to the bottom of the Canyon and back (on foot or by mule) is a two-day journey. Rim-to-rim hikers generally take three days one-way to get from the North Rim to the South Rim. A trip through Grand Canyon by raft can take two weeks or longer.

Chicken-Rice Salad with Artichokes

MARINADE:

½ teaspoon celery seed
1 clove garlic, minced
1 scallion, finely chopped
¼ teaspoon sugar
1 tablespoon freshly snipped
  parsley
¼ cup red wine vinegar
⅓ cup olive oil

2 (6-ounce) jars marinated
  artichoke hearts, sliced
1 (4-ounce) jar pimentos,
  chopped
2 celery stalks, thinly sliced
1 small green bell pepper,
  chopped

In medium bowl, combine celery seed, garlic, scallion, sugar, parsley, vinegar and oil. Blend well. Add artichokes (including marinade), pimentos, celery and green bell pepper. Coat well and marinate overnight.

SALAD:

2 (6-ounce) packages long-grain
  and wild rice
4 whole chicken breasts, cooked
  and diced

1 cup mayonnaise
1 pound mushrooms, sliced
1 head iceberg lettuce

Using ½ cup less water for each package, cook rice according to package directions. Combine rice, chicken, and mayonnaise. Add sliced mushrooms and Marinade. Stir and chill. Serve on lettuce cups. Serves 8–10.

Purple Sage and Other Pleasures

Wild Rice Salad

1 cup wild rice
3 cups chicken broth
1 (6-ounce) jar marinated artichoke
  hearts, quartered
15 pimento-stuffed olives, sliced

4 green onions, sliced
½ cup mayonnaise
1½ teaspoons curry powder
¼ cup chopped parsley

Cook wild rice in chicken broth in covered dish at 325° for 1½ hours. In mixing bowl, combine cooked rice, artichoke hearts, olives and onions. In small bowl, mix mayo, curry powder, and parsley. Stir into rice. Cover and refrigerate. You can add 3 cooked and diced chicken breasts to make this a main dish. Add to salad with vegetables. Serves 8–10.

Tostitos Fiesta Bowl Cookbook

Crystal Creek Crunchy Green Pea Salad

1 (10-ounce) package frozen peas, thawed
1 cup celery, sliced
1 cup cauliflower, chopped
¼ cup diced green onions
2 tablespoons pimento, sliced
1 cup roasted cashews

¼ cup bacon, cooked and crumbled
½ cup sour cream
1 cup ranch dressing
½ teaspoon Dijon mustard
1 small clove garlic, minced

Drain peas; combine vegetables, nuts and bacon with sour cream. Mix dressing, mustard, and garlic together. Pour over salad and toss gently. Serves 4.

Cowboy Cookin'

Roasted Pepper and Celery Salad with Tomato Vinaigrette

2 tablespoons olive oil
½ cup diced plum tomatoes
2 tablespoons tomato purée
¼ cup sherry vinegar
¼ cup raisins or currants, soaked in hot water until plump, drained

Salt and freshly ground black pepper to taste
3 large roasted red peppers, cut into ½-inch strips
6 ribs celery, strings removed, sliced thin on the diagonal

Mix oil, tomatoes, tomato purée, vinegar, and raisins in a bowl and mix together. Add salt and pepper to taste. Adjust sweet and sour ratio. If too tart, add a pinch of sugar. You may want a bit more vinegar or a squeeze of lemon juice. Toss the peppers and celery with the vinaigrette. Serves 6.

Variations: 2 large bulbs fennel, halved, cored, and sliced thin, can be substituted for the celery.

Cal 85; %Fat 51; Fat 5g; Sat Fat 0.7g; Chol 0mg; Sod 60mg; Carbo 11g; Prot 1g; Fiber 1g. Exchanges: Fruit ½, Vegetable 1, Fat 1

Arizona Heart Institute Foundation Cookbook

Green Beans and Walnuts in Basil Vinaigrette

1½ pounds crisp young green
  beans, trimmed
Basil Vinaigrette

2 green onions, thinly sliced
¼ cup chopped walnuts

Bring enough water to cover beans to a boil in saucepan. Add beans. Cook just until tender-crisp; do not overcook. Rinse in ice water and drain. Add Basil Vinaigrette; toss to mix well. Spoon into serving bowl lined with curly lettuce. Top with green onions and walnuts. Yields 6 servings.

BASIL VINAIGRETTE:

1 teaspoon pressed garlic
15 basil leaves
½ teaspoon salt
½ teaspoon freshly ground
  pepper

2 teaspoons Dijon mustard
¼ cup wine vinegar
½ cup olive oil

Combine garlic, basil, salt and pepper in blender container; process for 1 second. Add mustard and vinegar; process until smooth. Add olive oil in thin stream, processing constantly until smooth. Yields 1 cup.

Heard in the Kitchen

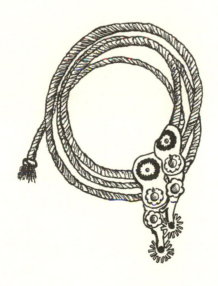

White Bean and Sun-Dried Tomato Salad

When you think of beans and Southwestern cuisine, you generally think of pinto or kidney beans, but white beans are often used for a different flavor. I developed this recipe from a dish I was served in Southern California. For a light summer meal, just serve this cold bean salad with a little cornbread and some steamed greens. Yum!

4 cups cooked navy or Great Northern beans
1 cup chopped hydrated sun-dried tomatoes
½ cup diagonally sliced shallots or scallions
¼ cup minced fresh cilantro
¼ cup olive oil
1 tablespoon balsamic vinegar
Freshly ground black pepper, to taste
Dash of tamari (optional)

Mix all the ingredients together and refrigerate to let all the flavors develop. Serve and enjoy! Yields 6 servings.

Variations: Substitute black or kidney beans (or a combination of beans), and use some chopped fresh basil in place of the cilantro. Add a clove or two of minced garlic.

Per serving: Calories 279; Protein 10g; Fat 9g; Carbohydrates 38g

Flavors of the Southwest

Colorful Black Bean Salad

2 (15-ounce) cans black beans,
    drained, rinsed
1 (11-ounce) can corn kernels,
    drained
1 medium red bell pepper,
    chopped
1 bunch green onions, chopped
¼ cup chopped red onion
3 cloves of garlic, minced

2 teaspoons chopped fresh basil
1½ teaspoons salt
1 teaspoon sugar
1 teaspoon pepper
⅓ cup red wine vinegar
¼ cup light olive oil
5–6 red or green bell peppers or
    tomatoes, halved, seeded

Combine the black beans, corn, red pepper, green onions, red onion, garlic and basil in a bowl; mix well. Combine the salt, sugar, pepper, wine vinegar and olive oil in a small bowl. Whisk until well mixed. Pour over the black bean mixture; toss to mix well. Spoon into the bell peppers or tomatoes. Serve immediately. Serves 10–12.

Reflections Under the Sun

Patio Potato Salad

⅓ cup Italian dressing
1 teaspoon instant minced
    onions
1 teaspoon salt
4 cups cubed cooked potatoes (about
    1½ pounds)

1½ cups cottage cheese
¾ cup chopped celery
1 hard-cooked egg, chopped
Tomato wedges

Combine dressing, onion and salt. Add to potatoes and toss lightly. Cover and chill to blend flavors. Add cottage cheese, celery and egg. Toss lightly. Garnish with tomato wedges.

Arizona Cook Book

The Sonoran Desert is the only place in the world where saguaro cactus grow. Saguaro National Park has the largest concentration of the cactus. The nation's largest national monument was established to protect the unique organ pipe cactus and its Sonoran Desert habitat. The monument supports over 30 other species of cactus as well as a multitude of wildlife.

Cornbread Salad

2 packages cornbread mix
10 slices bacon, cooked and
   crumbled
1 large onion, chopped

1 large bell pepper, chopped
2 medium tomatoes, chopped
1 cup mayonnaise
Salt and pepper to taste

Prepare cornbread according to directions on package. Cook and crumble.
Mix well with remaining ingredients and serve.

Tostitos Fiesta Bowl Cookbook

Chop Chop Salad

*With garlic toast and dessert, the perfect light but satisfying dinner for a warm
Arizona evening.*

DRESSING:
1 cup salad oil
¼ cup balsamic vinegar
⅛ cup sun dried tomatoes
⅛ cup fresh basil

1 teaspoon garlic, chopped
½ teaspoon sugar
Salt and pepper to taste

Blend all ingredients in food processor or blender.

2 cups mesclun salad mix (or
   your choice of lettuces)
½ pound salami, diced
½ pound mozzarella cheese,
   diced (reserve a few cubes)

4 canned artichoke hearts, diced
½ cup black olives, sliced
½ cup pepperocini, chopped
4 roma tomatoes, diced

Toss all ingredients with dressing to taste. Garnish with a few reserved
mozzarella cubes.

Contributed by Cafe Saguaro, Scottsdale
Arizona Chefs: Cooking at Home with 36 Arizona Chefs

Orange and Green Salad

DRESSING:

½ teaspoon salt

⅛ teaspoon freshly ground black
  pepper

¼ cup olive oil

2 tablespoons snipped fresh
  parsley

2 tablespoons sugar

2 tablespoons red wine vinegar

2–4 drops Tabasco sauce

Combine all dressing ingredients. Mix well. Cover and chill to allow flavors to blend while preparing remainder of ingredients.

GARNISH:

½ cup slivered almonds

3 tablespoons sugar

In a dry skillet, over medium heat, toast almonds and sugar lightly until sugar just melts. Set aside.

SALAD:

1 head iceberg lettuce

1 head romaine lettuce

2 celery stalks, thinly sliced

4 scallions, chopped

1 (11-ounce) can mandarin
  oranges, drained

To serve, tear greens into bite-size pieces and add celery, scallions and oranges. Pour dressing over greens. Toss well. Garnish with almonds. Serves 6.

Purple Sage and Other Pleasures

Pecan Praline Salad

Good served with baked or barbecued chicken.

¼ cup granulated sugar
½ cup pecan pieces
2 cups fresh spinach leaves
2 cups torn leaf lettuce
1 cup sliced mushrooms
1 green onion, thinly sliced
1 teaspoon dried tarragon leaves

3 tablespoons olive or salad oil
1 tablespoon white or red wine
   vinegar
¼–½ teaspoon salt
Freshly ground black pepper
1 (11-ounce) can mandarin
   oranges, drained

Put sugar into heavy skillet. Place on high heat. Stir until sugar melts and caramelizes. Add pecans; toss until nuts are coated. Turn onto buttered pieces of foil, separate nuts and let them cool.

Wash spinach and lettuce to remove all sand. Dry thoroughly. Place into salad bowl and top with mushrooms and onion. Sprinkle with tarragon leaves. Just before serving, drizzle oil evenly over leaves. Sprinkle with vinegar, salt and pepper. Toss, add mandarin oranges and top with caramelized pecans. Recipe may be halved or doubled.

Kids in the Kitchen

Jicama Strawberry Salad

1 pound spinach
1 head Bibb lettuce, torn
1 pint fresh strawberries, sliced

¼ cup chopped, toasted pecans
1 medium jicama, cut in julienne
   slices

Papaya, mango, and kiwi can be added, too.

DRESSING:
⅓ cup raspberry vinegar
⅓ cup sugar
1 tablespoon poppy seeds

2 teaspoons finely minced onion
¼ cup canola oil

Mix dressing. Add to salad ingredients. Mix together. Serve.

Vistoso Vittles II

Sedona Christmas Salad

This old-fashioned salad somehow seems right at home in the "new age" world of today's Sedona.

1 cup unpeeled and diced red apples	1 cup golden raisins
1 cup unpeeled and diced green apples	1 cup mayonnaise
1 cup pineapple chunks	½ cup dry white wine
½ cup diced celery	1 teaspoon crushed dried mint leaves
½ cup grated carrots	1 cup chopped pecans
	1 cup grated sharp Cheddar cheese

Place the fruits, vegetables and raisins in a salad bowl. Mix together mayonnaise, wine and mint leaves. Pour over the fruit mixture and toss lightly. Add pecans and cheese, and lightly toss again. Serves 6–8.

Christmas in Arizona Cook Book

Gazpacho Salad

2 envelopes plain gelatin	¼ cup green onions, sliced
2 cups tomato juice	1 small can pitted ripe olives
¼ cup red wine vinegar	1 cucumber, peeled, seeded, and diced
1 teaspoon salt	16 large butter lettuce leaves
2–3 drops Tabasco sauce	8 teaspoons non-fat mayonnaise
2 tomatoes, diced	
1 green pepper, diced	

Sprinkle gelatin over tomato juice to soften. Place over low heat and stir until dissolved. Remove from heat and stir in vinegar, salt, and Tabasco sauce. Cool until slightly thickened. Fold in tomatoes, green pepper, onions, olives, and cucumber. Place in sprayed or oiled ring mold. Chill several hours. Unmold on butter lettuce. Decorate with mayonnaise. Serves 8.

Bon Appétit

With a growing season of 300 days a year, the lush farmland around Phoenix is called The Valley of the Sun.

Delightful Orange Salad

2 small cans mandarin oranges
1 large can pineapple chunks
½ cup maraschino cherries
3 bananas, sliced
1 pint sour cream

1 medium-size Cool Whip
1 (3-ounce) package orange
  Jell-O
½ cup chopped nuts
2 cups miniature marshmallows

Drain fruits well. Mix sour cream, Cool Whip and dry Jell-O until blended. Fold in fruits, nuts and marshmallows. Chill in a 9x13-inch pan.

Heavenly Delights

Festive Prickly Pear Jellied Salad

2 envelopes unflavored gelatin
1 cup orange juice, divided
8–10 prickly pears
⅓ cup sugar
1 teaspoon salt

½ cup dry red wine
⅓ cup lemon juice
2 cups fresh fruit (grapes, diced
  orange sections, diced apples,
  diced pears, etc.)

Soften gelatin in ½ cup orange juice. Juice washed prickly pears in blender with about 1 cup water. Strain seeds, peel, and stickers through 3 layers of cheesecloth. Combine remaining orange juice and 1½ cups resulting prickly pear juice with the sugar and salt and heat almost to boiling. Add softened gelatin and stir to dissolve. Add wine and lemon juice. Chill until slightly thickened. Add the 2 cups fruit and pour into large ring mold sprayed with nonstick spray. Chill until set. Unmold on large round platter and garnish with salad greens and more fruit. Serve with sour cream or mayonnaise. Serves 8–10.

Fruits of the Desert Cookbook

Vegetables

At the base of sheer red cliffs in the canyon walls of Canyon de Chelly National Monument lies White House Ruins, a cliff dwelling built by native American Indians between 350 and 1300 A.D.

Calabacitas
(Sautéed Squash)

1 pound zucchini squash (or combined zucchini and summer squash), sliced lengthwise and cut into ½-inch pieces
½ onion, chopped
1 tablespoon olive oil

2 large tomatoes, diced
6 ounces green chiles
1 cup corn
Salt to taste
1 cup grated Cheddar cheese

Sauté squash and onions in oil, then add tomatoes, chiles and corn. Salt to taste. When squash is tender, add cheese and continue cooking until cheese melts.

Corazón Contento

Chile Cheese Squash

Squash was one of the earliest crops grown by the first inhabitants of the Sedona area.

1 pound squash (zucchini, summer or yellow), cut in ¼-inch pieces
½ cup mayonnaise (not salad dressing)

1 (4-ounce) can diced green chiles
½ cup Cheddar cheese, grated
½ cup bread crumbs

Cook squash until just tender. Drain well. Return to saucepan, stir in remaining ingredients. Serve hot. Serves 4.

Sedona Cook Book

Lynn's Squash and Cheese Bake

3 medium yellow squash, trimmed
   and sliced thin
6 tablespoons butter, divided
1 (10-ounce) package fresh
   spinach, washed and trimmed
2 cups cream-style cottage
   cheese

1½ cups coarsely crumbled Ritz
   crackers
¼ teaspoon oregano
¼ teaspoon basil
¼ teaspoon parsley
3 medium tomatoes, sliced
6 slices provolone cheese

Sauté squash slightly in 2 tablespoons butter. Remove from skillet and set aside. Repeat with spinach in 2 tablespoons butter. Mix cottage cheese, crackers and herbs in bowl. Spray 8x8-inch baking dish with cooking spray. Put squash in dish, layer ½ of cheese mixture over the squash, then spinach, and the remainder of the cheese mixture. Top with tomato slices. Place the provolone cheese slices in checkerboard fashion. Bake at 375° for 30 minutes. Serves 6.

Kids in the Kitchen

Yellow Squash Casserole

2 pounds squash (6 cups)
¼ cup chopped onion
1 can cream of chicken soup
1 cup sour cream

1 cup shredded carrots
1 (8-ounce) package herb-seasoned
   stuffing mix
½ cup margarine, melted

Cook squash and onion in salted boiling water for 5 minutes and drain. Combine soup and sour cream. Stir in carrots. Fold in squash and onion. Mix stuffing with margarine. Put half in baking dish. Put vegetable mixture over stuffing mixture. Cover with remainder of stuffing mixture. Bake at 350° for 25–30 minutes.

The Garden Patch

Stuffed Zucchini

8 medium (6-inch) zucchini
1 tablespoon salt dissolved in a
   large bowl of water
1 heaping cup ground lamb
1 cup short-grained white rice, well
   washed and drained
1½ teaspoons plus a pinch of salt

¼ teaspoon pepper
¾ teaspoon cinnamon
2 tablespoons butter, room
   temperature
1 (6-ounce) can tomato paste,
   divided
1 (16-ounce) can crushed tomatoes

Wash zucchini and cut off stalk ends. Hollow out interiors, taking care not to pierce sides or ends of squash. Place cored zucchini in salted water.

Combine lamb, rice, 1½ teaspoons salt, pepper, cinnamon, butter and a few spoonfuls of the tomato paste in a large bowl, mixing by hand.

Drain zucchini. Fill each one with lamb mixture, leaving ⅓ space free for expansion during cooking. Place stuffed zucchini in rows in a large pot. In a small bowl, mix tomatoes and remaining paste, and pour over squash. Add water to cover zucchini and sprinkle with a pinch of salt.

Place a plate upside down on top of stuffed zucchini. Cover with pot lid and cook on low heat about 1 hour or until rice is done. Serves 4.

Recipe by newscaster Hugh Downs, Scottsdale
The Arizona Celebrity Cookbook

Zucchini and Cheese Casserole

3 cups finely grated zucchini
1 cup cracker crumbs
1 cup grated Cheddar cheese
2 beaten eggs

2 tablespoons chopped onion
Salt
Pepper

Combine all ingredients and put in a well-buttered casserole. Bake at 350° for 1 hour.

St. Francis in the Foothills 30th Anniversary Cookbook

"Crab" Cakes

2 cups shredded zucchini
3 egg whites
2 tablespoons grated onion
1 tablespoon non-fat mayonnaise
4 tablespoons flour

1 cup seasoned bread crumbs
1 teaspoon Old Bay seasoning
¼ cup bread crumbs for
   dipping

Mix all ingredients except the ¼ cup bread crumbs together and form patties. Dip (or pat) in additional bread crumbs. Fry till brown on both sides in a sprayed nonstick pan. Makes 4–5 patties.

Bon Appétit

Hominy Casserole

2 large cans hominy (drain 1 can)
1 can diced green chiles
5 small green onions, chopped

1 medium carton sour cream
½ cup grated cheese

Mix together everything except grated cheese. Top with grated cheese and bake at 350° for 35 minutes.

Lion's Club of Globe Cookbook

Polenta and Pine Nut-Stuffed Red Peppers with Mole

4 cups water
1 tablespoon salt
2 teaspoons black pepper
1 tablespoon ground cumin
2 cups uncooked polenta
½ cup diced scallions
1 tablespoon chopped oregano
   (or 1½ teaspoons dried)
½ cup pine nuts, toasted
1 (4-ounce) can diced green chiles

1½ cups grated Monterey Jack
   cheese, divided
4 red bell peppers, tops removed
   and seeded
4–8 slices sweet onion (especially
   red, white, Vidalia, or Walla
   Wallas)
12 large zucchini, sliced
Vegetable oil to coat vegetables
Mole sauce

Bring water to boil, add salt, pepper, and cumin, then reduce heat and slowly add polenta, stirring constantly until all is added and water is absorbed. Remove from heat, stir in scallions, oregano, pine nuts, green chiles and 1 cup of the grated cheese.

Preheat oven to 350°. Fill red peppers with polenta mixture and place in a nonstick or oiled roasting pan. Bake for 20–25 minutes; remove and top with remaining cheese, then bake until cheese is melted. While peppers are baking, lightly oil onion and zucchini slices and grill. To serve, cover plate bottom with mole sauce, place one pepper in the center, and surround with grilled onions and zucchini. Serves 4.

Note: Prepared mole is available in many markets.

High Desert Inn, Bisbee, Arizona / **Vegetarian Southwest**

Incredibly Easy
Chile Rellenos

1 large (27-ounce) can green chile strips	12 eggs
1 pound sharp Cheddar cheese, cut in strips	½ teaspoon salt
	1½ cups milk

Wash chiles and remove seeds. Wrap chile strips around cheese strips. Place side by side in a shallow, 9x13-inch baking dish. Beat eggs with salt, then add milk and mix well. Pour over stuffed chiles. Bake 50–60 minutes in a 350° oven. Do not overbake, since it toughens the protein in both eggs and cheese. Serves 6–8.

Arizona Highways Heritage Cookbook

Chile Relleno Bake

½ pound hamburger	2 cups shredded Cheddar, divided
½ pound chorizo or pork sausage	4 eggs
1 cup chopped onion	¼ cup flour
2 cloves minced garlic	1½ cups milk
2 (4-ounce) cans whole green chiles	½ teaspoon salt
	Tabasco sauce

Brown beef and sausage. Add onion and garlic; cook till transparent. Drain. Line greased 9x9-inch pan with one can drained and seeded chiles. Top with 1½ cups cheese. Add meat mixture; top with remaining chiles. Beat eggs and flour till smooth, add milk, salt and Tabasco. Blend well and pour over casserole. Bake 60 minutes at 350° uncovered. Remove from oven, sprinkle with remaining cheese. Let stand for 5 minutes before serving.

Pleasures from the Good Earth

When storing fresh chiles, wash and dry the chiles, wrap them in paper towels and store in the crisper section of the refrigerator. Do not store in plastic bags as moisture will accumulate and hasten spoiling.

Chilaquila Casserole

Another Southwestern favorite! For a colorful touch, use a combination of yellow and blue corn tortillas.

1 tablespoon canola oil
1 small onion, chopped
4 medium zucchini, quartered
    lengthwise and cut in chunks
4 medium tomatoes, seeded and
    chopped
1½ teaspoons ground cumin
1 teaspoon dried basil
12 corn tortillas, divided

2 (4-ounce) cans diced green chiles,
    drained, divided
2 cups (8 ounces) shredded lowfat
    Monterey Jack cheese, divided
2 cups buttermilk
4 large eggs
¼ teaspoon ground black pepper
Black Bean, Corn, and Red Pepper
    Relish

THE NIGHT BEFORE:

Heat the canola oil in a large skillet over medium heat, add the chopped onion and sauté until soft and translucent, about 5 minutes. Add the chopped zucchini, sauté until tender, about 5 minutes more. Add chopped tomatoes, sprinkle with the cumin and basil, gently stir to mix; heat until just warm. Set aside to cool.

Spray a 9x13-inch pan with nonstick cooking spray. Tear 6 tortillas into bite-sized pieces and spread them evenly in the prepared pan. Spread 1 can of the chiles and 1 cup shredded cheese over the tortillas. Next, spread the cooled onion-zucchini-tomato mixture evenly over the cheese. Tear the remaining tortillas into bite-sized pieces and spread them over the vegetables. Follow with remaining chilies and cheese. Cover the casserole with foil and refrigerate until morning.

IN THE MORNING:

Preheat oven to 375°. Remove casserole from refrigerator and uncover. In a medium bowl, whisk together buttermilk, eggs, and ground black pepper. Slowly pour over the casserole. Bake uncovered for 35 minutes or until eggs are set. Serve hot, warm, or at room temperature with Black Bean, Corn and Red Pepper Relish.

BLACK BEAN, CORN, AND RED PEPPER RELISH:

1 (12-ounce) can black beans,
    drained, rinsed, and drained
    again
¾ cup frozen corn, thawed, rinsed,
    and drained
1 medium red bell pepper,
    minced

2 tablespoons olive or canola oil
2 tablespoons lime juice
¼ cup minced fresh cilantro
1 tablespoon dried parsley flakes or
    ¼ cup minced fresh parsley
⅛ teaspoon ground black
    pepper

(continued)

(continued)

In a medium bowl, toss together all of the ingredients. Let sit at room temperature for at least 30 minutes to allow flavors to develop. May be made the night before and stored in an airtight container in the refrigerator. Let come to room temperature before serving.

Mountain Mornings

Vegetable Paella

1 cup olive oil	2 cups cauliflower florets
2 leeks, white part only, chopped	½ pound shelled green peas
4 onions, chopped	5 cups vegetable stock (about 3
4 cloves garlic, chopped	13¾-ounce cans)
4 small tomatoes, chopped	Salt and pepper to taste
8 fresh artichoke hearts	4 teaspoons chopped fresh
4 red bell peppers, roasted, peeled,	cilantro
and julienned	1 pound short grain rice

In a casserole (preferably an earthenware casserole) over low heat, heat the oil. Add half of the leeks, onions, garlic and tomatoes. Cook for 2 minutes. Add artichoke hearts, bell peppers, cauliflower and peas. Add half of the vegetable stock and cook on low heat for 10 minutes; season with salt and pepper. Add the remainder of the leeks, onions, tomatoes, garlic, all the cilantro, the rice and the rest of the stock, and blend. Cook for another 20 minutes or so until rice is done. Add more stock if needed. Serves 6–8.

Note: This paella is very easy to assemble. The flavors of the fresh vegetables are so pronounced even non-vegetarians will rave.

The Wigwam Resort, Litchfield Park, Arizona / Vegetarian Southwest

Sloppy Josés

As good as or better than any Sloppy Joes you've ever tasted. Please don't let the amount of ingredients intimidate you; it's very simple. Serve with lots of napkins.

2 cups diced onions
1 cup diced red bell peppers
1 cup diced green bell peppers
3 cups chopped tomatoes
2 teaspoons extra-virgin olive oil
4–5 cloves garlic, minced
2 cups textured vegetable protein granules, hydrated in 1¾ cups boiling water
2 cups tomato purée

1½ tablespoons tamari
¼ cup lemon or lime juice
1 tablespoon chili powder
1 tablespoon cumin
2 teaspoons dry mustard
Pinch of cayenne
Pinch of cloves
Pinch of cinnamon
1 tablespoon sorghum or unsulfured molasses (optional)

In a large, heavy skillet, sauté the onions, peppers, and tomatoes in the oil over low heat until tender. Add the garlic and sauté another 2–3 minutes. Add the rest of the ingredients, cover, and cook over medium-low heat about 20–30 minutes. Uncover and cook another 10 minutes, or until the mixture is thick and the flavors have married well. Serve on whole-grain rolls with lettuce, tomato slices, and pickles or cucumber slices. Enjoy! Yields 8 servings.

Variations:

Substitute tempeh, tofu, or another variety of textured vegetable protein.

Shiitake mushrooms or diced zucchini are good additions. Add to the onions, peppers, and tomatoes.

A touch of orange juice may sound strange, but try adding it with or instead of lemon or lime juice. Chopped fresh cilantro adds an exotic touch.

Per serving: Calories 139; Protein 12g; Fat 1g; Carbohydrates 19g

Flavors of the Southwest

Stuffed Mushrooms

1 tablespoon minced onion
¼ pound butter
4 slices bulk sausage meat, cooked
½ cup dry bread crumbs

1 egg, lightly beaten
1 tablespoon chopped parsley
20 mushrooms

Sauté the onion in butter until soft. Chop the cooked sausage meat and mix with the bread crumbs, egg, parsley, and sautéed onion. Remove the stems of mushrooms and clean out caps. Wipe mushrooms with a damp cloth and arrange them upside down on a buttered baking dish. Fill each cap with stuffing. Dot with butter and bake in 375° oven for about 15 minutes. Baste during cooking with additional butter to keep mushrooms moist.

Dishes from the Deep

Mushroom Broccoli Strata

10 eggs
3½ cups milk
¼ teaspoon curry powder
½ teaspoon seasoned salt
2 cups grated Cheddar cheese,
  divided

8 slices stale bread, cubed
1 cup broccoli, chopped
½ cup mushrooms, sliced

Beat eggs, milk, curry powder, and salt with half of cheese. Cover bottom of 9x13-inch casserole with bread cubes. Top with broccoli and mushrooms. Pour milk mixture over all. Top with remaining cheese. Bake at 350° for 30 minutes until set. Let stand 10 minutes before serving. Yields 12 servings.

Note: Any combination of chopped fresh vegetables can be used.

What's Cooking Inn Arizona

Portobello Alla Maria

4 large portobello mushrooms
2 cups extra virgin olive oil
⅓ cup balsamic vinegar
Salt and pepper to taste

8 slices crusty Italian bread
4 leeks, cut horizontally then into
    ¼-inch pieces

Clean mushrooms, cut off stems, and scrape spores off bottoms with a spoon. Brush mushrooms with oil and vinegar. Season with salt and pepper. Brush bread slices with olive oil. Place mushrooms and bread on grill. Grill bread on both sides until golden. Remove from heat. Grill mushrooms about 3–5 minutes on each side or until cooked through. Meanwhile, heat remaining oil in sauté pan. Add leeks and cook until translucent. Remove from heat and add remaining vinegar. Adjust salt and pepper. Arrange 2 slices of bread on each plate and top with mushroom. Spoon ¼ oil /vinegar / leek mixture over each mushroom.

Contributed by Maria's When In Naples, Scottsdale
Arizona Chefs: Cooking at Home with 36 Arizona Chefs

Tarragon Sherry Carrots

1½ pounds carrots
½ cup water
1 teaspoon tarragon
½ cup chopped onion

2 tablespoons butter
3 tablespoons flour
¾ cup evaporated milk
⅓ cup sherry

Peel carrots and cut into 3-inch julienne strips to measure about 4 cups. Combine with water and tarragon in medium saucepan. Cook, covered, over medium-low heat for 10 minutes or until tender-crisp; do not drain. Sauté onion in butter in a large saucepan. Stir in flour and cook until bubbly. Stir in evaporated milk and wine gradually. Add undrained carrots and cook until mixture thickens, stirring constantly. Serves 8.

Wild Thyme and Other Temptations

Southern Arizona is a bird's paradise. At least 500 species of birds are reported in the Sonoran Desert, roughly half the known number of species in the continental US.

Honey Baked Onions

3 large red or yellow onions
⅓ cup honey
¼ cup water
3 tablespoons melted butter or
  margarine

1 teaspoon paprika
1 teaspoon ground coriander
⅛ teaspoon cayenne pepper

Peel and cut onions in half crosswise. Place cut-side-down in a foil baking pan. Sprinkle with water and cover tightly with foil. Place over medium coals and cook for about half an hour, or bake in a shallow baking pan at 350° for 30 minutes. In a small bowl, combine remaining ingredients. Remove onions from heat and spoon half the honey mixture over them. Return to heat for 15 minutes. Baste with remaining mixture and cook another 15 minutes or until the onions are tender.

License to Cook Arizona Style

Onion Pie

48 crushed saltine crackers
1 stick melted margarine
2–3 medium onions
2 tablespoons butter
½ pound Cheddar cheese or
  mozzarella

2 cups milk
3 eggs
Salt
Paprika

Roll crackers to make crumbs. Pour margarine over the crumbs. Mix well. Press ⅔ of mixture into a 9x13-inch pan.

Peel and slice onions. Sauté onions in butter until soft, not brown. Grate cheese. Place onions on top of cracker layer. Top with grated cheese. Heat milk almost to a boil. Beat eggs; add milk and salt. Pour over layers of crackers, onions, and cheese. Top with remaining cracker crumbs. Sprinkle with paprika. Bake at 350° for 30 minutes. Makes 10 servings.

Variations: I use olive oil instead of butter to sauté the onions. I have also added sautéed Ortega green chiles with the onions as well as artichokes purchased in a jar.

Kingman Welcome Wagon Club Cookbook

Swedish Green Potatoes

"This is best if made up and refrigerated, then baked the next day," says Janis Frieder, wife of ASU basketball coach Bill Frieder. "I serve it with grilled tenderloin, fresh asparagus, and a salad. Everyone loves it."

8 large potatoes, peeled and
   cut into 1-inch pieces
¾ cup sour cream
1 teaspoon sugar
4 tablespoons butter
2 teaspoons salt

¼ teaspoon pepper
2 tablespoons snipped dill
1 (10-ounce) package frozen
   chopped spinach, cooked and
   well drained
1 cup shredded Cheddar cheese

In a large pot, boil, drain, and mash potatoes. Add sour cream, sugar and butter, and beat until fluffy. Add remaining ingredients.

Preheat oven to 400°. Place potatoes in a greased baking dish. Bake 30 minutes or until bubbly. Serves 8.

The Arizona Celebrity Cookbook

Mashed Potato with Carrots and Caramelized Onion

1 teaspoon butter
1 small onion, chopped
1 large Idaho baking potato,
   peeled

2 medium carrots, peeled
¼ cup ricotta cheese
¼ teaspoon salt

Melt the butter in a small skillet over medium-high heat. Add the onion. Cook for 8–10 minutes or until golden brown, stirring frequently; set aside.

Cut the potato and carrots into pieces. Add to large saucepan of boiling water. Cook for 8–10 minutes or until the vegetables are tender; drain well.

Mash the potato and carrots together until the carrots are small chunks. Beat in the onion, ricotta cheese and salt. Serves 2.

Tucson Treasures

Mashed Potato Soufflé

4–6 potatoes, peeled and cut
1 (8-ounce) package cream
  cheese
1 egg

1 cup light cream
Salt and pepper to taste
Tabasco sauce to taste
¼ cup chopped scallions

Boil potatoes until tender. Drain. While still hot, whip potatoes with cream cheese, egg, and cream. Season to taste with salt, pepper, and Tabasco sauce. Fold in scallions. Pour into buttered casserole dish, leaving 2–3 inches at the top for "puffing." Bake at 350° for 45 minutes. Serves 6.

Note: Soufflé can be assembled and refrigerated until baking time.

Purple Sage and Other Pleasures

Sheepherder's Scalloped Potatoes

Home from the hill—the hunter finds a ready-to-eat gourmet dinner if he has had the forethought to prepare a Dutch oven meal early that morning.

Necessary are a dozen pork chops (or thick slices of ham or lamb chops) and a 14- or 16-inch Dutch oven.

Melt a little fat in the bottom of the oven and place meat in oven and brown lightly on both sides. Remove and place to one side.

Slice enough raw potatoes to half fill the oven. Slice two large onions and mix with potatoes. Leave the pork grease in bottom of the oven and put in layers of potatoes and onions with salt, pepper, and flour. Place all the pork chops on top and cover with milk (canned or powdered milk).

Dig hole large enough to hold about six inches of good hardwood coals. Place oven in hole and cover with hot coals. Foil or a small piece of tin placed on top of oven before adding coals will aid in removing later when done. Cover all with at least six inches of dirt.

Meat and potatoes will be done in four hours but can be left in hole for 8–10 hours if necessary. Do not remove until ready to eat.

Note: Can be baked in 350° oven for 1 hour.

Chuck Wagon Cookin'

Cheesy Potato Sticks

2 tablespoons butter
2 tablespoons all-purpose flour
¼ teaspoon salt
Dash pepper
1 cup milk

1 cup (4 ounces) shredded sharp
    Cheddar cheese, divided
1 (16-ounce) package frozen
    French-fried potatoes

Melt butter over low heat. Blend in flour, salt, and pepper. Add milk all at once. Cook quickly, stirring constantly until thickened and bubbling. Add half the shredded cheese. Stir until the cheese melts. Place potatoes in 10x6x1½-inch casserole dish. Pour milk mixture over top. Top with remaining cheese. Bake at 350° for 45 minutes.

Dishes from the Deep

Snackin' Good Potato Pancakes

If you like potato pancakes, you will love these!

3 pounds russet potatoes
    (about 5–6 spuds)
¾ cup shredded onions
¼ cup all-purpose flour
1 teaspoon salt

¼ teaspoon ground black
    pepper
1 teaspoon garlic powder
2 large eggs
½ tablespoon vegetable oil

Prepare frying pan by spraying with vegetable spray; heat on low setting. Shred potatoes by hand in a large bowl. Add shredded onions. Add flour, salt, pepper and garlic powder. Mix well. Add eggs and vegetable oil. Mix well again. Lightly drop mixture by rounded tablespoons into hot frying pan, forming cakes ¼ inch thick and about 3–4 inches in diameter. Fry 10 minutes or until golden brown on the bottom. Turn pancakes and fry 5–10 minutes longer or until golden brown. Transfer to platter. Do not overcook. Pancakes should appear underdone (soft) when fresh out of the fry pan. They firm as they cool. Makes 24 servings.

Kingman Welcome Wagon Club Cookbook

Sweet Potato Cakes

6 medium-sized sweet potatoes
3 well-beaten eggs, divided
1 tablespoon butter
2 tablespoons sugar

Pepper and salt to taste
Flour
Seasoned bread crumbs

Boil potatoes. When tender, mash very fine, add 2 beaten eggs, butter, sugar, and seasoning. Add flour to make a stiff dough, roll out, cut with biscuit cutter, dip in beaten egg, then crumbs, and fry in deep fat.

Chuck Wagon Cookin'

Potluck Spinach Squares

1 (10-ounce) package spinach,
  thawed and drained
1 cup cooked rice
1 cup grated sharp cheese
2 beaten eggs
½ cup milk
2 tablespoons chopped onion

½ teaspoon Worcestershire
  sauce
½ teaspoon salt
¼ teaspoon rosemary or
  tarragon
2 tablespoons softened butter

Mix all ingredients and pour into a 7x11-inch baking dish. Bake at 350° for 20–25 minutes. Cut into squares.

St. Francis in the Foothills 30th Anniversary Cookbook

Asparagus Stir Fry

1 bunch asparagus (15–20
  spears)
2 tablespoons olive oil

Lemon pepper, to taste
1 clove garlic, minced (optional)

Clean asparagus and cut off 1 inch of bottom. Cut spears into 2-inch pieces. Heat oil in a stir-fry pan; add asparagus and stir until crisp tender. Sprinkle with lemon pepper and serve. You will never serve it steamed again!

Hospice Hospitality

Broccoli and Rice Casserole

½ cup chopped onion
½ cup chopped celery
3 tablespoons butter
1 (16-ounce) package broccoli cuts
2 cups cooked rice
1 (4-ounce) can mushrooms, drained

1 can cream of chicken, celery, or
  mushroom soup
¼ cup milk
½ cup water
1 (8-ounce) jar Cheez Whiz

Sauté onion and celery in butter. Cook broccoli until slightly tender. Mix onion and celery, rice, mushrooms, and broccoli. Mix soup, milk, water, and Cheese Whiz and cook until cheese is melted. Add the cheese/soup mixture to broccoli. Pour into greased casserole and bake at 350° for 40–50 minutes.

St. Francis in the Foothills 30th Anniversary Cookbook

Broccoli Delight

2 (16-ounce) packages frozen
  broccoli, cooked and drained
1 can cream of mushroom soup
2 bunches chopped green onions

1 small can sliced water chestnuts,
  drained
2 cups grated Cheddar cheese
1 cup slivered almonds

Mix all ingredients together. Bake in a casserole dish at 350° for 30 minutes.

Cooking with Cops

Broccoli Puff

1 (10-ounce) box frozen broccoli
  cuts
1 can cream of mushroom soup
2 ounces grated sharp Cheddar
  (about ½ cup)

¼ cup milk
¼ cup mayonnaise
1 beaten egg
Bread crumbs

Cook frozen broccoli, omitting salt. Drain. Place in baking dish. Stir together soup and cheese. Add milk, mayonnaise and egg. Blend thoroughly. Pour over broccoli. Sprinkle with bread crumbs. Bake at 350° for 45 minutes.

Dishes from the Deep

Baked Beans

2 pounds white beans
½ pound salt pork
2 onions, chopped
2 cups molasses
¼ cup brown sugar
½ cup catsup

2 tablespoons dry mustard
2 tablespoons vinegar
3 tablespoons Worcestershire
  sauce
1 cup dark beer, optional
1 pound bacon or ham, chopped

Soak beans overnight. Add salt pork, bring to a boil; turn heat low, cover and simmer 1 hour. Drain all but two cups of broth (save). Add remaining ingredients.

Bake at 200° for 6–9 hours, adding more broth or beer as needed. Uncover pot for the last hour. Makes 20 servings.

Pioneer Family Recipes

Company Beans

¼ pound ground beef
1 cup chopped onion
1 (15-ounce) can garbanzo beans,
  drained
1 (15-ounce) can kidney beans,
  drained
1 (15-ounce) can pork and beans,
  drained

¾ cup brown sugar
¼ cup ketchup
¼ cup barbecue sauce
2 teaspoons vinegar
1 teaspoon brown mustard

Brown ground beef with onions. Add garbanzo beans, kidney beans, pork and beans, brown sugar, ketchup, barbecue sauce, vinegar and brown mustard. Bake in 3-quart casserole at 350° for 1 hour. Can also be put in a crockpot and cooked on low for 3 hours. Add bacon, if desired.

Favorites for All Seasons

Scalloped Green Beans

1 cup margarine, divided
⅓ cup flour
Milk, to make a thick white sauce
8 slices American cheese, or
  ½ cup Velveeta cheese

3 cans drained green beans, whole
  or French-cut
8–10 slices bread

In pan, melt ½ cup margarine; add flour and mix; add milk while stirring, enough for thick white sauce. Add cheese while cooking. Put beans in baking dish. Pour cheese sauce over. Melt remaining margarine in saucepan. Break bread into bite-sized pieces. Add all at once to melted margarine and stir to coat. Spread bread over top of beans and bake in slow oven at 325° for 45 minutes to 1 hour, until bread is golden brown.

Note: Do not bake too fast or sauce will curdle.

The Garden Patch

Greek-Style Green Beans

4 medium white onions, chopped
3 garlic cloves, crushed
1 tablespoon olive oil
4 large tomatoes, peeled, sliced

Pepper to taste
2 pounds fresh green beans,
  trimmed
Salt to taste

Sauté onions and garlic in olive oil in skillet until light brown. Add tomatoes and season with pepper.

Cook beans in salted water in a saucepan for 5 minutes; drain. Add tomato mixture and cover. Simmer 30–60 minutes or until done to taste, removing cover toward end of cooking time. Adjust seasonings. Serves 6.

Wild Thyme and Other Temptations

Kartchner Caverns, the most recently discovered cave in Arizona, is a living one, meaning that its formations are still growing. The massive column known as Kubla Khan found in the Throne Room stretches 58 feet to the ceiling.

Mexican Corn Pudding

2 cups water
2 cups evaporated milk
1½ cups yellow cornmeal
1 teaspoon salt
1 tablespoon sugar
1 cup corn kernels
½ chopped red pepper
2 tablespoons melted butter

½ cup grated Cheddar cheese
2 tablespoons chopped cilantro
5 eggs
1 tablespoon baking powder
2 tablespoons chopped chile
  (your choice)
Salt to taste
Pepper to taste

Combine water and milk and bring to a boil. Add cornmeal, salt and sugar. Reduce heat to medium low and whisk until thickened. (If mixture becomes too thick, add more milk, up to ½ cup.) Remove from heat and add corn kernels, red pepper, butter, cheese and cilantro. Set aside.

Whisk eggs together with baking powder until frothy. Add chile and whisk in cornmeal mixture. Blend well. Add salt and pepper to taste and pour into a greased casserole or skillet. Bake at 425° for 30 minutes or until golden brown.

Vistoso Vittles II

Pasta, Rice, Etc.

Monument Valley, a Navajo Nation tribal park, as seen through the Tear Drop window. The stark sandstone buttes of Monument Valley rise a thousand feet above the valley floor.

Chile Cheese Rice Casserole

1½ cups steamed rice
½ large white onion, diced
¼ cup oil
1 pint cottage cheese

1 pint sour cream
½ round Longhorn cheese, grated
3 small cans diced green chiles

Follow instructions on package of rice for steaming. Brown chopped onion in oil until golden brown, using an extra large skillet. After rice is steamed, drain off any excess water and add to onion in skillet then add cottage cheese and sour cream. Blend mixture well.

In 9x13-inch greased baking dish, place ½ rice mixture, then add 1½ cans green chiles followed by ½ grated cheese, being sure to cover the entire surface of first layer. Repeat the same procedure with remaining ingredients, ending with grated cheese on top. Bake at 375° for 20–30 minutes (just to melt the cheese between layers).

Lion's Club of Globe Cookbook

Black Bean and Rice Tostadas

Cooking spray
1 cup chopped onion
2 cloves garlic, minced
1 cup long-grain rice, cooked
1 (15-ounce) can black beans, rinsed and drained
1 (14.5-ounce) can Mexican-style stewed tomatoes with jalapeño peppers and spices, undrained
1 (7-ounce) can corn with red and green peppers, drained

1 (4.5-ounce) can chopped green chiles
2 tablespoons lime juice
½ teaspoon dried oregano
½ teaspoon ground cumin
½ teaspoon chili powder
¼ teaspoon ground red pepper
4 (6-inch) flour tortillas
½ cup finely shredded sharp Cheddar cheese
¼ cup fat-free sour cream

Coat a large nonstick skillet with cooking spray. Place over medium-high heat until hot. Add onion and garlic and sauté 4 minutes or until tender. Stir in rice, black beans, stewed tomatoes, corn, green chiles, lime juice, oregano, cumin, chili powder and red pepper. Cook 3 minutes, stirring frequently. Place tortillas on a baking sheet. Bake at 350° in preheated oven for 6 minutes, turning after 3 minutes. Spoon rice mixture onto tortillas. Top with cheese and sour cream. Makes 4 servings.

Par Excellence

Spanish Rice

3 cloves garlic
1 medium onion
Small amount oil
1 cup rice (not instant)
Pinch saffron

1 can consommé
3 cans hot water (using consommé can)
1 small jar pimientos
1 jar mushrooms

Chop garlic and onion. Sauté in small amount of oil. Add rice and stir a few minutes to pick up the flavor. Add saffron, consommé, water, pimientos and mushrooms. Bring to a boil and bake covered in a 10-inch Dutch oven for 1 hour over low (13 coals on bottom, 6 coals on top) heat.

Note: See page 50 for Dutch oven cooking instructions and chart.

Dutch Oven and Campfire Cookbook

Spanish Rice Nº 2

This is a good Dutch oven dish, also.

Put two frying pans on the stove, and in each put one teaspoonful of bacon fat. Take one onion and four green chilies, chop very fine, and sprinkle with a little salt; put this in one frying pan and cook until softened without browning. In the other pan put in 1 cup rice, washed and dried; stir and let cook to a light brown; add the onion and chilies and 1 cup of canned tomatoes; then fill the frying pan with boiling water and let cook until rice is dry. Black pepper may be added to taste.

Chuck Wagon Cookin'

Pan-Fried Rice

¼ cup chopped green onions
6–8 mushrooms, sliced
½ cup diced ham
6 tablespoons oil, divided

3 eggs
4 cups cooked rice
4 tablespoons soy sauce

Stir-fry green onions, mushrooms and ham in 2 tablespoons oil. Scramble eggs in remaining oil. Add eggs, rice and soy sauce to stir-fry and cook at low heat, stirring occasionally, for at least 20 minutes.

The Garden Patch

Firehouse Bubble Pizza

4 (7½-ounce) cans refrigerator
  biscuits
1 (16-ounce) jar pizza sauce
½ cup green peppers, chopped
½ cup mushrooms, sliced
½ cup black olives, chopped

½ cup onions, chopped
½–1 pound of your choice of
  pizza ingredients: Italian sausage,
  pepperoni, hamburger, Canadian
  bacon
8–12 ounces mozzarella cheese

Cut refrigerator biscuits into halves or quarters. Stir together in a large bowl with pizza sauce. Add vegetables and desired pizza ingredients and mix well. Spray a 9x13-inch pan with vegetable spray. Pour in pizza mix. Bake for 10 minutes at 450°. Sprinkle with cheese and return to oven for additional 10–15 minutes. Feeds 6–8 firefighters.

The National Firefighters Recipe Book

Operated by the National Optical Astronomy Observatory, Kitt Peak has the world's greatest concentration of telescopes for stellar, solar and planetary research.

Pancho Villa's Favorite Quiche

¼ cup chopped onion
1 tablespoon oil
1 pie shell (can be pre-made kind)
3 eggs
1 cup evaporated milk
½ teaspoon (or more if you like it) ground cumin

1½ cups grated Jack cheese (although Mormon cheese from Chihuahua works best)
1 cup grated mild Cheddar cheese
1 (4-ounce) can chopped green chiles

Preheat oven to 325°. Sauté onion in oil. Line quiche or pie pan with pie crust. Brush crust with beaten egg white, then lightly beat remaining eggs with onion and other ingredients. Pour into pie crust. Form a collar around the edge of the pie crust by crimping aluminum foil (this keeps edges from burning). Bake at 325° for 40 minutes, or until knife inserted in center comes out clean. Makes 4 generous servings or 8 cocktail-size servings.

Padre Kino's Favorite Meatloaf

Quiche

3 cups shredded potatoes
3 tablespoons oil

Salt and pepper to taste

Mix potatoes with oil, salt and pepper and spread in bottom and sides of 9x13-inch greased pan and bake at 375° for about 10–15 minutes until it starts to brown. Set aside.

MIX:

½ pound crisp bacon, or diced ham or both
1½ cups grated Swiss or Cheddar, grated
1 cup cottage cheese
1 cup Monterey or Gruyère cheese

2 (4-ounce) cans green chiles, diced
½ teaspoon salt
½ teaspoon cayenne pepper
¼ cup butter, melted
6 large eggs, well beaten

After potatoes are brown, mix all other ingredients together. Pour over potatoes and bake until knife or toothpick comes out clean. Bake at 375° for 45–55 minutes. This can be baked ahead of time and just warmed in the microwave for one or two minutes. Keeps well in fridge for a week.

Lion's Club of Globe Cookbook

Chili Mac

3 cups chopped onion
3 cloves garlic, minced
2 (15½-ounce) cans pinto beans, undrained
2 (14½-ounce) cans stewed tomatoes, undrained and chopped
1½ tablespoons chili powder

2 tablespoons no-salt-added tomato paste
2 teapoons ground cumin
1 cup cooked elbow macaroni
½ cup no-salt-added tomato juice
½ cup shredded lowfat Cheddar cheese

Sauté onion and garlic until tender. Add remaining ingredients, except cheese, and stir well. Reduce heat and simmer, uncovered, for 15 minutes, stirring frequently. Add a little water or tomato juice if mixture is too thick. Top individual servings with grated cheese. Serves 8.

Cal 257; %Fat 17; Fat 5g; Sat Fat 1.4g; Chol 4mg; Sod 316mg; Carbo 44g; Prot 12g; Fiber 9g.
Exchanges: Starch 2, Vegetable 3, Fat 1

Arizona Heart Institute Foundation Cookbook

John Wayne Cheese Casserole

2 (4-ounce) cans whole green chiles, drained, seeded
4 cups shredded Monterey Jack cheese
4 cups shredded Cheddar cheese
4 eggs, separated

1 (5-ounce) can evaporated milk
1 tablespoon flour
½ teaspoon salt
⅛ teaspoon pepper
2 medium tomatoes, sliced

Chop the green chiles and place them in a large bowl. Add the Monterey Jack cheese and Cheddar cheese and mix lightly. Spoon into a greased shallow 2-quart casserole.

Beat the egg whites in a mixer bowl until stiff peaks form. Whisk the egg yolks and evaporated milk in a bowl until well blended. Stir in the flour, salt, and pepper. Fold the egg whites into the egg yolk mixture. Pour over the cheese mixture in the casserole.

Pierce the layers with a fork to allow the cheese mixture to absorb some of the egg mixture.

Bake at 325° for 30 minutes. Remove from the oven. Arrange the tomato slices around the edge of the casserole. Bake for 30 minutes longer or until a knife inserted in the center comes out clean. Serves 8.

Tucson Treasures

Tortilla Casserole

1½ pounds lean ground beef
1 large onion, chopped
Olive oil
1 cup mushrooms, sliced
1 can chopped black olives
1 (14-ounce) can enchilada sauce
1 (15-ounce) can Hunt's tomato sauce
½ cup water
½ teaspoon basil
½ teaspoon oregano
1 package four tortillas (for 2 layers, use large size)
2 cups Jack cheese, grated
2 cups mozzarella cheese, grated

Brown ground beef and onion in a little olive oil and drain. Add mushrooms and olives. Mix well. Set aside. In a saucepan mix enchilada sauce, tomato sauce, water, basil, and oregano. Bring to a boil. Put aside. Rub bottom and sides of 9x13x2-inch glass Pyrex casserole with oil. Add a little sauce in bottom. Place one layer of tortillas on bottom. Add half of the meat mixture, half of the Jack and mozzarella cheese and half of the sauce. Repeat one more layer. Bake 35 minutes, uncovered at 350°. Let cool 5 minutes. Serves 6.

Favorites for All Seasons

Six Shooter Casserole

1 (2-pound) package thawed hash brown potatoes
1 pound chopped ham, sausage, or bacon, cooked and crumbled
1 (8-ounce) can chopped green chiles
12–14 eggs
1 teaspoon salt
½ teaspoon pepper
⅓ teaspoon dry mustard
½ cup milk
1 cup grated Cheddar cheese

Layer potatoes, meat, and chiles in greased 9x13-inch baking dish or evenly into individual ramekins. Beat together eggs, salt, pepper, dry mustard, and milk. Pour over top of casserole. Sprinkle with grated cheese. Bake at 350° for 1 hour. Can be prepared and refrigerated overnight. Garnish with salsa. Makes 12 servings.

What's Cooking Inn Arizona

Sister Marla's Dirty Rice

1 cup uncooked rice
⅓ cup chopped green onion
¼ cup diced red pepper
2 tablespoons bacon drippings
   (may substitute cooking spray
   or butter)

1 tablespoon Worcestershire sauce
½ tablespoon liquid smoke
¾ teaspoon cumin
Salt and pepper
2 cups beef broth

Sauté rice, onion and red pepper in bacon drippings until golden. Stir in remaining ingredients and bring to boil. Cover tightly and reduce heat. Cook slowly for 20 minutes without lifting lid. Serves 4.

First Baptist Favorites

Frito Pie

1 pound ground beef
1 package taco seasoning
2 cans chili (hot or mild according
   to your taste)

1 package Fritos (dip size)
1 medium-sized onion, chopped
3 cups grated cheese (Mexican
   three cheeses or Cheddar)

Preheat oven to 400°. Prepare meat according to directions on taco mix packet. Heat chili in saucepan. Spray a large casserole dish or stoneware dish with nonstick cooking spray and layer ingredients in the following order. Layer of Fritos, lightly mashed to settle, layer of prepared meat. Sprinkle onion over layer and spoon chili over layer. Cover layer with cheese. Repeat layering until all ingredients are added (usually 2 or 3 layers). The Fritos should be soaked, but firm and crisp at serving. Bake covered for 20 minutes. Serve with salad, avocados, and salsa.

Note: Moisture is the key to this dish. Do not cook the meat too dry and a ¼ cup water in the chili will add enough moisture.

Dishes from the Deep

Greek Macaroni-Meat Pie
(Pastitso)

2–2½ cups elbow or shell
  macaroni
2 tablespoons margarine
⅛ teaspoon nutmeg
Salt and pepper to taste
2 eggs, beaten
1 tablespoon margarine
½ onion, chopped
1 garlic clove, crushed
¾ pound ground meat
1½ tablespoons tomato paste

¼ cup wine
¼ cup beef bouillon
1 tablespoon parsley, chopped
¼ teaspoon sugar
2½ tablespoons margarine
¼ cup flour
1½ cups non-dairy creamer
⅛ teaspoon nutmeg
1 egg
1 tablespoon margarine pieces
Paprika

Preheat oven to 350°. Place water (about 2 quarts) in a saucepan. Add macaroni to boiling water with salt. Cook until tender, drain, and set aside in bowl. Add 2 tablespoons margarine, nutmeg, salt and pepper on macaroni and toss. Let cool. When cool, add 2 eggs, toss and set aside.

Heat margarine in a frying pan. Sauté onion and garlic until onion is soft. Add meat and brown. Add tomato paste, wine, bouillon, parsley, sugar, salt and pepper. Cover and simmer 20 minutes.

Melt 2½ tablespoons margarine in saucepan. Stir in flour to make a roux. Cook 2 minutes. Add non-dairy creamer and bring to a boil. Cook 1 minute. Add nutmeg, salt and pepper. Set aside to cool. Add egg. Add ¼ of the sauce to the meat mixture and stir. Grease a casserole. Spoon half the macaroni, all the meat sauce, rest of the macaroni, and top with cream sauce. Scatter margarine pieces on top. Sprinkle with paprika. Bake in a 350° oven for 50 minutes.

Kosher Kettle

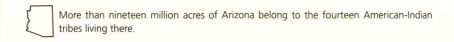

More than nineteen million acres of Arizona belong to the fourteen American-Indian tribes living there.

Los Olivos' Sonora Enchiladas

RED CHILE SAUCE:

10 dried red chiles
Water for boiling
4 tablespoons shortening

2 cloves garlic, minced
1½ tablespoons flour
½ tablespoon salt

Remove stems and seeds from red chiles. Boil chiles in enough water to cover, about 4 cups, for approximately 15 minutes or until chiles are tender. Remove from heat and let stand until cool enough to touch. Pour chiles and liquid into blender container and purée. Heat shortening in saucepan over medium-high heat. Add garlic and cook until light brown. Add flour and stir constantly until browned. Add salt and chile purée. Simmer and stir until thickened. If sauce gets too thick, add water to thin to desired consistency. Makes about 2½ cups.

ENCHILADAS:

2 pounds corn masa
½ pound Cheddar or longhorn cheese, shredded
1½ tablespoons salt
1 tablespoon baking powder
1 cup instant mashed potato flakes

2 cups water
Oil for frying
2 cups shredded cheese
2 cups chopped green onions
Shredded lettuce
Chopped tomato
Sliced black olives

In large bowl, mix corn masa, Cheddar or longhorn cheese, salt, baking powder, instant mashed potato flakes and water together into a rough dough. Knead a few times to soften. Separate dough into 6 or 8 balls. Flatten balls with hands or rolling pin into patties about ½-inch thick. Heat 1 inch of oil in skillet. Place patties in oil, one at a time, and cook until both sides are golden brown. Add more oil to pan as needed. Drain patties on paper towels. Place each patty on ovenproof serving plate and cover with Red Chile Sauce. Sprinkle shredded cheese and chopped onions over top of patty and put in hot oven until cheese is melted. Top with lettuce, tomato and olive slices before serving. Serves 6–8.

Arizona's Historic Restaurants and their Recipes

Nogales Pie

This hearty southern Arizona favorite is our improved variation of the long-popular Tijuana Pie. For busy folks like us, this dandy dish is perfect; we let it simmer all day while we're away at work or play (mostly work).

1½ pounds ground beef	1 (8-ounce) can tomato sauce
2 cloves garlic, minced	2 (16-ounce) cans chili-seasoned
1 onion, chopped	beans
Salt and pepper to taste	1 (16-ounce) can corn, drained
8 corn tortillas, cut into wedges	1 (6-ounce) can olives, drained
¾ pound Cheddar cheese, grated	

Brown beef, garlic, and onion, then season with salt and pepper. Put 2 tortillas in bottom of crockpot. Add ¼ beef mixture and cheese. Add 2 more tortillas. Top with ¼ beans, cheese, corn, and olives. Repeat layering until all ingredients are in pot, ending with some cheese and olives on top. Cook on low 5–7 hours.

Coronado's Favorite Trail Mix

Mexican Casserole

1 teaspoon margarine	1 can cream of chicken soup
1 teaspoon seasoning salt	1 (8-ounce) can cream-style corn
12–16 ounces lean ground beef	1 dozen corn tortillas
1 tablespoon onion soup mix	¼ cup Cheddar, longhorn or
Garlic powder to taste	Monterey Jack cheese
1 (1⅞-ounce) can green chiles	Cornflake crumbs or crumbled
(sliced, or whole chiles, drained	Fritos
and seeded)	Paprika

Melt margarine and sprinkle seasoning salt into it. Brown meat until crumbly. Add onion soup mix and garlic powder. Add chiles and soup. Mix well. Add corn. Simmer 30 minutes.

In greased 2-quart casserole, layer a small amount of meat mixture, then a layer of tortillas, ending with meat.

Sprinkle cheese over top, then cornflake crumbs or crumbled Fritos, and finally paprika. Can be refrigerated and baked later. Cover and bake at 350° for 45 minutes. Remove cover and bake another 15 minutes to brown top.

The Dog-Gone Delicious Cookbook

Mexican Polenta Casserole

2 cups shredded Jack cheese, divided (I use reduced-fat cheese and often mix in a little Cheddar or yellow cheese for flavor)
1 cup commercial salsa (your favorite medium-hot)
½ cup chopped, fresh cilantro leaves, lightly packed
½ teaspoon chili powder
½–1 teaspoon cumin (to taste)
¼ teaspoon dried minced garlic
1 (15-ounce) can black beans, drained
Basic Polenta (1 recipe)
1 cup onion, chopped
Vegetable cooking spray

Combine 1 cup cheese, salsa, cilantro, chili powder, cumin, garlic and black beans in a bowl, and set aside. Prepare Basic Polenta recipe. When cooked, add remaining 1 cup cheese and onions, stirring until cheese melts. Spray 9x13x2-inch baking dish with cooking oil. Spread ½ the cornmeal mixture over bottom of the dish. Spread bean mixture evenly over top. Spread remaining cornmeal mixture over bean mixture. Bake at 350° for 35 minutes, or until lightly browned. Let stand 15 minutes before serving. Cut into 6 squares.

BASIC POLENTA:
1¼ cups yellow cornmeal
½ teaspoon salt
½ teaspoon chili powder
4 cups water

Place cornmeal, salt, and chili powder in a large saucepan. Gradually add water, stirring constantly with wire whisk. Bring to a boil. Reduce heat and cook, uncovered, 15 minutes. Stir frequently; add a little water if it gets too thick. Makes 4 cups.

To serve, cut into portions. Top each portion with chopped lettuce, chopped tomato, and a bit more shredded cheese. Avocado slices, sliced olives and sour cream also make good additional toppings, but be careful if you are watching fat calories!

Coronado's Favorite Trail Mix

Chinese Vegetables with Pasta

¾ pound pasta
2½ large carrots
¾ pound Chinese pea pods
1½ teaspoons ground ginger
¾ pound fresh mushrooms, sliced

⅓ cup soy sauce
1½ cups + 1-2 tablespoons fat-free
   chicken broth
1 cup water
¼ teaspoon crushed red pepper

Prepare pasta according to package directions. Slice carrots into thin strips. Remove stems and strings along sides of pea pods.

Heat 1–2 tablespoons chicken broth in large nonstick skillet over medium-high heat; add ginger and mushrooms and cook until lightly browned. Stir in soy sauce and cook, stirring constantly, until mushrooms are tender and liquid is absorbed. Stir in carrots and pea pods and cook about 3 minutes, or until vegetables are tender-crisp.

Add 1½ cups chicken broth and water to vegetables and cook over high heat to boiling. Stir in cooked pasta and toss with vegetable mixture. Sprinkle with red pepper. Serves 6.

Nutritional Analysis Per Serving: Cal 168; Prot 8g; Carbo 32g; Chol 0mg; Sod 839mg; Dietary Fiber 0g. Exchanges 1½ starch; 2 veg.

Recipes for Fat Free Living Cookbook

Spyros Pasta

1 small red onion, chopped
2 cloves garlic, chopped
2 ounces wild mushrooms (oyster,
   portabello), sliced
1 tablespoon olive oil
2 ounces sun-dried tomatoes,
   reconstituted according to
   package directions

¼ cup white wine
½ cup chicken stock
½ cup chopped fresh spinach
2⅔ tablespoons chopped fresh basil
¼ cup plus 2 tablespoons grated
   Parmesan cheese
Salt and pepper to taste
8 ounces linguine, cooked

Sauté onion, garlic, and mushrooms in olive oil. Add sun-dried tomatoes. Add white wine to deglaze, scraping any particles from the pan, and reduce until almost dry. Add chicken stock, spinach, basil, cheese, and salt and pepper to taste. Toss with linguine to serve. Serves 4.

Approximate values per serving: Cal 310; Fat 7g; Chol 6mg; Carbo 48g; Soc 530mg; Cal from Fat 21%

By Request

Pesto Pasta

8 ounces thin spaghetti
1 handful fresh basil leaves
3–4 sprigs fresh thyme, stems
   removed

2 tablespoons olive oil
¼ cup Parmesan cheese, grated

Cook spaghetti according to package directions and drain. Blend basil, thyme and olive oil in a food processor until leaves are finely chopped. Stir spaghetti and pesto together and toss with Parmesan cheese.

Hospice Hospitality

Susan's White Spaghetti

2 whole large chicken breasts,
   boned and skinned
1 tablespoon cooking or dry
   sherry
2 teaspoons cornstarch
Salt
4 tablespoons salad oil, divided
2 medium zucchini, thinly sliced

1 (4-ounce) package sliced ham,
   cut into ¼-inch strips
⅓ cup half-and-half
3 tablespoons butter
¼ teaspoon pepper
2 tablespoons grated Parmesan
1 (8-ounce) package angel hair
   pasta

Mix chicken, cut into bite-sized pieces, in mixture of sherry, cornstarch, and salt. Set aside. In 1 tablespoon oil over medium heat, cook zucchini and ¼ teaspoon salt until tender crisp. Remove with slotted spoon. Add 3 tablespoons oil to pan and sauté chicken. Mix chicken with zucchini. Cook pasta, drain, then add chicken, ham, half-and-half, butter, pepper and cheese. Toss and serve.

St. Francis in the Foothills 30th Anniversary Cookbook

Chicken Tequila Fettuccine

1 pound spinach fettuccine
½ cup chopped fresh cilantro,
   divided
2 tablespoons minced garlic
2 tablespoons minced jalapeños
3 tablespoons butter, divided
½ cup chicken stock
2 tablespoons gold tequila

2 tablespoons lime juice
3 tablespoons soy sauce
1¼ pounds chicken breasts, diced
¼ medium red onion, thinly sliced
½ medium red bell pepper
½ medium green bell pepper
1½ cups heavy cream

Cook pasta al dente according to package. Cook ⅓ cup cilantro, garlic and jalapeños in 2 tablespoons butter over medium heat for 5 minutes. Add stock, tequila, and lime juice. Bring mixture to a boil and cook till paste-like; set aside. Pour soy sauce over diced chicken; set aside for 5 minutes. Meanwhile, cook onion and peppers with remaining butter till limp. Add chicken and soy sauce, then add reserved tequila/lime paste and cream. Boil sauce till chicken is cooked through, and sauce is thick. Serve sauce over fettuccine on serving dishes. Serve with cilantro and jalapeños as garnish. Makes 4–6 servings.

Pleasures from the Good Earth

Penne Arrabiata

4 (6-ounce) boneless, skinless
 chicken breasts
2 red bell peppers, cut in ½-inch
 strips
1½ teaspoons cayenne pepper
1½ pounds penne pasta
2 teaspoons olive oil
4 tablespoons minced shallots (or
 any other onion)

1 tablespoon fresh garlic, minced
2 cups white wine
1 cup sun-dried tomatoes, julienned
½ cup prepared pesto sauce
2 cups heavy cream
Salt and pepper to taste
⅓ cup Parmesan cheese
Basil leaves for garnish (optional)

Preheat broiler. Place chickens on broiler pan and red pepper strips on a baking sheet. Sprinkle peppers with cayenne. Broil chicken until golden brown and done, and peppers until they are fork tender (about 20 minutes). Set aside. At this point begin cooking pasta in boiling salted water until al dente. In a saucepan, heat olive oil and sauté onion and garlic . Deglaze pan with white wine and reduce the liquid, adding the tomatoes and cooking 3–4 minutes. Then add pesto, cream and seasonings and stir until fully incorporated. Add drained pasta to sauce and toss. Divide mixture among 4 warm plates. Top each with a chicken breast, red peppers, Parmesan and basil leaves.

Contributed by Armadillo Grill, Phoenix
Arizona Chefs: Dine-In Dine-Out Cookbook

Ricotta Stuffed Shells

1 onion, chopped
1 clove garlic, minced
3 tablespoons low-fat oleo
1 package frozen chopped spinach
Egg substitute equal to 2 eggs
2 cups ricotta cheese
¼ cup non-fat Parmesan, grated

1 tablespoon chopped parsley
½ teaspoon oregano
½ teaspoon salt
⅛ teaspoon pepper
24 giant pasta shells
4 cups spaghetti sauce

Sauté onion and garlic in oleo until limp. Add thawed drained spinach and cook 3 minutes. Stir eggs and ricotta cheese together well. Stir into spinach mixture. Stir in Parmesan, parsley, oregano, salt and pepper. Stuff shells. Pour spaghetti sauce in baking dish and over shells. Bake covered at 350° about 30 minutes. Serves 8.

Bon Appétit

Chicken Stroganoff Fettucini

4 bacon slices
1 large onion, diced
1 pound mushrooms, sliced
2 large garlic cloves, minced
2 pounds boneless, skinless
  chicken, cut into ¾-inch pieces
1 cup dry red wine

1 cup chicken broth
1 teaspoon dried oregano
1 teaspoon dried basil
Salt and pepper
4 tablespoons butter
4 tablespoons flour
1 pound fettucini

In a 12-inch frying pan, fry bacon. Retain grease; drain and crumble bacon and set aside. In bacon grease, sauté onion, mushrooms and garlic until tender. Transfer to a 4-quart pot and add bacon.

Using the same frying pan, sauté chicken cubes until just done (add a little oil, if necessary). Transfer chicken to pot. Add wine, chicken broth, oregano and basil.

Bring to a boil and reduce heat to simmer. Add salt and pepper to taste. Simmer over low heat for 30 minutes, stirring occasionally.

Cook fettucini according to directions. Drain. Time to finish with the stroganoff.

In a small pan, melt butter over low heat. Add flour slowly, stirring until smooth. Add to pot and stir into mixture until it thickens. Pour over fettucini. Makes 4 generous servings.

Portal's Best Little Cookbook

Spicy Shrimp Noodles

This is a terrific hot weather meal!

½ pound dried egg noodles
1 tablespoon oil
4 ounces fresh snow peas, sliced
diagonally
½ pound bean sprouts

1 carrot, cut into matchstick-size
pieces
4 ounces precooked shrimp
1 egg, beaten, cooked into a sheet
and shredded

SAUCE:
5 tablespoons soy sauce
½–1 teaspoon hot sesame chili
oil to taste
1½ tablespoons sugar
½ tablespoon sugar

1 tablespoon black vinegar
(optional)
2 tablespoons rice vinegar
3 green onions, minced
1 tablespoon grated gingeroot

Boil noodles in water for about 10 minutes. Rinse in colander; add oil to prevent sticking and mix well. Set aside to cool and thoroughly drain. Boil a few cups of water and immerse the snow peas, bean sprouts and carrot briefly, then rinse with cold water. Chill the ingredients. Place noodles, shrimp, vegetables, and egg in a bowl; pour prepared Sauce over all and toss lightly before serving.

Tostitos Fiesta Bowl Cookbook

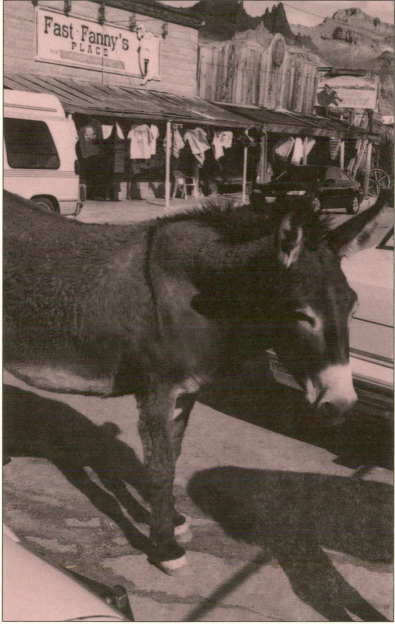

Burros roam the main street of Oatman looking for handouts, and gunfighters re-create wild west shootouts in the old mining town, located on historic Route 66.

Sweet and Sour Beef

2 pounds lean beef, cubed
2 (8-ounce) cans tomato sauce
Juice of 1 lemon

½ cup sugar
Salt and pepper to taste

Sear beef cubes on all sides in skillet; remove to 2½-quart baking dish. Combine tomato sauce, lemon juice, sugar, salt and pepper in bowl; mix well. Pour over beef. Bake, covered, at 325° for 3 hours. Serve over hot cooked rice or noodles. Yields 8 servings.

Heard in the Kitchen

Bronc Rider Beef Strips

2 pounds beef sirloin (cut in strips)
¼ cup plus 1 tablespoon soy sauce, divided
1½ teaspoons sugar
½ medium onion, chopped

1 teaspoon garlic powder
2 tablespoons sliced ginger
1 teaspoon chili powder
2 tablespoons cooking oil
1½ tablespoons toasted sesame seeds

Marinate sirloin by combining ¼ cup soy sauce, sugar, onion, garlic powder, ginger, chili powder and beef sirloin. Let set in refrigerator, covered, 1 hour. Drain meat and brown in oil in skillet. Remove from pan and coat with remaining soy sauce and sesame seeds. Serves 6.

Cowboy Cookin'

Dutch Oven Swiss Steak

3 pounds steak (at least 1 inch thick)
½ cup flour
Salt and pepper

2 tablespoons fat
Boiling water
Bit of bay leaf, if desired

Pound the steak until the fiber is thoroughly broken up; add the flour with salt and pepper while pounding. When the steak is tender, the flour should be thoroughly absorbed into the steaks. Melt fat in Dutch oven; put in the meat and let brown on one side, then turn and brown on the other. Add boiling water to cover steak and let simmer until tender (maybe as much as 2 hours or more). The bay leaf, if used, should be crumbled and added with the water.

Chuck Wagon Cookin'

Beef Fajitas

5½ pounds steak (flank lean)
1 medium onion, sliced
1 medium green pepper, cut in strips
1 medium sweet red pepper, cut into strips
1 raw jalapeño pepper, chopped
1 tablespoon cilantro, chopped
2 medium garlic cloves, minced
1 teaspoon chili powder
1 teaspoon cumin seed, ground

1 teaspoon coriander, ground
½ teaspoon salt
2 large tomatoes, chopped and seeded
12 (8-inch) flour tortilla pieces
1 pint sour cream
1 (8-ounce) package Cheddar cheese, shredded
2 large avocados (guacamole)
1 jar medium salsa

Cut flank steak into 6 portions. In any size crockpot, combine meat, onion, green pepper, red pepper, jalapeño pepper, cilantro, garlic, chili powder, cumin, coriander and salt. Add tomatoes. Cover and cook on LOW for 8–10 hours or on HIGH 4–5 hours. Remove meat from crockpot and stir. To serve fajitas, spread meat mixture into flour tortillas; add favorite toppings. Roll up tortillas. Makes 8 one-cup servings.

Vistoso Vittles II

Steak Rolls à la Lydia

2 pounds round steak	**3–4 carrots, cut in strips**
Flour for dredging	**1 medium onion, cut in strips**
Salt and pepper to taste	**1 large green pepper, cut in strips**
½ pound bacon, cut into thirds	

Preheat oven to 350°. Cut steak in ¼-inch thick wedges. Coat with flour, salt and pepper. Place ⅓ bacon strip on steak wedge. Add carrots, onion and green pepper. Roll up and secure with a toothpick. Brown steak rolls in skillet. Place in casserole dish.

GRAVY:

2 tablespoons melted butter	**¼ cup mushrooms, sliced**
2 tablespoons flour	**1 tablespoon parsley**
Salt and pepper to taste	**1 teaspoon Worcestershire sauce**
2 cups milk	

In saucepan, combine butter, flour, salt and pepper. Heat until bubbles form. Remove from heat and add milk. Return to heat until thickened. Add mushrooms, parsley and Worcestershire sauce. Pour gravy over steak rolls. Bake 1 hour. Feeds 4 firefighters.

The National Firefighters Recipe Book

Beach-Style Carne Asada

1 (14-ounce) can tomatoes
1 (4-ounce) can chopped green
   chiles
1 bunch green onions, chopped
3 tablespoons vegetable oil
1 tablespoon vinegar
1 tablespoon leaf oregano

1–2 sprigs of cilantro
1 teaspoon ground oregano
1 teaspoon coriander
½ teaspoon onion salt or garlic
   salt
1 (1½–2-pound) flank steak
8 small flour tortillas, warmed

Mash the tomatoes in a bowl. Add the green chiles, green onions, oil, vinegar, dried leaf oregano, and cilantro; mix well. Chill the salsa for several hours to blend the flavors.

Combine the ground oregano, coriander, and onion salt in a small bowl; mix well. Rub the mixture into both sides of the steak. Place the steak on a grill over hot coals. Grill for 7 minutes on each side or until done to taste. Do not overcook. Remove to a cutting board. Cut across the grain into ½-inch strips. Place a few strips on each flour tortilla. Top with salsa. Fold each tortilla to enclose the steak. Serves 4.

Reflections Under the Sun

Cupboard Casserole

1½ pounds hamburger
1 teaspoon pepper
1 teaspoon salt
1 (28-ounce) can crushed
   tomatoes
4 tablespoons dry oregano

1 teaspoon garlic salt
2 cans green beans
1 can cream-style corn
1 can whole kernel corn
1 (15-ounce) box cornbread mix

Brown hamburger; season with salt and pepper. Drain off fat. Add crushed tomatoes, oregano, garlic salt, canned beans, and corns. Bring to a boil. Turn down to simmer. Mix up cornbread batter per package directions. Pour meat mixture into a 9x13-inch pan; top with cornbread mix. Bake at 400° until cornbread is done, approximately 30–35 minutes.

Cooking with Cops

Bírria
(Shredded Beef)

This Mexican beef is often served at weddings. In preparation, my dad would dig a hole in the back yard, line it with rocks, and light a fire. The meat with all its seasonings would be placed in a cast iron Dutch oven and the lid put on firmly. When the coals were red hot and glowing, Dad would place the pan on the coals and cover the entire hole with a piece of tin. Then he would cover the tin lid with mud to seal it, and would leave the meat to cook overnight. Some of the old-timers would wrap the beef in banana leaves and wet burlap instead of using a Dutch oven.

4–5 pounds chuck roast or flank steak
2 bay leaves
2 large cloves garlic
1 can beer
2 jalapeños, seeds and veins removed
1 teaspoon oregano
1 large onion, sliced

Put all ingredients into a Dutch oven or other heavy pan with a lid, and cook in oven at 300° for 4–6 hours. Beef is ready when it is so tender it falls apart when pulled with a fork. Put the meat in a bowl and shred it while it's still warm. Remove the bay leaves from the beef juice, and store in the refrigerator for a few hours until the fat congeals on the surface. Remove the congealed fat, then warm the remaining juice and serve as a light sauce to accompany your bírria.

This dish is usually served with Spanish rice, charro beans, finely shredded cabbage or lettuce, and tortillas of choice. Serves 8–12.

Corazón Contento

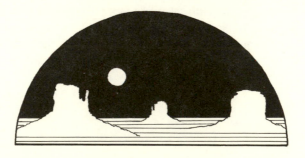

Picadillo
(Spiced Meat Filling)

2 tablespoons olive oil or
  vegetable oil
½ pound ground beef
½ pound ground pork
1 cup chopped onion
1 clove garlic, finely chopped
1 (16-ounce) can whole tomatoes,
  drained and chopped
1 tart apple, chopped (1 cup)
¼ cup golden raisins
¼ cup chopped green pepper
½–1 teaspoon salt
½ teaspoon pepper
¼ teaspoon oregano leaves,
  crushed
¼ teaspoon ground cumin

In large skillet, heat oil over medium to high heat. Sauté beef, pork, onion and garlic until meat is no longer pink, and onion is tender. Stir in remaining ingredients and cook mixture 15–20 minutes, or until apple and green pepper are tender. Use to stuff tacos, tamales, or whole green chiles. Yields about 4 cups.

Recipes from Arizona with Love

Prime Rib Hash

1½ pounds cooked prime rib,
  medium to medium-rare, cut
  into ½-inch cubes
3 pounds small red potatoes,
  parboiled and cubed
1 large leek, sliced into ¼-inch
  rings
1 red sweet bell pepper, diced
1 green sweet bell pepper, diced
Salt and pepper, to taste
4 tablespoons olive oil
6–8 poached eggs
¾ cup hollandaise sauce (your
  favorite made-from-scratch
  recipe)
¼ cup chopped fresh parsley
Lemon wedge

Sauté prime rib, potatoes, leek, bell peppers, and salt and pepper in olive oil in large cast iron skillet or griddle. You may have to hold the sauté mixture in a 250° oven. Divide sauté mixture into 6–8 ounce portions. Top each portion with a poached egg, and 2 ounces of hollandaise sauce. Sprinkle with chopped parsley and garnish with lemon wedge. Makes 6–8 servings.

What's Cooking Inn Arizona

Soft Tacos

2½ pounds hamburger
2 tablespoons garlic salt
2 teaspoons pepper
½ cup diced onions
18-count package soft taco tortillas

16 ounces shredded longhorn
  cheese
½ head lettuce, shredded
2 diced tomatoes
Salsa

In a skillet, brown hamburger; season during browning. Last 5 minutes, add onions. Heat flat skillet. In ½ tortilla, add couple spoonfuls of meat mixture and sprinkle with cheese. Fold other side over. Grill each side until lightly brown. Place lettuce and tomatoes inside of each. Top with salsa. Makes approximately 14 tacos.

Cooking with Cops

Real Mexican Tacos

2 pounds round steak
1½ onions, chopped
3 garlic cloves, chopped
1 tablespoon green chiles
1 bell pepper, sliced
⅛ teaspoon cumin

¼ teaspoon salt
2 tablespoons shortening
1 (8-ounce) can tomato sauce
18 corn tortillas
Tomato chunks, shredded lettuce,
  grated cheese

Boil meat until well done, reserving stock. Grind meat in grinder. Mix ground beef, onions, garlic, chiles, pepper, cumin and salt in skillet with shortening over low heat. Add tomato sauce and stock (about 1–1½ cups). Cook down for 1 hour. Fry corn tortillas and fill with meat mixture. Garnish with tomato chunks, shredded lettuce and grated cheese.

Cowboy Cookin'

Southern Arizona and Sonora are truly beef country. You can cook your beef over a grill, and it becomes carne asada; chop your beef into cubes and cook it with red chile sauce and you have carne de chile colorado; cut your beef into thin strips, dry it, shred it, and cook it up with chiles, onions, garlic and tomatoes and you have machaca, a wonderful dish also called carne seca or "dry meat."

Taco Ring

½+ pound ground beef, cooked
  and drained
1 package taco seasoning mix
4 ounces Cheddar cheese,
  shredded
2 tablespoons water
2 (8-ounce) packages refrigerated
  crescent rolls

1 medium green pepper
½ head lettuce, shredded
1 medium tomato, cubed
1 small onion, chopped
½ cup whole black olives, sliced
1 cup salsa
Sour cream

Preheat oven to 375°. Mix together meat, taco seasoning, cheese and water. Arrange uncooked crescent roll triangles in a circle on a 13-inch baking sheet, overlapping in center, with points to the outside. (Leave at least a 5-inch hole in the center of the dough.) Arrange meat on dough and fold triangles over meat, tucking under at center. Bake 20–25 minutes until golden brown. Cut top off green pepper and remove seeds; fill with salsa. Arrange lettuce, tomato, onion and olives in center of ring and nestle green pepper in center of lettuce. Garnish with sour cream.

Hospice Hospitality

Cypress Chimichangas

A favorite of the Southwest, chimichangas are filled and rolled or folded tortillas which are baked or deep fried.

1 pound ground beef
1 (15-ounce) can refried beans
⅓ cup onions, chopped
1 tablespoon ground chili powder
¼ teaspoon garlic powder

1 (7-ounce) can diced green chiles
12 (10- or 12-inch) flour tortillas
2 (15-ounce) cans tomato sauce
1 teaspoon ground cumin
2 cups Cheddar cheese, grated

Sauté beef until cooked; drain well. Return to skillet and add beans, onions, chili powder, garlic powder and green chiles. Spoon equal amounts of beef mixture into center of each tortilla. Roll tortillas and place, seam side down, in large baking pan. Bake in 350° oven for 30 minutes. In medium saucepan, heat tomato sauce and cumin together. When chimichangas are done, top with tomato sauce and grated cheese. Serves 6 (2 chimichangas per serving).

Sedona Cook Book

Hungarian Stuffed Cabbage

2 medium-sized heads cabbage
Water (1–2 cups)
2 pounds onion, chopped
Vegetable shortening

2½–3 pounds ground beef
1½ cups long grain rice
Salt and pepper to taste
1 (46-ounce) can tomato juice

Trim and core cabbage. In large pot, bring water to boil. Add cabbage heads. Lower heat to simmer 15 minutes on each side until cabbage is softened. Carefully detach leaves. Meanwhile sauté onions in shortening. Put beef in large bowl; add sautéed onion, rice and seasonings. Stuff cabbage leaves with mixture. Roll leaves loosely. Put in large roaster, cover with chopped leftover cabbage and onion. Pour on the tomato juice. Cover and cook slowly at 350° about 1–1¼ hours. Serves 12.

That Hungarian's in My Kitchen

Souvlakia

Salt and pepper
⅓ cup lemon juice
Juice of 1 orange
Oregano
1 cup olive oil
½ cup red wine

2 cloves garlic, minced
2 bay leaves
Leg of lamb, cut into 1-inch cubes
1 green pepper, cut into 1½-inch
  cubes
Small white onions, parboiled

Combine salt, pepper, lemon and orange juice, oregano, olive oil, wine, garlic and bay leaves with the meat. Place in a bowl and cover. Allow to marinate for 5 hours, turning occasionally. Drain the meat; thread on skewers. Alternate meat with peppers and onions. Broil on a grill or under broiler, turning the skewers often.

Recipes from Our Mothers' Kitchens

Shepherd's Beef Pie

4 cups of cooked beef, cubed
2½ cups leftover gravy
2 or 3 cups leftover vegetables
   (potatoes, carrots, string beans,
   peas, etc.)

1 small onion, minced
Parsley flakes
Salt and pepper
3 cups hot mashed potatoes
1 egg, well beaten

Combine meat, gravy, vegetables, onion, parsley flakes, salt and pepper. Heat to boiling point, stirring often. Put mixture in Dutch oven or baking dish. Combine mashed potatoes and egg in bowl; mix thoroughly. Cover top of casserole with potatoes or drop in spoonfuls. Bake in hot oven, 425°, for 15 or 20 minutes or until brown.

Chuck Wagon Cookin'

E Z Shepherd's Pie

1 onion, chopped
3 pounds ground beef
2 cups instant potato flakes
2 cups milk

4 tablespoons margarine
4 cans peas or corn, drained
Salt and pepper to taste
12 slices Cheddar cheese

Brown onion in 14-inch Dutch oven. Add beef and brown. Drain excess grease off. Mix potato flakes, milk and margarine according to package directions. Let stand for 1 minute. Spread peas evenly on top of meat mixture. Spread potatoes on top. Season to taste. Place lid on oven and cook 30 minutes with 12 coals on top and 18 coals on bottom. Top with cheese and cook for 10 additional minutes.

Note: See page 50 for Dutch oven cooking instructions and chart.

Dutch Oven and Campfire Cookbook

Beaver Street Burgers

2 cups boiling water
⅔ cup sun-dried tomatoes
4 pounds beef chuck or ground chuck
2 tablespoons fresh basil leaves, finely chopped
2 tablespoons minced fresh garlic
2 teaspoons kosher salt

1 tablespoon freshly ground black pepper
8 slices Havarti cheese
Basil Pesto Mayonnaise
8 leaves romaine lettuce
8 slices red onion
8 French rolls

Pour about 2 cups boiling water over the dried tomatoes to reconstitute. Cover and soak until the tomatoes are soft, about 30 minutes. Drain off the remaining water, reserving 2 tablespoons of the tomato "liquor," and chop tomatoes.

If using beef chuck roast, cut meat into 1-inch strips. Grind in a meat grinder using the biggest hole grinder plate (⅜-inch).

Preheat a grill.

In a medium bowl, combine the ground chuck or ground beef, basil, garlic, reconstituted tomatoes, salt, pepper, and sun-dried tomato liquor. Combine well and grind, using the smallest hole on the grinder plate, and form into eight patties.

Grill over hot coals to desired doneness and serve with sliced Havarti cheese, Basil Pesto Mayonnaise, lettuce, onion slices, and crusty French rolls. Serves 8.

BASIL PESTO MAYONNAISE:

¼ cup mayonnaise
2 tablespoons basil pesto

Combine mayonnaise and pesto well. Makes ¼ cup.

Approximate values per serving: Cal 887; Fat 61g; Chol 168mg; Carbo 36g; Sod 1,219mg; Cal from Fat 62%

By Request

Magnificent Meatloaf ✗

2 eggs, beaten
½ cup sour cream ⎫ OR ✗
½ cup catsup ⎭
1¼ cups fine bread crumbs
4 large carrots, finely shredded
1 (4-ounce) can sliced mushrooms, drained (optional)
1 rib celery with leaves, finely chopped

1½ tablespoons finely chopped onion
2 tablespoons grated Parmesan cheese
½ teaspoon garlic salt
¼ teaspoon thyme
¼ teaspoon pepper
2 pounds ground sirloin

+1 can wild mushroom soup

Combine the eggs, sour cream and catsup in a large bowl. Add the bread crumbs, carrots, mushrooms, celery, onion, Parmesan cheese, garlic salt, thyme and pepper. Mix until well blended. Add the ground sirloin and mix lightly.

Shape into a loaf in a shallow baking dish or press into a 5x9-inch baking pan. Bake at 350° for 1¼ to 1½ hours or until cooked through. Remove from the oven. Let stand for 5 minutes before slicing to serve. Serves 8.

Note: May process the bread slices in a food processor or blender container to get the measured amount of crumbs. Place the carrots and celery in the food processor or blender container to shred and chop.

Tucson Treasures

Padre Kino's Favorite Meatloaf

2 cups chopped onion
2 tablespoons oil
2 pounds extra lean, double ground beef
1 pound lean chorizo
1 cup seasoned bread crumbs (Italian)
½ cup beef bouillon

2 eggs, lightly beaten
⅔ cup grated Cheddar cheese
1 teaspoon pepper
1 tablespoon salt
2 teaspoons thyme
2 teaspoons paprika
1 teaspoon allspice
1 teaspoon crushed, dried oregano

Preheat oven to 350°. Sauté onions in oil. Mix with other ingredients well. Shape into a loaf (not too high) and bake in a large pan at 350° for 1½ hours. If your oven runs hot, shape a tin foil tent over it to keep it moist. Serves 10.

Padre Kino's Favorite Meatloaf

Applesauce Meatloaf

It makes a great sandwich the following day, too. Of course, around here a good meatloaf goes so fast you have to sneak a couple of slices into the fridge before everyone gets to the table for dinner.

2 pounds lean hamburger	**1 (24-ounce) jar applesauce**
1 pound pork sausage	**1½ teaspoons ginger**
1 large onion, chopped	**Salt and pepper to taste**
1 large green pepper, chopped	**1 bag unseasoned croutons**

Preheat oven to 350°. Combine all ingredients in a large bowl, adding croutons last. Form meat mixture into a loaf in a roasting pan. Bake uncovered 45 minutes. Pour off excess grease and bake an additional 45 minutes. Feeds 4–6 firefighters.

The National Firefighters Recipe Book

Cabbage-Potato Meatloaf

8 potatoes	**2 eggs**
Salt and pepper	**10–15 saltine crackers**
1 head cabbage, sliced	**½ cup chopped onion**
1½–2 pounds ground round	**1½–2 cups water**

Spray Dutch oven with vegetable cooking spray. Peel and slice half the potatoes and layer on bottom of Dutch oven. Sprinkle with salt and pepper. Add a layer of sliced cabbage. Mix ground round, eggs, saltine crackers and chopped onion. Make a large patty and place on top of cabbage. Cover with another layer of cabbage and then another layer of remaining potatoes. Sprinkle with more salt and pepper. Add water; bring to a boil, then cover and simmer 45–50 minutes.

Heavenly Delights

The Yuma Crossing, mapped in 1699 by Father Eusebio Francisco Kino, was the first land route to California. Otherwise it took about 100 days to reach Southern California by sea from Mexico.

Ham, Champagne Sauce

This recipe is a good way to serve leftover ham. If you are using leftovers, skip to Champagne Sauce recipe.

1 (5 to 7-pound) ham   **½ cup white wine**
½ cup brown sugar   **Whole cloves, about 30**

Score ham ¼ inch deep and 1 inch apart. Place ham in a baking pan, fat-side-up. Mix brown sugar and wine in a small bowl and spread over ham, reserving some of the mixture. Push the cloves into the ham where you have scored it. Bake at 350° for 3½ hours, basting occasionally with sugar mixture. Check with a meat thermometer to ensure doneness. Slice ham and serve with Champagne Sauce.

CHAMPAGNE SAUCE:
¼ cup butter   **6 peppercorns**
¼ cup chopped carrot   **5 tablespoons flour**
¼ cup sliced onion   **2 cups beef stock**
1 bay leaf   **½ cup champagne**
1 sprig thyme   **1 tablespoon powdered sugar**
¼ cup chopped fresh parsley

Melt butter in a large saucepan over medium heat. Sauté vegetables and seasonings until lightly browned. Add flour and cook until it starts to brown. Gradually add stock and cook until slightly thickened. Strain sauce and discard vegetables. Return sauce to heat and cook for 5 minutes. Add champagne and sugar; heat through and serve.

Taste of Tombstone

Posole

1 package (#2) frozen posole
    (hominy) or 1 (#10) can hominy
4–5 pounds pork shoulder roast
6 chicken bouillon cubes
2 medium onions, coarsely
    chopped

2 teaspoons sweet basil
1 teaspoon cilantro
3 cloves fresh garlic, crushed
4 tablespoons mild red chili powder
    (more or less, according to taste)
Salt to taste

Place posole (hominy) in large heavy stockpot and add 2 quarts water. Cover with lid. Simmer SLOWLY for about 2 hours, adding water as need-ed. (If using canned hominy, you just need to heat up.) Cut large pieces of pork off the bone and add both to pot. Add chicken bouillon, onions, sweet basil, cilantro, and garlic. Continue to simmer SLOWLY for 3–4 hours, until pork is tender and falling off bone and posole is tender. Remove pork bone and pork meat from pot. Pick meat off bone and shred all the pork and place back in the stockpot. Add the red chili powder and salt to taste. Make a paste of cornstarch and water to thicken slightly. Serve with warm flour tortillas. Serves 8–10 hearty appetities.

Portal's Best Little Cookbook

Chalupa

3 pounds pork loin roast or
    boneless shoulder
1 pound pinto beans
2 cloves garlic, chopped
2 tablespoons chili powder
1 tablespoon cumin, ground
1 teaspoon oregano
1 (27-ounce) can green chiles,
    chopped

3 teaspoons salt or to taste
Fritos
Grated cheese
Shredded lettuce
Onions
Diced tomatoes
Diced avocados
Salsa to taste

In a large pot, put pork roast, pinto beans, garlic, chili powder, cumin, oregano, chopped chiles and salt. Cover with water; cook for 6 hours or until beans are tender. Remove roast and all fat and bone. Shred meat. Put meat back in bean mixture, cook for 1 hour longer without lid to thick-en. Serve over Fritos with grated cheese, shredded lettuce, onions, diced tomatoes, diced avocados and salsa to taste. Leftover chalupa can be used for burritos, dip, or cheese crisp.

Par Excellence

Dorothee's Kahlúa Kabobs

CHUTNEY-KAHLÚA SAUCE:

½ cup chutney	**1 tablespoon vinegar**
¼ cup coffee-flavored liqueur	**3 tablespoons salad oil**
1 tablespoon soy sauce	**½ teaspoon coarse-ground pepper**

Mince or mash your favorite chutney. Combine it thoroughly with liqueur—Kahlúa or any coffee liqueur. Add soy sauce, vinegar, oil and pepper. Put all ingredients into blender and process at high speed until thick and smooth.

KABOBS:

4 pounds lean pork loin cut into 1½-inch cubes	**Whole pimentos**
Green pepper strips	**Parboiled onions**
	Fresh pineapple chunks

Alternate pork cubes on skewers with strips of green pepper, whole pimentos, parboiled onions and fresh pineapple chunks. Grill kabobs 20 minutes, then brush with sauce every few minutes, grilling until tender. Makes eight bronze-glazed portions.

Outdoor Cooking

Emma's Hungarian Goulash

2 large onions, diced	**1 teaspoon paprika**
4 tablespoons Crisco, divided	**1 teaspoon black pepper**
2½ pounds beef, diced	**2 teaspoons salt**
Boiling water	**1 teaspoon garlic salt**
1 tablespoon chopped parsley	**6 large red potatoes, diced**
6 medium carrots, sliced round	**2 teaspoons flour**

In a large pot, sauté onions in 2 tablespoons of the shortening; add beef; brown for 20 minutes. Add enough boiling water to cover the meat, plus 1 inch. Add parsley, sliced carrots and spices. Cook about 2½ hours or until done. Add potatoes after about 2 hours and cook until they are done. In fry pan, make sauce of the remaining 2 tablespoons shortening and flour (cook until medium brown). Add sauce to goulash. Mix well and serve. Serves 8.

That Hungarian's in My Kitchen

Pork Loin Roast for Four with Cinnamon Applesauce and Roasted Potatoes

PORK LOIN ROAST FOR FOUR:

2 pounds boneless pork loin roast **1 clove garlic (reduced to paste)**
1 sprig rosemary **Salt and pepper to taste**
1 sprig thyme

Preheat oven to 500°. Rub roast with herbs and seasonings. Place in a roasting pan with fat-side-up and cook for 20 minutes. Reduce heat to 350° and cook for 30–40 minutes or until internal temperature is 160°. Continually baste roast with excess pork juices while cooking to maintain moistness.

CINNAMON APPLESAUCE FOR FOUR:

4 Golden Delicious apples **¼ cup sugar**
1 cinnamon stick **¼ cup water**

Peel and core apples, then cut into medium-sized pieces. Add apples and cinnamon stick to sugar and water and bring to a boil. Reduce to a simmer for 15–20 minutes or until apples are very soft. Remove cinnamon stick and process apples through a food mill. Then return to stove and simmer for another 5 minutes adding water to desired consistency.

HERB ROASTED POTATOES FOR FOUR:

4 Yukon Gold potatoes **½ tablespoon fresh basil**
1 tablespoon olive oil **½ tablespoon fresh chives**
½ tablespoon rosemary leaves **Salt and pepper to taste**
½ tablespoon fresh parsley

Preheat oven to 350°. Quarter potatoes lengthwise. Combine oil and herbs in mixing bowl and rub potatoes until evenly coated. Bake for 45 minutes or until soft when pierced with fork.

License to Cook Arizona Style

Empañaditas, a popular holiday food in the Southwest, are a smaller version of empañadas. The pastry dough is filled with a mixture of dried fruits, pork, and piñon nuts, a southwestern style of mincemeat, and fried in oil or shortening.

Marinated Pork Loin with Creamy Sun-Dried Tomato Pesto

MARINADE:

½ cup balsamic vinegar
1½ cups extra virgin olive oil
½ teaspoon salt
½ teaspoon black pepper
½ teaspoon thyme
1 tablespoon oregano

1 tablespoon parsley, minced
2 garlic cloves, minced
1 cup onions, finely diced
3 tablespoons Dijon mustard
2 (1-pound) pork loins

Combine all ingredients and marinate pork 24 hours.

CREAMY SUN-DRIED TOMATO PESTO:

1 cup sun-dried tomatoes
¼ cup white wine
2 cloves garlic
¾ cup grated Parmigiana cheese,
 divided
¼ cup pine nuts
1 cup fresh basil, chopped (reserve
 a few leaves for garnish)

1 cup olive oil
Salt and pepper
2 cups heavy cream
1 stick (4 ounces) butter
¼ pound mushrooms, cleaned and
 sliced
1 pound penne pasta

Rehydrate sun-dried tomatoes in white wine. Place in food processor with garlic, ¼ cup cheese, pine nuts, basil, olive oil, salt and pepper. Purée. In saucepan, reduce cream and butter by half. Add ½ cup Parmigiana and stir until melted. Meanwhile sauté mushrooms in a little olive oil. Combine pesto, cream mixture and mushrooms. Keep warm.

Prepare pasta according to package directions. Grill pork loins to desired doneness. Cut each piece of pork in half and into a fan (sliced on the diagonal not quite through the bottom). Drain pasta and divide among 4 plates, top with pesto sauce, slice and fan pork and garnish with fresh basil.

Note: The Creamy Sun-Dried Tomato Pesto also works well with grilled chicken or shrimp. The meat marinade can be used with steaks or poultry.

Contributed by Anzio Landing, Mesa
Arizona Chefs: Cooking at Home with 36 Arizona Chefs

Cracked Black Peppercorn Crusted Pork Loin with Pommery Mustard Sauce

ENTRÉE:

2 pounds pork loin
2 tablespoons black pepper
Salt to taste

Pommery Mustard Sauce
Vegetable Ragout

Preheat oven to 350°. Coat pork with pepper and salt. Sear in a sauté pan until golden brown on all sides. Transfer pork to a baking dish and finish cooking for about 25 minutes or until 140° internal temperature. Remove from oven and let sit about 10 minutes.

POMMERY MUSTARD SAUCE:

½ cup dry white wine
½ cup chicken broth
1 stalk celery, chopped
5 small whole white mushrooms

1½ tablespoons Pommery or
  whole grain mustard
2 cups heavy cream

In a medium saucepot, combine first 5 ingredients. Place on medium high heat and reduce liquid until almost dry. Add cream and reduce again by ⅓ or to a sauce consistency. Keep warm.

VEGETABLE RAGOUT:

2 tablespoons olive oil
8 Red Bliss potatoes, quartered
  and blanched
½ pound small white mushrooms,
  quartered
1 clove garlic, minced

1 bunch asparagus, peeled,
  trimmed, blanched in boiling
  salted water about 3 minutes
  and shocked in ice
Salt and pepper to taste
4 sprigs thyme (garnish)

In a medium size sauté pan, add olive oil and heat until smoking. Add potatoes and cook until golden brown (6 minutes). Add mushrooms and garlic and stir until mushrooms start to darken. Add asparagus tips and heat through. Divide the vegetable ragout among 4 heated plates. Spoon mustard sauce around vegetables and place 3 slices of pork on top.

Contributed by A.J.'s, Scottsdale
Arizona Chefs: Dine-In Dine-Out Cookbook

Sausage, Peppers, and Onions with Polenta

MARINARA SAUCE:

¼ cup olive oil
1 large white onion, finely diced
3 gloves garlic, minced
1 large can crushed tomatoes
1 tablespoon dried basil

2 bay leaves
¼ teaspoon fennel seeds
½ tablespoon salt
¼ teaspoon red pepper flakes
Salt and pepper to taste

Heat oil in heavy-bottomed saucepan over medium heat. Add onion and garlic and sauté until translucent, about 5 minutes. Add the remaining ingredients. Bring to a boil, reduce heat, and simmer 45 minutes. Stir and taste occasionally. The sauce should thicken and lose its acidic taste. Adjust seasonings. Set aside.

SAUSAGES:

6 Italian sausages (about 1½ pounds)
2 tablespoons oil
1 large white onion, sliced vertically

2 large green peppers, stemmed, seeded, and cut into ½-inch strips
Marinara Sauce

Cut sausages in half. Heat oil in heavy skillet. Add sausages and begin to brown. When partly browned, add onion and peppers. When sausages are fully browned, add marinara and simmer 30 minutes, reducing heat, if necessary. Meanwhile, prepare Polenta.

POLENTA:

5 cups water
1 tablespoon salt

1 cup yellow cornmeal
¼ cup Parmigiana cheese, grated

Bring water to a boil and add salt. Add cornmeal slowly while whisking constantly. Once all cornmeal is added, stir frequently until the polenta thickens and pulls away from sides of pan. Add cheese and stir to incorporate. Polenta will be fairly soft.

Note: Sausages and polenta can be served separately or together with the sausages surrounding or topping the polenta.

Contributed by Tucchetti, Phoenix
Arizona Chefs: Cooking at Home with 36 Arizona Chefs

Sausage-Chile Rellenos Casserole

1 pound bulk pork sausage
3 (4-ounce) cans whole green
   chiles, drained, cut in ½
   lengthwise
4 cups (16 ounces) Colby cheese,
   shredded

4 cups (16 ounces) Monterey Jack
   cheese, shredded
6 eggs, beaten
1 can evaporated milk
2 tablespoons flour

Cook sausage over medium heat until browned. Stir to crumble and drain well. Layer chiles in a greased 9x13x2-inch casserole. Sprinkle with sausage and cheeses. Combine eggs, milk, and flour, mixing well. Pour over sausage and cheese. Bake, uncovered, at 325° for 45 minutes. Serve with picante sauce, flour tortillas, or refried beans. Serves 10.

The Dog-Gone Delicious Cookbook

Chorizo
(Hot Sausage)

5 ounces whole dry red chiles,
   seeded
9 ounces ground red chile (extra
   hot)
2 heads garlic, separated, peeled,
   and finely chopped
3 tablespoons dried oregano
   leaves, crushed

2 tablespoons white distilled
   vinegar
5 teaspoons salt
1 teaspoon pepper
½ teaspoon ground cloves
6 pounds pork roast, ground with
   some fat

In large saucepan, cover dry chiles with water and boil until soft. Drain, reserving liquid. In blender or food processor, purée chiles. Add ground red chile and enough of the reserved liquid to make thick sauce. Stir in garlic, oregano, vinegar, salt, pepper and cloves. Mix well with ground pork. Fry a small amount of sausage and taste for seasoning. Refrigerate three days. Package sausage in sealed plastic bags and freeze until ready to use. Serve with fried eggs, beans, potatoes, or part of fillings for burritos and tacos. Makes about 6 pounds.

Recipes from Arizona with Love

Pork Chop Skillet Dinner

4 pork chops
1 tablespoon shortening
4 tablespoons rice, uncooked
4 slices onion

4 slices green pepper
1 (16-ounce) can tomatoes
1 teaspoon salt
½ teaspoon pepper

Brown chops in medium skillet in heated shortening. Pour off excess fat. On each chop, place a tablespoon of rice, a slice of onion and green pepper, and a portion of tomatoes. Add seasonings and cover with liquid from tomatoes. Cover. Cook over low heat until chops are tender, about 1 hour. Serves 4.

Dishes from the Deep

Pork Chops and Potatoes

6 medium potatoes, peeled and
  sliced
1 can mushroom soup, condensed
1 large can evaporated milk or
  1 cup whole milk

2 tablespoons dry onion
Salt and pepper to taste
6 pork chops, thinly sliced

Heat oven to 350°. Grease oblong baking dish. Mix potatoes, soup, milk, dry onions, and salt and pepper. Put in baking dish. Arrange pork chops on top of mixture and bake, uncovered, for 1 hour.

The Dog-Gone Delicious Cookbook

Lamb Noisettes Janos

DUXELLES:

12 ounces domestic mushrooms
6 ounces shallots
1½ cups dry white wine

Salt and freshly ground pepper to
taste

In food processor fitted with a stainless-steel blade, finely chop mushrooms and shallots. Transfer to a medium saucepan. Add wine, salt and pepper, bring to a boil, and reduce until liquid has almost evaporated. Set aside.

LAMB:

1 boneless lamb loin (1½ pounds)
Salt and freshly ground pepper to
taste

Clarified butter for sautéing
1½ cups Mousseline Sauce*

Preheat oven to 375°. Sprinkle lamb with salt and pepper. Coat a sauté pan with clarified butter and when pan is very hot, sear lamb on all sides. It should be well browned.

Slice lamb into 16 equal slices, or noisettes. Place in one layer on a cookie pan and mound duxelles onto each slice. Cook in oven for 5 minutes, or until meat is medium-rare.

Preheat broiler. Top each noisette with Mousseline Sauce and place pan 2 inches under broiler. Broil until Mousseline is nicely browned. Divide noisettes among 4 warm dinner plates and serve. Serves 4.

*Mousseline Sauce is simply Hollandaise that has been lightened and enriched by the addition of whipped cream.

Janos: Recipes and Tales from a Southwest Restaurant

The Wishing Shrine is the only shrine in the U.S. dedicated to sinners. Legend tells of the death of a young herder who was involved in a love triangle. Because he was buried in unconsecrated ground, people lit candles on this spot. It is said that if you light a candle and it burns all night, your wish will come true.

Lamb Chops St. Basil

This was an award winner.

½ cup vegetable oil	**¼ teaspoon onion salt**
1 teaspoon black pepper	**1 can or bottle of beer**
¼ cup Dijon mustard	**1 teaspoon rosemary**
1 teaspoon Worcestershire sauce	**1 tablespoon basil**
1 teaspoon minced garlic	**2 loin lamb chops, ½-inch thick**

Prepare marinade with oil, pepper, mustard, Worcestershire sauce, garlic, and onion salt in a medium container. Slowly add beer while stirring. Sprinkle rosemary and basil and stir in. Rinse and pierce chops and place in marinade. Cover and refrigerate several hours. Grill over low to medium heat ½ hour, turning and basting frequently. Use up all of marinade.

Favorites for All Seasons

Dry Rub

Use this spicy dry rub on chicken, ribs, or beef the night before grilling.

1 tablespoon ground black pepper	**1 tablespoon garlic powder**
1 tablespoon ground white pepper	**1 tablespoon brown sugar**
1 tablespoon sugar	**1 tablespoon ground oregano**
2 tablespoons ground cayenne chiles	**4 tablespoons sweet paprika**
	1 teaspoon dry mustard
2 tablespoons chili powder	**1 tablespoon celery salt**
1 tablespoon cumin	**1 tablespoon salt**

Thoroughly combine all ingredients. Rub mixture into the meat of your choice. Wrap coated meat tightly in plastic wrap and refrigerate overnight or for at least 8 hours. Store remaining mixture in a jar in the refrigerator or freezer.

License to Cook Arizona Style

Mary Ann's Magnifico Meatballs and Spaghetti Sauce

SPAGHETTI SAUCE:

¾ cup chopped onion
3 tablespoons olive oil
1 cup water
1 tablespoon sugar
1½ teaspoons crushed oregano
1 bay leaf, optional

1 clove garlic, minced
2 (6-ounce) cans tomato paste
2 (1-pound) cans tomatoes
1½ teaspoons salt
½ teaspoon pepper

Sauté onion in oil until tender; stir in remaining ingredients. Simmer uncovered 30 minutes. Add Meatballs; cook 30 minutes longer.

MEATBALLS:

4 slices dry bread
2 eggs
2 tablespoons chopped parsley
1 clove garlic, minced
1 pound ground beef
Dash pepper

1 teaspoon salt
½ cup grated Parmesan or Romano
  cheese
1 teaspoon crushed oregano or basil
2 tablespoons olive oil

Soak bread in water 2 or 3 minutes; squeeze out moisture. Combine bread with remaining ingredients except oil, mixing well. Form small balls (about 20). Brown slowly in hot oil. Add to spaghetti sauce; cook 30 minutes. Serve over hot spaghetti.

First Baptist Favorites

Poultry

Arizona's state symbol is the saguaro cactus, which is the largest and one of the slowest growing of all cacti, reaching up to fifteen meters high and living for several centuries. Plants can weigh up to eight tons.

El Presidio
Pan-Fried Chicken

4 boneless, skinless chicken breasts
3 egg whites
1 Anaheim chile, peeled, seeded, and chopped
1 cup (4 ounces) grated Cheddar cheese
2 tomatoes, peeled, seeded, and chopped

4 scallions, finely chopped
1 tablespoon finely chopped garlic
2 sprigs cilantro, chopped
½ cup heavy cream
Salt and freshly ground pepper to taste

Cut breasts into chunks and quickly process in a food processor along with egg whites. Do not purée; chicken should be fairly coarse. Fold in chile, cheese, tomatoes, scallions, garlic, chopped cilantro, and cream; season with salt and pepper. Shape mixture into patties about 1½ inches thick.

BREADING:
2 cups all-purpose flour
1 cup milk
4 cups coarse bread crumbs

Vegetable oil or shortening for frying
Sprigs of cilantro for garnish

Preheat oven to 350°. Set out individual containers of flour, milk, and bread crumbs. Dust patties with flour, dip in milk, and coat with bread crumbs, handling carefully so that they maintain their shape. Heat ¼ inch oil or shortening in a sauté pan. Add patties and fry until golden brown, turning once. Finish in oven, 7 minutes. Garnish with cilantro and serve immediately.

Janos: Recipes and Tales from a Southwest Restaurant

Grilled Chicken
with Macadamia Nuts

1 pound skinless, boneless chicken
breasts, cut into bite-size pieces
¼ cup chopped green onion
1 cup roughly chopped honey-
roasted macadamia nuts

½ cup fresh orange sections
2 tablespoons finely diced or
julienned red bell pepper
Ginger Chili Vinaigrette

Grill chicken, or bake in a 350° oven for 20 minutes, until chicken is no longer pink. Cool. In a medium salad bowl, combine cooled chicken, green onion, nuts, orange sections, and bell pepper. Serve with Ginger Chili Vinaigrette. Serves 4–6.

GINGER CHILI VINAIGRETTE:

½ teaspoon fresh, minced ginger
¾ teaspoon chopped chipotle
pepper
¼ teaspoon chopped onion
¼ teaspoon chopped garlic
1½ teaspoons chopped pimientos
Pinch of salt

Pinch of black pepper
1 tablespoon chopped fresh parsley
1 tablespoon pasteurized egg
substitute
¼ cup tarragon vinegar
¼ cup fresh orange juice
½ cup corn oil

In a blender, combine ginger, chipotle pepper, onion, garlic, pimientos, salt, pepper, parsley, egg substitute, vinegar and orange juice. Blend well. Slowly add oil, blending until well combined. Chill before serving. Makes about 1 cup.

Approximate values per serving (salad with 2 tablespoons Ginger Chili Vinaigrette): Cal 329; Fat 22g; Chol 66mg; Carbo 6g; Prot 27g; Sod 98mg; Cal from Fat 60%

By Request

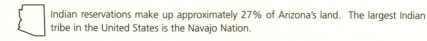

Indian reservations make up approximately 27% of Arizona's land. The largest Indian tribe in the United States is the Navajo Nation.

Spanish Chicken Casserole with Saffron Rice

1 (3 to 3½-pound) frying chicken
Salted water
1 cup (maybe more) chicken stock
¼ teaspoon saffron
1 cup raw long grain rice
2 onions, 1 chopped and 1 cut in rings

2 green bell peppers, 1 chopped and one cut in rings
2 cups chopped fresh tomatoes
Salt and freshly ground pepper
2 tablespoons coarsely chopped cilantro

Preheat oven to 350°. Clean and cut up chicken, removing all fat. Give chicken a cleansing bath in salt water for 15 minutes. Drain on paper towels. Use a large casserole or flat baking pan to bake chicken 45 minutes to an hour, until browned (turn pieces at least once). Remove half of chicken to plate and pour off excess fat. Add saffron to chicken stock and mix thoroughly, then add to pan. Scrape bottom and sides of pan to loosen any brownings, and mix with stock.

Add rice to bottom of pan around chicken, then a layer of chopped onion and chopped bell peppers. Return the rest of chicken pieces to dish. Layer tomatoes over chicken. Then add onion and bell pepper rings on top. Salt and pepper to taste; sprinkle with cilantro.

Cover tightly and bake 1 hour and 15 minutes, until rice has browned sufficiently. Let rest short time before serving. Serves 6.

Gourmet Gringo

Mission SanXavier del Bac, the stunningly beautiful adobe church located on the Tohono O'odham Indian Reservation southwest of Tucson, has been called the "Sistine Chapel of North America" for the fine artwork that has emerged from an international restoration effort. Constructed in the 1780s, the church continues as an active Catholic church.

Fiesta Tortilla Stack

1 (9-ounce) can bean dip
½ cup plus 2 tablespoons sour cream, divided
1 tablespoon plus ½ teaspoon Mexican seasoning mix, divided
2 cups chopped, cooked chicken
1 medium red pepper, chopped
½ cup thinly sliced green onions with tops
¾ cup sliced olives, divided
¼ cup snipped cilantro, divided
5 (10-inch) flour tortillas
8 ounces mild Cheddar cheese, shredded
2 medium tomatoes, seeded and chopped
Salsa (optional)

Heat oven to 375°. In a 1-quart glass bowl, combine dip, 2 tablespoons sour cream, and 1 tablespoon seasoning mix. Mix well. Place chicken and bell pepper in bowl. Add green onions, ½ cup olive slices, and 2 tablespoons cilantro. Mix gently. Place one tortilla in a 13-inch round baking dish. Top tortilla with two scoops of bean mixture, spread chopped chicken evenly over mixture and top with grated cheese. Repeat layers three more times. Top with remaining tortilla and spray with vegetable oil. Bake 25–30 minutes or until top of tortilla is golden brown. Place remaining mixture on top of warm tortilla. Add remaining olives, tomatoes, and remaining cilantro for garnish.

Kids in the Kitchen

Pomegranate-Sauced Chicken

3 pounds favorite chicken parts
Oil
½ teaspoon poultry seasoning

1 large onion, chopped
1 cup coarsely chopped pecans
Pomegranate seeds

Brown chicken pieces in oil, remove from pan, and keep warm. Drain all but 2 tablespoons drippings from pan and stir in poultry seasoning and onion. Cook until transparent. Stir in nuts and cook until lightly brown. Serve chicken topped with Pomegranate Sauce and garnished with pomegranate seeds. Serves 6.

POMEGRANATE SAUCE:

2 tablespoons tomato sauce
1½ cups water, divided
1 teaspoon salt
½ teaspoon ground cinnamon

1 cup orange juice
1 cup pomegranate juice
1 tablespoon cornstarch

Combine tomato sauce with 1¼ cups water, salt, cinnamon, orange juice and pomegranate juice; bring to a boil and simmer for 20 minutes. Return chicken pieces to pan, cover and simmer until tender. Remove chicken. Combine cornstarch with remaining ¼ cup water and stir into sauce. Cook and stir until thickened.

Fruits of the Desert Cookbook

Pollo en Chile Colorado
(Chicken in Red Chile)

8 chicken breasts
2 cloves garlic
3 tablespoons flour
2 teaspoons salt, or to taste

2 bay leaves
Sprinkle of vinegar
3 cups Red Chile Sauce

In a 2-quart pot, put chicken breasts and garlic in 2 cups of water and cook over medium heat 20–30 minutes. Reserve broth. Remove skin, debone chicken, cut meat into cubes, and let cool. Put chicken into a bag with a mixture of the flour and salt, and toss to coat. Warm the Red Chile Sauce, add chicken and the bay leaves, and enough chicken broth to give you the consistency you want. Cook on low for about another 30 minutes.

CHILE COLORADO (RED CHILE SAUCE):

In our area, red chiles are available in a variety of forms and under different labels. Among the canned chiles, Las Palmas brand is my favorite; for frozen chiles, I prefer the Baca label; and for powdered chile, I like Santa Cruz chile. But my all-time favorite chile sauce is made with dried chiles from your own ristra or chile string.

10–12 red chiles
3 cups water

Salt to taste

Homemade red chile sauce is made from the pulp of dried red chile peppers. The chiles must be washed and seeded, and their stems removed. Place the chiles in 3 cups of water and bring to a boil. Turn off the heat and leave the pan with the chiles to cool.

When cool, put the chiles in a blender with enough water from the boiling pot to make a thin paste. Add more liquid as necessary. Use a strainer to remove any particles of the outer skin of the chile that have not been liquefied. Red Chile Sauce freezes well. This recipe makes 3 cups. I usually freeze it in 1-cup amounts, which is enough for most meals.

When you're ready to use this beautiful orange-red mixture for a recipe, heat a couple of tablespoons of oil in a pan and sauté a couple of garlic cloves. Add 3 tablespoons of flour and stir while cooking slightly. Add chile paste and stir. Add more water or broth to bring chile sauce to desired thickness.

Don't forget: A few drops of vinegar will round off the flavors.

Corazón Contento

Chicken Fricassee

4 tablespoons butter
1 teaspoon oil
3 pounds chicken, cut up
Salt and pepper to taste
½ teaspoon tarragon
1 onion, quartered

4 tablespoons flour
2 cups dry white wine
2 cups chicken stock
½ pound mushrooms, quartered
½ cup heavy cream
Juice of ½ lemon

Melt butter and oil in large stockpot over medium heat. Sprinkle chicken with salt and pepper; add to pot. Cook chicken until it is firm and lightly golden. Sprinkle meat with tarragon and add the onion. Cover pot and simmer for 10–15 minutes. Uncover and sprinkle chicken and onions with flour. Turn chicken to coat evenly. Cook an additional 15 minutes. Gradually stir in wine and stock. The chicken should be almost covered, if not, add more stock. Cover and simmer for 35 minutes. Add mushrooms and cream; simmer for an additional 10 minutes. Add the lemon juice. Check the seasonings; adjust, if needed. Serve over rice.

Taste of Tombstone

Malka's Chinese Chicken "Spare Ribs"

7 tablespoons brown sugar
7 tablespoons soy sauce
7 tablespoons water

1–2 garlic cloves, crushed
2 pounds chicken wings

Preheat oven to 350°. In a bowl, combine sugar, soy sauce, water, and garlic. Place chicken wings in a greased casserole. Pour sauce on top. Bake in a 350° oven for 1½ hours, basting occasionally. Yields 4 servings.

Kosher Kettle

Kung Pao Chicken

1¼ pounds skinless, boneless
  chicken breasts, cut into ½-inch
  pieces
1 egg white
1 tablespoon plus 1 teaspoon
  cornstarch
1 teaspoon Szechuan chili paste
2 tablespoons soy sauce
1 teaspoon dry sherry

1 teaspoon red wine vinegar
¼ cup chicken broth
1 teaspoon Oriental sesame oil
3 tablespoons vegetable oil
½ cup raw peanuts
4 scallions, in ½-inch pieces
2 garlic cloves, chopped
½ teaspoon crushed hot pepper

In a small bowl, combine chicken pieces with egg white and 1 tablespoon cornstarch. Toss to coat and set aside. In another small bowl, blend chili paste with soy sauce, sherry, vinegar, broth, 1 teaspoon cornstarch and sesame oil. Set sauce aside.

Heat oil in a wok or large frying pan over medium-high heat. Add chicken and stir-fry until it separates and turns white, about 4 minutes. Remove with a slotted spoon and drain on paper towels. Deep fry peanuts in oil over medium heat until they are golden brown, about 3 minutes. Remove and drain. Remove all but 2 tablespoons oil from wok. Stir-fry scallions, garlic, and hot pepper for 30 seconds. Add chicken. Stir-fry over high heat for 1 minute. Add sauce. Stir-fry until heated through and thickened. Add peanuts. Stir to mix. Serve over rice. Serves 4.

Pleasures from the Good Earth

Spinach-Stuffed Chicken Rolls

1 cup frozen, chopped spinach,
   thawed and drained
2 teaspoons onion powder
⅓ cup fat-free Parmesan cheese
1½ tablespoons + 1 teaspoon
   garlic powder
2 teaspoons dried basil

1½ cups fat-free seasoned
   croutons, crushed
⅓ cup fat-free mayonnaise
¾ teaspoon Tabasco sauce
2 pounds fat-free chicken breasts
2 tablespoons reconstituted Butter
   Buds

Prepare medium-hot grill and lightly spray with nonfat cooking spray. Combine spinach, onion powder, Parmesan cheese, 1½ tablespoons garlic powder, basil, croutons, mayonnaise and Tabasco sauce in medium bowl and mix until blended. In small bowl, combine Butter Buds and 1 teaspoon garlic powder and mix until blended.

Lay chicken breasts flat on work surface; divide spinach mixture evenly and spoon down the center of each chicken breast. Fold chicken breast and roll around filling and secure with toothpick.

Brush chicken breasts with garlic-butter mixture and place on grill. Grill chicken 10–15 minutes, turning 1–2 times, until no longer pink and cooked through. Serves 6.

Nutritional Analysis Per Serving: Cal 196; Carbo 12g; Chol 95mg; Dietary Fiber ,2g; Fat <1g; Prot 35g; Sod 542mg; Exchanges 2 veg; 4 meat

The Fat Free Living Family Cookbook

Stuffed Chicken in Phyllo with Asparagus and Tomatoes

4 (8-ounce) skinless, boneless
   chicken breasts
Vegetable oil
Salt and pepper to taste
2 cups water
8 asparagus stalks, diced

1 cup boursin cheese
2 tomatoes, seeded and diced
1 egg
12 sheets phyllo dough
6 ounces melted butter

Heat sauté pan; add oil to cover bottom. Sprinkle chicken with salt and pepper. Sear chicken on both sides until about ¾ cooked. Set aside to cool. In medium pot, boil water. Cook asparagus until semi-soft. Cool. Set aside.

In mixing bowl, add cheese, asparagus, tomatoes and 1 egg. Mix thoroughly. Preheat oven to 350°. Slice chicken breasts in half lengthwise. Divide cheese into 4 portions. Place ¼ cheese mixture on 4 chicken halves, topping with the other half. Set aside. Lay out one sheet phyllo dough and brush all over with melted butter. Lay two more sheets over the first, repeating the buttering process. Lay chicken in center of triple sheet and wrap. Repeat with other breasts. Brush outside of each packet and bake 20–25 minutes or until phyllo is golden brown.

Contributed by Quill Creek Cafe, Scottsdale
Arizona Chefs: Dine-In Dine-Out Cookbook

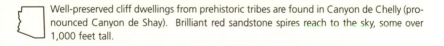

Well-preserved cliff dwellings from prehistoric tribes are found in Canyon de Chelly (pronounced Canyon de Shay). Brilliant red sandstone spires reach to the sky, some over 1,000 feet tall.

Chicken Dijon in Phyllo

3 whole chicken breasts
½ teaspoon salt
¼ teaspoon white pepper
4 tablespoons butter
½ cup Dijon mustard
2 cups heavy cream

8 phyllo pastry sheets
12 tablespoons butter, melted
¼ cup bread crumbs
1 egg
1 teaspoon water

Skin, bone, and cut chicken into 1-inch strips. Sprinkle with salt and pepper. Sauté in 4 tablespoons butter until strips are no longer pink, about 5 minutes. Transfer to platter and keep warm.

Add mustard to skillet, scraping pan. Whisk in cream, blending thoroughly. Reduce heat and simmer until sauce is slightly thickened and reduced. Stir in any juices from the chicken. Strain sauce over chicken.

Lay 1 sheet of phyllo on a damp dish towel. Brush liberally with melted butter and sprinkle with 1–2 pinches bread crumbs. Layer 6 more sheets of phyllo on top, preparing each with butter and bread crumbs. Top with last sheet of phyllo, brushing only the borders with melted butter. Arrange chicken over lower third of long side of dough, leaving a 2-inch border along outside edges, partially enclosing chicken. Roll up jelly-roll fashion. Place seam-side-down on lightly greased baking sheet. Beat egg with water and brush over dough to glaze. Bake at 450° until phyllo is crisp and golden brown, about 12–15 minutes. Cut into 2-inch slices. Serves 6.

Purple Sage and Other Pleasures

Weekender Party Pleaser

2 cups diced cooked chicken
½ cup shredded carrots
½ cup chopped fresh broccoli
½ cup chopped sweet red
  pepper
1 cup sharp cheese, shredded
½ cup mayonnaise

2 cloves of garlic, chopped
¼ teaspoon salt
Pepper
2 (8-ounce) tubes refrigerated
  crescent rolls
1 egg white, beaten
2 tablespoons slivered almonds

In a bowl, mix chicken, carrots, broccoli, red pepper, cheese, mayonnaise, garlic, salt and pepper; mix well. Unroll crescent roll dough and place on cookie sheet, side-by-side, pressing out perforations and making a 15x12-inch rectangle (dough will hang over pan). Spread filling down center of dough. On each side, cut wide strips. Start at one end and alternate strips, twisting the ends across the filling. Seal ends. Brush with egg white and top with almonds. Bake at 375° 30–35 minutes. Makes 12 servings.

Kingman Welcome Wagon Club Cookbook

Santa Cruz Chicken Casserole

1 cup diced, cooked chicken
1 cup sliced celery
2 teaspoons chopped onion
½ cup chopped walnuts
1½ cups cooked rice
1 (10½-ounce) can cream of
  chicken soup

½ teaspoon salt
¼ teaspoon pepper
1 tablespoon lemon juice
¾ cup mayonnaise
¼ cup water
1 hard-boiled egg, diced
8 soda crackers

Combine first nine ingredients. Mix mayonnaise with water then add to first nine ingredients. Gently stir in egg. Pour into greased 9-inch square pan. Top with crushed crackers. Bake at 450° for 15 minutes. Serves 6.

Cowboy Cookin'

Montezuma Chicken Bake

6 cups cooked, cubed chicken
Green Sauce
2 cups (16 ounces) dairy sour
cream

12 (6-inch) corn tortillas, cut in
1½-inch pieces
1½ pounds Monterey Jack cheese,
shredded

Heat oven to 375°. In shallow rectangular baking dish, 9x13x2-inch, arrange alternating layers of half of chicken, Green Sauce, sour cream, tortillas and cheese. Repeat layers, ending with cheese. Cover with aluminum foil. Can be made ahead up to this point and refrigerated. Bake for 30–35 minutes or until heated through and bubbly (uncover for last 8–10 minutes). If made ahead and just out of refrigerator, bake 40–45 minutes. Makes 10–12 servings.

GREEN SAUCE:
1 (14-ounce) can Mexican
tomatillos, drained
½ cup chopped onion
½ cup packed fresh cilantro
leaves or parsley

1 (4-ounce) can green chiles
2 cloves garlic, crushed
1 teaspoon salt
½ teaspoon sugar

In blender container or food processor, combine all ingredients. Blend until smooth.

Recipes from Arizona with Love

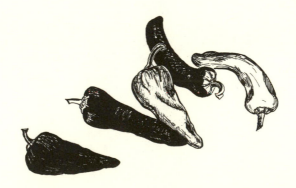

Chicken or Turkey Tortillas Casserole

½ cup onion, chopped
½ cup chicken broth
¼ cup celery, chopped
3 cups cooked chicken or turkey
10–12 corn tortillas, torn in
   bite-size pieces
1 (4-ounce) can diced green chiles

1 can cream of mushroom soup
1 teaspoon pepper
1 cup Cheddar cheese, shredded
   and divided
1 cup Monterey Jack cheese,
   shredded and divided
1 cup salsa

In medium pan, combine onion, broth, and celery. Bring to a boil and simmer, covered, for 5–6 minutes until vegetables are tender. In a large bowl, stir together the undrained vegetable mixture, cooked chicken or turkey, corn tortillas, green chiles, soup, and pepper. Reserve ½ cup of each cheese and set aside. Stir remaining cheese into tortilla mixture. Transfer mixture to a lightly greased 9x13x2-inch baking dish. Top with salsa and reserved cheeses. Bake at 350° for 30 minutes. Let stand 5 minutes before serving. Serves 10–12.

Par Excellence

Quick Chicken Casserole

3 chicken breasts, cut in halves
½ teaspoon salt
¼ teaspoon pepper
½ teaspoon Accent (optional)
¾ cup Bisquick
¼ cup peanut oil

1 cup instant rice
1 (10-ounce) can cream of chicken
   soup (low salt)
¾ cup half-and-half (mocha flavor)
   or canned evaporated milk

Wipe the chicken breasts with paper toweling. Sprinkle with a portion of the salt, pepper and Accent. Place the pancake mix in a paper sack, then coat each piece of chicken with the mix by shaking up and down vigorously. Heat oil in skillet; brown each piece of chicken on both sides.

    Cook rice according to directions on package. Stir cream of chicken soup and half-and-half into cooked rice. Put soup and rice mixture into a buttered casserole, then put the pieces of chicken on the top. Place in a 350° oven for 35 minutes. Serve piping hot. Serves 6.

Heavenly Delights

Sandra's Cream Taco Casserole

This is a rousing way to use up leftover turkey.

12 corn tortillas	4 ounces diced green chiles
2 tablespoons corn oil, heated	½ cup taco sauce
Salt	Butter
1 onion, finely chopped	3 cups cooked, diced chicken
1½ cups light cream or	8 ounces sharp Cheddar cheese,
half-and-half	grated

Dip tortillas in hot oil just enough to soften. Drain and cool on paper towels or paper bag. Salt tortillas and tear into quarters. Set aside.

Sauté chopped onion in remaining oil. Add the cream—skim milk will never give the desired satiny sauce—and stir over low heat 5 minutes. Add chiles and taco sauce and stir to blend. Have ready a buttered, 2-quart casserole. Layer into it the torn tortillas, chicken, sauce, and cheese, in that order. Bake, uncovered, about 45 minutes at 350°. Serves 6.

Arizona Highways Heritage Cookbook

Chicken Taco Bake

1 pound chicken, cut into cubes	6 flour tortillas cut into 1-inch
1 can tomato soup	pieces
1 cup salsa	1 cup shredded Cheddar cheese,
½ cup milk	divided
1 can refried beans	

Preheat oven to 400°. In skillet over medium heat, cook chicken until brown and juices run clear; pour off fat. Add soup, salsa, milk, refried beans, tortillas and half of the cheese. Spoon into a 2-quart shallow baking dish. Cover and bake about 20 minutes until hot. Sprinkle with remaining cheese. Quick and easy!

Kids in the Kitchen

Chicken Enchilada Casserole

6 whole chicken breasts
1 can cream of mushroom soup
1 can cream of chicken soup
1 cup milk
1 onion, grated

1 can diced green chiles
1 can green chile salsa
12 corn tortillas, cut in squares
1 pound Longhorn cheese, grated

Boil chicken breasts and remove bones. Cut meat into pieces. Mix soups, milk, onion, chiles and salsa. Butter a large, shallow baking dish. Pour in small amount of chicken broth. Make a layer of tortillas, a layer of chicken and a layer of soup mix, then sprinkle small amount of cheese. Continue layering with cheese on top. Bake at 375° until cheese is bubbly, about 35 minutes.

Lion's Club of Globe Cookbook

Stuffed Peppers à la Phoenix

¾ pound ground turkey breast
¼ cup chopped scallions
1 tablespoon chopped cilantro
Freshly ground black pepper to
    taste

1 cup shredded part-skim
    mozzarella cheese
4 Anaheim or Poblano peppers,
    seeded and halved
1 tablespoon chopped parsley

Cook turkey, scallions, cilantro, and pepper over medium heat until the turkey is no longer pink. Stir in half of the cheese. Spoon mix into the pepper halves. Arrange the peppers in a casserole dish lightly coated with vegetable spray. Bake at 350° for 15 minutes. Sprinkle remaining cheese and parsley over the peppers and bake until cheese is melted, about 10 minutes. Serves 4.

Variation: Two medium bell peppers can be substituted for the Anaheim or Poblano peppers.

Cal 163; %Fat 28; Fat 5g; Sat Fat 2.3g; Chol 58mg; Sod 125mg; Carbo 4g; Prot 24g; Fiber 1g. Exchanges: Vegetable 1, Low-fat protein 3

Arizona Heart Institute Foundation Cookbook

Chicken Catchatuelle

1 bunch green onions, diced
2 large celery stalks, diced
1 small green pepper, diced
½ teaspoon garlic powder
3 tablespoons margarine
6 ounces mushrooms, chopped, divided
½ teaspoon basil
½ teaspoon thyme
½ pound ham, chopped or ground
6 chicken breasts, boned, skin on
Salt, pepper and Lawry's seasoning salt, to taste
1 large can stewed tomatoes
1 cup cooking sherry

Sauté onions, celery and green pepper with garlic powder in margarine. Add 5 ounces mushrooms, basil and thyme. Add chopped ham. Stuff chicken breasts with mixture (2-3 spoonfuls), roll and place skin-up in baking dish (place so that pieces don't touch together).

Sprinkle with seasoning salt and bake at 425° for ½ hour. In a blender, blend stewed tomatoes, 1 ounce mushrooms and cooking sherry. Pour over chicken and bake at 350° for 1 hour.

First Baptist Favorites

Stuffed Wild Goose

1 wild goose, plucked
Juice of 1 lemon
Salt and pepper to taste
2 tablespoons butter
1 onion, chopped
1 apple, chopped
2 tablespoons apricot preserves
2 cups soft bread crumbs or cubed bread
4–6 slices bacon

Rub the cleaned bird inside and out with lemon juice, then sprinkle with salt and pepper.

For the stuffing, melt the butter in a skillet and sauté the onion until soft and clear. Mix in the apple, apricot preserves, bread crumbs, and a bit of salt and pepper. Spoon stuffing into cavity. Close opening with skewers or string. Place bacon slices over the bird. Add 1 cup water to the roasting pan with the bird. Cover and roast in 325° oven, allowing 25 minutes per pound. Cook until tender. Baste frequently with pan drippings.

Arizona Small Game and Fish Recipes

Stuffed Game Hens with Raspberry Sauce

¼ teaspoon pepper
¼ teaspoon garlic powder
2 rock cornish game hens
1 package long-grain and wild rice, cooked

¼ cup butter
¼ cup honey

Combine pepper and garlic powder in a bowl. Pat hens dry inside and out and season cavities with half the pepper mixture. Fill the hens with rice and close with skewers. Tuck wings under. Melt butter and combine with honey. Place hens in a preheated (350°) 12-inch Dutch oven. Brush butter and honey over hens. Sprinkle with remaining pepper mixture. Turn and baste frequently with butter and honey mixture. Bake hens until the juices run clear when the thigh is pierced in the thickest part. Use 12 briquets on bottom and 14 on the lid. Cook for about 40 minutes or until thigh meat is done.

RASPBERRY SAUCE:

1 (10-ounce) package frozen raspberries (sieved, if desired)
2 tablespoons sugar

¼ cup water
¼ cup honey
1 teaspoon lemon zest

Combine raspberries, sugar, water, honey and lemon zest in a saucepan over medium heat. Cook until sauce thickens, stirring frequently, about 10 minutes. Transfer hens to cutting board and split in half. Place on plates and spoon sauce over.

Note: See page 50 for Dutch oven cooking instructions and chart.

Dutch Oven and Campfire Cookbook

Traditional Orange Duck

2 wild ducks
4 tablespoons butter, divided
1 teapoon garlic powder
Salt and pepper
4 slices bacon, divided
1 cup water
Flour for dusting

1 small onion, chopped fine
Grated rind and juice of 1 orange
1 cup beef bouillon
¼ cup red wine
Dash of cayenne
1 teaspoon flour

Spread 1 tablespoon butter inside and out of each bird. Dust with garlic powder, salt and pepper. Lay 2 strips of bacon over each bird. Heat remaining butter in roasting pan. Place ducks in pan and baste with the hot butter. Add 1 cup of water to pan. Roast in a 400° oven for 30–35 minutes. Remove bacon from breasts and dust ducks with flour, baste with butter and cook 10 minutes more or until brown and crisp. Remove birds and keep warm.

Add onion to the juice and cook until golden. Add orange rind, juice, and bouillon. Simmer 10 minutes and strain. Return liquid to pan and add wine, cayenne, salt and pepper. Bring to a boil. Thicken slightly with a teaspoon of flour.

Note: Birds will be slightly rare and pink inside.

Arizona Small Game and Fish Recipes

Seafood

The London Bridge was purchased in 1968, when it was "falling down" and moved 10,000 miles to Lake Havasu City. The bridge was rebuilt on land, then water was diverted from the lake through the Bridgewater Channel.

Easy Tasty Bass

4 tablespoons butter
1 clove garlic, crushed
1 green onion, chopped fine
3 sprigs parsley, chopped

1 teaspoon tarragon
1 large or 2 small bass
Salt and pepper to taste
2 tablespoons lemon juice

In a skillet, melt the butter and add the garlic, onion, parsley and tarragon. Simmer for 2 minutes. Season fish with salt and pepper and cook gently in the herb-butter mixture until fish flakes. Remove bass to a serving dish. Add lemon juice to the sauce in the skillet, heat 1 minute, then pour over the fish.

Arizona Small Game and Fish Recipes

Orange Roughy with Tomatoes

2 large onions, sliced
1 medium bell pepper, sliced
1 clove garlic, minced
1 (1-pound) can no-salt-added
  stewed tomatoes, crushed
1 teaspoon oregano

1 pound orange roughy, cut into 4
  serving-size pieces
1 lemon, sliced
Freshly ground black pepper to
  taste

Sauté onions and bell pepper until tender. Stir in garlic, tomatoes and oregano, cooking for 1 minute. Place fish in a single layer in a nonstick baking dish. Top with lemon slices and pepper; add vegetable mixture. Bake, uncovered, at 350° for 45 minutes. Fish is done when it is opaque and flakes easily with fork. Serves 4.

Cal 290; %Fat 31; Fat 10g; Sat Fat 1.9g; Chol 45mg; Sod 143mg; Carbo 22g; Prot 28g; Fiber 4g. Exchanges: Starch ½, Vegetable 3, Lowfat protein 4

Arizona Heart Institute Foundation Cookbook

Mount Lemmon is the southernmost ski area in the continental United States and is the only U.S. peak named for the woman who first climbed it.

Seasoned Catfish

1 teaspoon onion powder
1 teaspoon garlic salt
1 teaspoon ground red pepper
1 teaspoon dried basil
½ teaspoon thyme

¼ teaspoon sage
4 catfish fillets
¼ cup margarine or butter, melted
Lemon slices

In a shallow dish combine all seasonings. Brush both sides of fish with some of the melted margarine or butter. Coat both sides of fish with the seasoning mixture.

Grill fish or use a nonstick frying pan with 2 teaspoons margarine or butter and quick-fry them.

Arizona Small Game and Fish Recipes

Filet of Sole à L' Orange

This wonderfully delicate fish dish makes a great holiday offering either on a buffet or for a special luncheon. You can substitute pollack or any other tender white fish filets, if you wish.

1½–2 pounds filet of sole or other
    white fish
1½ cups chicken broth, divided
3 medium-size green onions,
    chopped
1 tablespoon fresh chopped
    parsley

1 teaspoon cornstarch
½ cup fresh orange juice
1 tablespoon orange-flavored
    liqueur
1 teaspoon orange peel
Orange slices
Cilantro sprigs

Arrange the filets in a microwave-safe cooking dish. Pour ½ cup of chicken broth over fish, sprinkle onions and parsley on top, cover with plastic wrap and cook in the microwave on HIGH for 6–8 minutes or until fish tests done when tested with a fork. While the fish is cooking, dissolve cornstarch in orange juice in a saucepan. Add remaining 1 cup of chicken broth. Stir in orange liqueur and orange peel and cook over medium heat until sauce has thickened.

Remove fish from microwave, drain off liquid and arrange on warm plates or serving platter. Spoon orange sauce over fish, arrange orange slices and cilantro around fish and serve. Serves 4.

Christmas in Arizona Cook Book

Cattle Drover's Salmon and Wild Herbs

2½ cups chardonnay wine
2 cups water
1 teaspoon basil, divided
1 teaspoon sage, divided
1 teaspoon parsley, divided
1 teaspoon oregano, divided
1 teaspoon thyme, divided
1 teaspoon marjoram, minced, divided
Dash salt and pepper
4 salmon fillets
1 lemon, sliced

Place wine, water, and ½ of the 6 herbs in pan and simmer 4 minutes. Pat salmon with salt and pepper and place in liquid and cover. Cook over low heat 5 minutes. Remove salmon from pan and pat dry with paper towels. Sprinkle remaining dry herbs on salmon and serve with lemon slices.

Cowboy Cookin'

Red Snapper Fiesta

1 pound (about 4 fillets) red snapper
Salt and pepper
¾ cup chopped onion
¾ cup chopped tomato
¼ cup chopped green pepper
1 (4-ounce) can mushroom pieces, drained
1–2 tablespoons butter or margarine
1 cup Cheddar cheese, shredded

Check fillets for bones, and remove any you find. Place snapper in a 10x10-inch microwave-safe baking dish that has been coated with nonstick cooking spray. Sprinkle with salt and pepper. Sprinkle onion, tomato, green pepper, and mushrooms on top of fillets. Dot with butter.

Cook, uncovered, in microwave oven at full power for 3 minutes. Turn dish halfway and cook another 3 minutes. Turn dish halfway and cook another 3 minutes or until fish flakes when tested with fork. Sprinkle cheese over fish. Cook another 2 more minutes or until cheese has melted. Makes 4 servings.

Savory Southwest

Red Snapper Vera Cruz

1 pound red snapper fillets
1½ cups milk
2 teaspoons oregano leaves, crushed
¼ teaspoon pepper
1 teaspoon each vegetable oil and butter
1 cup thinly sliced onion
2 cloves garlic, finely chopped
4 cups chopped tomatoes

2½ cups green pepper, cut in 1-inch matchsticks
1 cup medium pitted ripe olives
¼ cup plus 2 tablespoons dry red wine
¼ cup lemon juice
1 teaspoon ground cumin
¾ teaspoon salt
Hot pepper sauce to taste
Lemon wedges and sour cream

Place fillets in a 9x13x2-inch pan. Pour milk over and sprinkle with oregano and pepper. Cover and refrigerate 1 hour. Turn fillets after ½ hour.

Heat oven to 350°. In large skillet, heat oil and butter over medium-high heat. Sauté onion and garlic until onion is tender. Add remaining ingredients except fillets; simmer about 15 minutes, or until mixture is thickened. Set sauce aside.

Remove fish from milk and discard milk. Divide fish among 4 large squares of aluminum foil. Spoon sauce evenly among packets; fold over and seal. Place in a 15½x10½x1-inch jellyroll pan. Bake for 30 minutes, or until fish is opaque. Serve with lemon wedges and dairy sour cream. Serves 4.

Recipes from Arizona with Love

Robert's Baked Fish

Recipe is superb using any large fish.

2 thinly sliced onions
1 large bass (3–5 pounds),
  cleaned
6 whole peppercorns
2 bay leaves

2 quartered cloves of garlic
2 sprigs fresh parsley
1 cup dry vermouth
1 tablespoon ginger, grated fresh
Salt, thyme, and rosemary to taste

Arrange onions on large baking dish. Place fish on onions. Add remaining ingredients. Cover and bake 2 hours or until flake-tender but not overdone in 350° oven.

Arizona Highways Heritage Cookbook

Salmon, Baked à la Richeleau

2 pounds salmon, cut into serving
  pieces
½ teaspoon salt
¼ teaspoon freshly ground
  pepper

3 eggs, beaten
1 cup dry bread crumbs
4 tablespoons butter
1 tablespoon oil

Season salmon with salt and pepper. Dip salmon pieces in beaten eggs and then in bread crumbs. Melt butter and oil in ovenproof skillet (cast iron works great) over high heat. When butter bubbles, add salmon and quickly brown on both sides. Place skillet in 450° oven and bake for about 5–8 minutes, depending on thickness of salmon. When done, a fork should pierce the center of the salmon easily. Place salmon on a platter and serve with Maitre d' Hôtel Sauce.

MAITRE D' HÔTEL SAUCE:
1 cup butter
1 teaspoon chopped parsley
Juice of 1 lemon

⅛ teaspoon cayenne pepper
¼ teaspoon salt

Combine all ingredients in medium saucepan and cook over medium-low heat until butter has melted. Allow to simmer for 1 minute.

Taste of Tombstone

Oysters Michelina

8 medium-sized oysters in shell

FILLING:

1½ cups fresh spinach, chopped	**¼ cup grated Parmesan cheese**
1 egg	**½ cup grated mozzarella cheese**
½ tablespoon fresh garlic, chopped	

In a small bowl combine all ingredients.

SAUCE:

1½ cups heavy cream	**¼ teaspoon fresh garlic,**
⅓ cup bay shrimp	**chopped**
1 teaspoon fresh parsley, chopped	**¼ cup grated Parmesan cheese**
1 tablespoon butter	**Paprika**

Combine all ingredients except paprika.

Clean oysters and open shell. Divide filling between each oyster and stuff. Place oysters in a sauté pan and add sauce. Sprinkle with paprika and cook over medium heat about 7–8 minutes. Sauce will thicken. Serve warm. (Oysters and filling may be prepared a day ahead and cooked in sauce when needed.)

Contributed by Michelina's, Phoenix
Arizona Chefs: Dine-In Dine-Out Cookbook

Crab Enchiladas
(Enchiladas de Cangrejo)

¾ cup unsalted butter, as needed
24 corn tortillas
3 pounds crabmeat
2 cups Flavored Sour Cream

2 cups Salsa de Tomatillo
2 cups shredded Monterey Jack
  cheese

Heat 3 tablespoons butter in medium-sized skillet over medium heat. Soften corn tortillas by lightly heating them in the butter, one at a time. Stack tortillas and set aside. (Use more butter as necessary, a little at a time.) In a large skillet, heat 6 tablespoons butter over medium heat until hot, and quickly cook crabmeat, stirring until just cooked through.

Take one softened tortilla at a time and thinly spread with Flavored Sour Cream. Next cover with a thin layer of Salsa de Tomatillo, then 2 table-spoons crabmeat in the center. Sprinkle with cheese and roll up fairly tight. As you are rolling them, the enchiladas can be placed in an unbuttered 9x13-inch baking pan or 2 smaller casserole dishes. Preheat oven to 350°. Spread remaining tomatillo sauce evenly over the enchiladas, cover with remaining Flavored Sour Cream and top with shredded cheese. Bake until cheese is melted and enchiladas are heated through, approximately 30 minutes.

FLAVORED SOUR CREAM:
½ cup finely chopped onion
1 small clove garlic, minced
2 cups sour cream

2 tablespoons finely chopped fresh
  cilantro
Salt to taste

Combine all ingredients and let rest 5 minutes to blend flavors. Can be made ahead of time and stored for 2 days.

SALSA DE TOMATILLO:
18–20 large tomatillos
¾ cup chopped onion
2 cloves garlic, peeled
1 corn tortilla
2–3 fresh jalapeños, tops removed
  but not seeded

1 cup fresh cilantro, loosely packed
1 teaspoon sugar
2 tablespoons unsalted butter or
  vegetable oil

Place tomatillos in a medium-size saucepan and add water to cover. Bring to a boil and cook, uncovered, over high heat about 5 minutes, stirring occasionally. Drain, saving 1 cup of the cooking liquid. Heat a little oil in a small pan and lightly fry the corn tortilla; drain on paper towel and break into small pieces when cool. Combine all ingredients, except butter, in a

(continued)

(continued)

blender and purée. Heat butter on high heat in a medium-sized saucepan. When hot, add tomatillo mixture, reduce heat to medium, and cook, stirring occasionally, until thickened (6–8 minutes). This can also be made ahead and refrigerated for about 2 days.

Hospice Hospitality

El Tovar Dining Room's Black Bean and Crabmeat Cakes with Avocado Salsa

1 pound black beans	1 cup lump crabmeat
4 cups water	2 tablespoons Tabasco
1 medium onion, chopped	1 tablespoon salt
2 tablespoons garlic, minced	Flour
2 cups chicken stock	Cooking oil or butter
1 bunch fresh cilantro	Avocado Salsa

Soak beans overnight in water. Drain beans and discard soaking water. Cook beans, onion and garlic in chicken stock over low heat until tender, about 1½ hours. Drain and cool. Run through a grinder on large die with cilantro. Add crabmeat and seasonings. Form into 16 equal patties. Dust with flour. Sauté a few minutes on each side until heated throughout. Top with Avocado Salsa. Makes 16 cakes or 8 servings.

AVOCADO SALSA:

2 avocados, diced	½ bunch green onions, chopped
½ medium red onion, diced small	⅓ bunch fresh cilantro, chopped
1 medium red pepper, diced small	1 tablespoon fresh lemon juice
1 medium yellow pepper, diced small	¼ cup olive oil
	2 tablespoons rice wine vinegar

Mix all ingredients together. Allow to sit for 1 hour before serving.

Arizona's Historic Restaurants and their Recipes

Lobster and Brie Chiles Rellenos

BEER BATTER:

2 egg whites
1 whole egg

1 cup all-purpose flour
½ cup beer

Beat egg whites in a mixer until they form faintly stiff peaks but are not dry. In a stainless-steel bowl, lightly beat the whole egg and slowly whip in the flour, forming a batter-like consistency. Whip in beer to form a smooth liquid with no lumps. Gently fold in egg whites and refrigerate for ½ hour.

1 recipe Beer Batter
4 Anaheim chiles, prepared for stuffing
8 ounces raw lobster meat, roughly chopped
2 tablespoons brandy
2 tablespoons Pernod liqueur

½ teaspoon chopped garlic
4 ounces Brie cheese
4 ounces cream cheese
Vegetable oil or clarified butter for frying
2 cups Lobster Sauce
Salsa, for garnish

Refrigerate Beer Batter for ½ hour. It must be cold when you use it. Peel roasted chiles, make a slit down one side and remove seeds, leaving chiles otherwise intact. Set aside. Preheat oven to 375°.

Combine lobster, brandy, Pernod, and garlic in a sauté pan. Ignite with a match, shaking pan until flames subside. Continue cooking until lobster is cooked through, about 3 minutes. Purée lobster and cheeses in a food processor until thoroughly blended. Using a large, plain-tipped pastry bag, pipe filling into each chile, allowing edges of slit to seal.

In a large skillet, heat enough oil or butter to coat pan. Holding chiles by the stem, individually dip them in batter, coating completely except for the stem. Place in skillet, leaving space between them, and brown well on both sides, turning once. When done, place on a cookie sheet and bake in oven for about 5 minutes, just enough to melt cheese. Meanwhile, heat Lobster Sauce and divide evenly among 4 dishes. Serve chiles on sauce, garnished with salsa.

LOBSTER SAUCE:

¼ cup chopped shallots
¼ cup chopped garlic
6 tablespoons brandy
2 tablespoons anisette

2 cups lobster stock
2 cups heavy cream
Salt and freshly ground pepper to taste

(continued)

(continued)

In a heavy medium saucepot, combine shallots and garlic over high heat, shaking pot to prevent them from burning. Add brandy and anisette and, when warm, ignite with a match. When flames subside, add stock and reduce to 1 cup. Add cream and reduce to 2 cups. Strain through a fine mesh strainer and season with salt and pepper.

Janos: Recipes and Tales from a Southwest Restaurant

Babci's Lobster Thermidor

1 (2-pound) lobster	½ pint heavy cream
1 teaspoon peppercorns	1 teaspoon dry mustard
¼ cup chopped celery	1 tablespoon cooking sherry
½ cup chopped mushrooms	¼ cup Parmesan cheese
2 tablespoons butter	

Boil lobster with peppercorns and celery just until lobster is opaque; drain, reserving peppercorns and celery. Remove shell from lobster and cut meat into 1-inch chunks. Set aside.

Preheat oven to 350°. Sauté the mushrooms in butter. In a large casserole dish, mix reserved peppercorns and celery, mushrooms, cream, mustard and sherry. Add lobster chunks. Top with cheese and bake 20 minutes. Serves 2.

Recipe by TV host Tara Hitchcock
The Arizona Celebrity Cookbook

Montezuma Castle, the 5-story structure built into a recess in a white stone cliff about 70 feet from the ground, was first thought to be of Aztec origin. But it is now known to belong to the Sinagua Indians who farmed the surrounding land between the 12th and 14th centuries. It is near Camp Verde.

Shrimp Quesadillas

4 (16–20 count) shrimp, peeled
   and deveined
1 green chile, roasted, peeled
   seeded and diced
1 tablespoon cilantro
1 teaspoon Southwestern Spice

2 tablespoons butter
1 (10-inch) flour tortilla
3 ounces Jack and Cheddar cheese,
   shredded and mixed together
2 ounces salsa
Parsley

Cook shrimp in butter with green chile, cilantro and Southwestern Spice. When cooked, dice shrimp. Heat 2 tablespoons of butter in large frying pan. Add flour tortilla. Sprinkle cheese and shrimp over half of tortilla. Fold over and turn. Cook until both sides are golden brown. Cut into 4 pieces. Serve with salsa and garnish with parsley.

SOUTHWESTERN SPICE:
¼ cup chili powder
4 teaspoons ground cumin

½ tablespoon ground oregano
1 teaspoon ground basil

Combine in small bowl and stir well.

Sedona Cook Book

Baked Shrimp with Feta Cheese

2 medium onions, chopped
½ cup olive oil
2 (32-ounce) cans tomatoes, peeled
   and chopped
Chopped parsley to taste
2 teaspoons salt

¼ teaspoon freshly ground pepper
2 cloves garlic, minced
2 pounds large shrimp, shelled and
   deveined
½ pound feta cheese

Sauté onions in olive oil until tender. Add tomatoes, parsley, salt, pepper, and garlic. Cover; simmer for 1 hour, stirring occasionally. Place sauce and shrimp in baking dish; crumble feta over top. Bake, uncovered, in 400° oven for 10–15 minutes, or until shrimp is cooked and cheese is melted. Garnish with parsley, if desired. Makes 6 servings.

Recipes from Our Mothers' Kitchens

Camarones Veracruz
(Veracruz-style Shrimp)

1 tablespoon butter or margarine
1 tablespoon vegetable oil
2 medium onions, thinly sliced and cut in half-rings
1 large garlic clove, thinly sliced
2 large green bell peppers, seeded and deveined, thinly sliced into rings

2 serrano chiles, seeded and deveined, cut in thin strips
2 large (about 1 pound) fresh tomatoes
Salt and freshly ground pepper
1 pound raw medium shrimp, peeled and deveined
1 cup green olives

Use an extra large (12-inch) skillet to melt butter or margarine with oil, and sauté onion rings and garlic until soft. Add bell pepper rings and chile strips; cook only until they begin to soften.

Meanwhile, place washed tomatoes in a shallow pan, set on rack 5–6 inches from heat and broil 5 minutes, then turn over and broil another 2–3 minutes. Remove to cool, then core, peel, and coarsely chop, saving all juices. Add tomatoes and juices to skillet, breaking up further as you stir them into other ingredients. Salt and pepper to taste.

Cover and simmer 15 minutes. Stir shrimp and olives into sauce to completely cover; simmer an additional 5 minutes. Can be served with sauce either over rice or offer rice on the side. Serves 6.

Gourmet Gringo

Cheesy Seafood Lasagna Rolls

15 ounces ricotta cheese
1 cup shredded mozzarella cheese
¼ cup grated Parmesan cheese
1 (10½-ounce) package chopped
   frozen spinach, thawed and
   drained

1 pound bay shrimp
1 pound crabmeat, shredded
Salt and pepper to taste
12 lasagna noodles, cooked
   according to package directions

In a medium bowl, mix the cheeses, spinach, shrimp, and crab together. Season with salt and pepper. Lay noodles out on a work surface. Spread an even layer of filling on each and roll up. Place the rolls in a 9x11-inch baking pan coated with cooking spray. (At this point, you may refrigerate for convenience. Just wait to pour the sauce over until right before baking and add an extra 10 minutes to baking time.)

SAUCE:
4 tablespoons butter
4 tablespoons flour
3 cups half-and-half
⅓ cup chopped onion

¼ cup sherry
1 teaspoon chopped dried basil
1 teaspoon chopped dried oregano
Salt and pepper to taste

Melt butter in a saucepan. Whisk in flour. Add the remaining ingredients and cook over medium-high heat, stirring often, until reduced and slightly thickened.

Pour sauce over the lasagna rolls, and bake at 350° for 20–25 minutes. Makes 12 servings.

Savory Southwest

Seafood Lasagna

½ cup butter
½ cup flour
1 quart half-and-half
1 package Primo seafood
  seasoning sauce
Salt
Pepper

9 lasagna noodles, cooked and
  cooled
2 packages frozen, chopped
  spinach, thawed and drained
1 pound shrimp
1 pound sea scallops or crabmeat
Grated cheese

Make white sauce base in saucepan over medium heat with butter and flour. Stir in half-and-half. When thickened, add Primo sauce, salt, and pepper. Put small amount of sauce in 9x13-inch pan. Add three noodles. Cover with ⅓ sauce, spinach, shrimp, and scallops. Repeat until all noodles are used. Cover with sauce and remaining spinach, shrimp, scallops and grated cheese. Bake at 300° until bubbly (35-45 minutes).

Red, White & Blue Favorites

Hot Seafood Salad

2 cups cut-up, cooked shrimp
  (1-pound frozen package)
2 cups cubed brick cheese
  (Monterey Jack)
1 cup chopped celery
¼ cup toasted, slivered
  almonds
¼ cup chopped green pepper

1 cup sour cream
2 tablespoons minced onion
2 tablespoons fresh lemon juice
1 teaspoon salt
2 tablespoons margarine, melted
½ cup cornflake crumbs or bread
  crumbs

Combine shrimp, cheese, celery, almonds and green pepper. Set aside. Blend sour cream, onion, lemon juice and salt. Blend 2 mixtures well. Spoon about 1 cup onto individual baking shells or ramekins. Combine margarine and crumbs. Sprinkle over top. Bake at 300° for 10–15 minutes, until just heated. Garnish with lemon wedges.

The Garden Patch

Encrusted Salmon

PECAN CRUST:

½ pound pecans, finely chopped
1 tablespoon Parmesan cheese, grated
1 teaspoon salt
1 teaspoon black pepper
1 tablespoon fresh or dried oregano

Combine ingredients.

4 (5-ounce) salmon fillets
¼ cup flour
2 egg whites, beaten
2 tablespoons olive oil

Dip salmon fillets in flour, egg whites, and Pecan Crust mixture. Sauté in heated olive oil, 1-2 minutes on each side, and set aside.

SAUCE:

1 teaspoon shallots, chopped
1 teaspoon fresh garlic, chopped
4 tablespoons capers
1 tablespoon olive oil
¼ cup lemon juice
1 cup fresh tomato juice
Salt and pepper, to taste

In hot pan add shallots, garlic, capers, and olive oil. Add lemon juice and tomato juice. Bring to a boil and stir constantly until thick. Season to taste. Pour sauce on individual plates.

To serve, place encrusted salmon portions on sauce and accompany with your favorite vegetables. Yields 4 servings.

Tucson Cooks!

The Petrified Forest National Park is home to some of the most visually astonishing land formations in the United States, and features one of the world's largest and most colorful concentrations of petrified wood.

Cafe Mexicana Cheesecake

CRUST:

¼ cup chocolate wafer crumbs
¼ cup butter, melted

1 tablespoon sugar
¼ teaspoon cinnamon

Combine crumbs, butter, sugar and cinnamon in small bowl. Press evenly over bottom of a buttered 9-inch springform pan. Refrigerate.

FILLING:

4 (8-ounce) packages cream
  cheese, softened
1½ cups sugar
4 large eggs
1 cup sour cream
¼ cup coffee-flavored liqueur
1 teaspoon vanilla

1 cup whipping cream
1 cup semisweet chocolate chips,
  melted
½ teaspoon cinnamon
Sweetened whipped cream
Candy coffee beans

Beat cream cheese until smooth. Gradually beat in 1½ cups sugar; add eggs, one at a time, beating well. Stir in sour cream, liqueur, vanilla, whipping cream, melted chocolate and cinnamon. Blend well. Pour into crust-lined pan. Bake at 325° for 1 hour and 15 minutes. Do not open oven door. Turn oven off and leave cheesecake in another hour. Remove and cool slightly, then refrigerate. To serve, remove cake from pan. Garnish with sweetened whipped-cream rosettes, sprinkled lightly with cinnamon and topped with candy coffee beans. Makes 8–12 servings.

Savory Southwest

Lemon Cheesecake with Berry Topping

¾ cup fat-free granola
16 ounces fat-free cottage
   cheese
8 ounces fat-free cream cheese
¼ cup plus ½ tablespoon flour
1¼ cups sugar

4 egg whites, beaten
1 tablespoon lemon juice
1 tablespoon grated lemon rind
¼ cup blueberries
¼ cup strawberries
¼ cup raspberries

Preheat oven to 325°. Place granola in food processor or blender, and blend until slightly ground. Lightly spray 8-inch springform pan with cooking spray and place ground granola in pan.

Combine cottage cheese and cream cheese in food processor or blender, and process until smooth. Add flour, sugar, egg whites, lemon juice, and lemon rind to cheese mixture. Pour into prepared pan and bake in preheated oven for 50 minutes. Turn oven off and let the cheesecake remain in oven for another hour, with the door slightly open. Remove pan from oven and allow cheesecake to cool completely before removing sides of pan. Top cheesecake with mixed berries and serve. Serves 12.

Nutritional Analysis Per Serving: Cal 151; Prot 9g; Carbo 29g; Chol 5mg; Sod 228mg; Dietary Fiber < 1 gram; Exchanges: 2 starch; ½ meat

Recipes for Fat Free Living Cookbook

Ginny's Apple Cake

5 cups chopped apples tossed
   with 1 tablespoon lemon juice
½ cup salad or olive oil
2 cups sugar (brown, white, or
   both)
1 teaspoon vanilla
2 eggs, slightly beaten

2 cups flour
½ teaspoon salt
1 heaping teaspoon baking soda
2 teaspoons cinnamon
½ cup chopped nuts, raisins, or
   cranberries (optional)

Mix apples, oil, sugar, vanilla, and eggs. Sift dry ingredients together and add to apple mixture. Add nuts, raisins, or cranberries, if desired. Spread in a 9x13-inch, lightly oiled pan. Bake about 30 minutes at 350°; cake is done when edges are brown and pull away from pan.

Portal's Best Little Cookbook

Fresh Apple Cake

3 cups flour
2 cups sugar
1 teaspoon baking soda
1 teaspoon salt
1 teaspoon cinnamon
3 cups shredded apples (do not
   peel the apples)

1 cup vegetable oil
2 eggs
1 teaspoon vanilla
1 cup nuts, finely chopped (pecans
   or walnuts)

Sift flour, sugar, baking soda, salt and cinnamon 3 times. Add apples to all of the above ingredients. Stir oil, vanilla and nuts into all of the above. Mix well. After mixing of all ingredients, pour into greased and floured Bundt baking pan. Bake at 325° for 1½ hours. Press maraschino cherries into top of cake right after taking out of oven. Enjoy.

Lion's Club of Globe Cookbook

The March Hare's
Brownie Chocolate Chip
Cheesecake

1 small (10-ounce) package
   fudge-brownie mix
3 (8-ounce) packages cream
   cheese, softened
1 (11-ounce) can sweetened
   condensed milk

3 eggs
2 teaspoons vanilla
½ cup mini chocolate chips

Preheat oven to 350°. Grease bottom of 9-inch springform pan. Prepare brownie mix as package directs. Spread in pan and bake 35 minutes, or until set. Remove from oven and set aside.

While brownie mix is baking, beat cream cheese in large mixing bowl until fluffy. Gradually add condensed milk, mixing well. Add eggs and vanilla, mixing until well blended. Stir in chips. Pour mixture over brownie shell. Reduce oven temperature to 300°. Bake 50–60 minutes, or until center is set. Allow to cool, then chill thoroughly in refrigerator.

Arizona's Historic Restaurants and their Recipes

Pat's Arizona
Chocolate Turtle Cheesecake

3 cups chocolate cookie crumbs
5 tablespoons melted margarine
14 ounces caramels (approximately
   51)
5 ounces evaporated milk
½ cup chopped, toasted Arizona
   nuts

16 ounces softened cream cheese
½ cup sugar
1 teaspoon vanilla
2 large eggs
½ cup melted semisweet chocolate
   pieces

Combine crumbs and margarine. Press into sides and bottom of 9-inch springform pan. Bake 10 minutes at 350°.

In heavy pan, melt caramels with milk over low heat. Stir frequently until smooth. It takes a while. They scorch easily; don't get on the phone. Pour over crust and top with nuts. Combine cream cheese, sugar, and vanilla. Mix at medium speed on electric mixer until well blended. Add eggs, one at a time, mixing well. Blend in chocolate. Pour over nut-topped crust. Bake 40 minutes at 350°. When done, the top will crack gently at the outside edge. Take it out of the oven. Do not overbake. Loosen cake from rim of pan. Cool before removing rim. Chill. Garnish with whipped cream, if desired.

Outdoor Cooking

Phoenix is named for the mythical Egyptian bird that rose from the ashes of its open funeral pyre, reborn to a new life. Modern Phoenix was built over the ruins of an advanced prehistoric civilization that we call the Hohokam. The Hohokam flourished here in the inhospitable desert for centuries, then mysteriously vanished.

Poorman's Cake

Contains no eggs or milk.

1 cup raisins	**1 teaspoon baking powder**
2 cups water	**½ teaspoon soda**
1 cup shortening	**1 teaspoon each: allspice, cloves,**
1 cup white sugar	** nutmeg, and cinnamon**
1 cup brown sugar	**½ teaspoon salt**
4 cups flour	

Put raisins in saucepan with water. Cook about 15 minutes. While still warm, add shortening and sugars. Let cool. Then add flour, baking powder, soda, and allspice, cloves, nutmeg, and cinnamon with salt. Put in greased and floured pan and cook in slow 325° oven at least 45 minutes or until done.

Variations: You can substitute molasses for brown sugar. You can add any cooked fruit you may have on hand—such as applesauce or any cooked dried fruit. Be sure it is drained before adding to batter.

You can add a cup of chopped nuts and 1 cup of diced pineapple, but if you have nuts and pineapple, you're not a poorman!

Cooked prunes can be added instead of raisins. Using prunes doesn't disqualify you as a poorman.

Chuck Wagon Cookin'

Pineapple Upside-Down Cake

½ stick margarine
1 cup brown sugar
1 can pineapple rings (medium-size can), reserve juice
1 small jar maraschino cherries, reserve juice

1 yellow cake mix
3 eggs
1 cup reserved pineapple juice
⅓ cup reserved maraschino cherry juice

Melt margarine in bottom of 12-inch Dutch oven. Sprinkle brown sugar evenly over margarine (do not stir). Place pineapple rings in a circle, with a de-stemmed cherry in the center of each ring on top of the brown sugar. Prepare cake mix, using eggs and juices. Spoon batter over pineapple rings. Spread evenly. Bake 30 minutes with 12 coals on top and 10 coals on bottom. While hot, turn out onto a foil-covered board or plate.

Note: See page 50 for Dutch oven cooking instructions and chart.

Dutch Oven and Campfire Cookbook

Date Cake

2 cups boiling water
1½ cups cut-up dates
1½ teaspoons soda
3 tablespoons soft butter
2 small (or 1 extra-large) eggs

1½ cups sugar
2 cups flour
1½ teaspoons baking powder
½–¾ cup nuts (optional)

Pour water over dates, soda and butter. Let stand until cool. Beat together eggs and sugar. Mix flour and baking powder together; add egg/sugar mixture and date mixture. Mix well; add nuts, if desired. Bake in 350° oven 40–45 minutes, or until done when tested.

DATE SAUCE TOPPING:
½ cup cut-up dates
½ cup nuts
¾ cup water

¼ cup sugar (more or less, depending on sweetness desired)

Boil until thick and spread on Date Cake while it is still warm.

Pioneer Family Recipes

Party Cake Elegante

1 (2-layer) package yellow cake mix
1½ cups plain yogurt
1 (6-ounce) can frozen lemonade concentrate, thawed
1 (14-ounce) can sweetened condensed milk
4 kiwi fruit, peeled, sliced
1 pint fresh strawberries or raspberries, sliced

Prepare and bake cake mix using package directions for two 9-inch cake pans. Remove layers to wire rack to cool. Split layers horizontally into halves. Combine yogurt, lemonade concentrate and condensed milk in bowl; mix well. Spread mixture over cake layers. Stack cake layers with fruit between, alternating kiwi fruit and strawberries. Spread remaining lemonade mixture over top of cake; mixture will run down sides of cake. Decorate top of cake with concentric rings of remaining fruit. Chill until serving time. Yields 10–12 servings.

Heard in the Kitchen

Tomato Soup Cake

Have fun surprising people when they find out the secret ingredient.

1 cup sugar
½ cup margarine, melted
2 cups flour
1 teaspoon salt
1 teaspoon cloves
1 teaspoon nutmeg
2 teaspoons baking powder
1 teaspoon cinnamon
1 teaspoon baking soda
1 can tomato soup
½ cup chopped nuts

Preheat oven to 350°. In a mixing bowl, cream sugar and margarine. In a second bowl, combine flour, salt, cloves, nutmeg, baking powder and cinnamon. Add baking soda to tomato soup and stir. Blend creamed mixture with dry mixture. Add tomato soup and blend. Add nuts. Pour into a greased (9-inch) cake pan and bake in a 350° oven for 35–45 minutes. Yields 10–12 servings.

Kosher Kettle

Butterscotch Toffee Heavenly Delight

1½ cups whipping cream	½ teaspoon vanilla
1 (5½-ounce) can butterscotch syrup	1 angel food cake
	1 pound English toffee, crushed

Whip cream until it starts to thicken. Add butterscotch syrup and vanilla slowly. Continue beating until thick. Cut cake into 3 layers. Spread whipped cream mixture on layers. Sprinkle each layer generously with toffee. Stack layers on top of each other. Frost sides and sprinkle with toffee. Chill cake for a minimum of 6 hours.

Tostitos Fiesta Bowl Cookbook

Coffee Torte

⅓ cup strong coffee, divided	1 cup flour
4 eggs, separated	¼ teaspoon baking powder
1 cup sugar	Powdered sugar
½ teaspoon vanilla	1 pint whipping cream

Boil 1 cup of strong coffee. Let cool. Beat egg whites until stiff. In a separate bowl, beat egg yolks. Add sugar and vanilla; beat. Add 1 tablespoon coffee; beat. Add flour and baking powder, beating until smooth. Fold into egg whites. Bake in 2 (9-inch) greased cake pans about 15 minutes at 400°. Let cool in pans slightly. Turn out onto waxed paper. Let cool.

Make thin frosting with coffee and powdered sugar. Frost only one layer. Whip cream. Add powdered sugar to taste and frost second layer with it. Put together, coffee frosted layer on top. Refrigerate until serving.

Red, White & Blue Favorites

Arizona became the 48th state on February 14, 1912. The battleship USS *Arizona* was named in honor of the state. It was commisssioned in 1913 and launched in 1915 from the Brooklyn Navy Yard.

Strawberry Chocolate Mousse Cake

1 cup chocolate cookie crumbs
3 tablespoons butter, melted
2 pints strawberries, stemmed and halved
12 ounces semisweet chocolate chips

2 tablespoons light corn syrup
½ cup orange liqueur
2½ cups whipping cream, divided
1 tablespoon powdered sugar

In a 9-inch springform pan, mix the cookie crumbs and butter thoroughly. Press evenly into the bottom of the pan. Stand strawberry halves around pan, touching, side-by-side, pointed ends up, with cut sides against the side of pan. Set aside. Place chocolate chips, corn syrup, and orange liqueur in bowl. Microwave for 1 minute or until the mixture is smooth when stirred. Beat 1½ cups of cream until it forms stiff peaks. Fold the cooled chocolate mixture into the cream. Pour into strawberry-lined bowl. Refrigerate. When ready to serve, unmold the dessert and whip the remaining cream with 1 tablespoon powdered sugar. Arrange cream on top of dessert and top with the remaining strawberries. Serves 12.

Favorites for All Seasons

Guilt-Free Chocolate Cake

1¾ cups flour
2 cups sugar
¾ cup baking cocoa
1½ teaspoons baking soda
1½ teaspoons baking powder
4 egg whites

1 cup skim milk
½ cup unsweetened applesauce
2 teaspoons vanilla extract
1 cup boiling water
¼ cup confectioners' sugar

Combine flour, sugar, baking cocoa, baking soda and baking powder in mixing bowl and mix well. Add egg whites, skim milk, applesauce and vanilla. Beat at medium speed for 2 minutes. Stir in boiling water. Pour into a 9x13-inch baking pan sprayed with nonstick cooking spray.

Bake at 350° for 35–40 minutes or until a wooden pick inserted in center comes out clean. Cool on wire rack. Sift confectioners' sugar over cake. Serves 16.

Wild Thyme and Other Temptations

Grandma Lesher's Chocolate Birthday Cake and Brown Sugar Sauce

CAKE:

2 cups sugar
2 cups flour
1 cup cocoa
2 beaten eggs

1 cup Crisco
2 scant cups brewed coffee
1 teaspoon baking soda

Mix together sugar, flour, cocoa, and then mix in eggs. Boil together Crisco and coffee. Stir in soda and add to above mixture. Mix well. Bake in greased 9-inch square pan at 350° for 40 minutes. Pour Sauce over cake or on individual serving plates.

SAUCE:

2 cups brown sugar
1 small can evaporated milk

1 tablespoon butter
½ teaspoon vanilla

Cook in top of double boiler; do not boil.

Coronado's Favorite Trail Mix

Oops! Forgot Dessert

2 (1-pound) pound cakes
2 cans cherry pie filling
2 large containers Cool Whip,
thawed

Fresh fruit (such as kiwi,
strawberries, raspberries,
blueberries, blackberries, etc.)

Slice pound cake into ¼-inch slices. Lay the entire bottom of 11x15-inch pan with slices of pound cake. Spread pie filling over cake. Spread a layer of Cool Whip, then layer more pound cake over Cool Whip. Layer more Cool Whip over cake; decorate top of cake with sliced fresh fruit. Serve or chill.

Lion's Club of Globe Cookbook

The Arizona-Sonora Desert Museum is rated one of the top zoos in the country by *The New York Times* and *Parade* magazine. The museum is not only a renowned zoo, but also a natural history museum and a botanical garden all in one.

Chocolate Kahlúa Cake

¼ cup dried cherries (optional)
⅓ cup Kahlúa
1 box chocolate cake mix with
   pudding in mix
12 ounces chocolate chips

2 cups sour cream
2 eggs
¼ cup oil
Powdered sugar

Soak cherries a few minutes in Kahlúa. Combine cake mix, chocolate chips, sour cream, eggs, oil, Kahlúa and cherries and mix by hand. Pour into a greased Bundt pan. Bake at 350° for 45–50 minutes. Let stand 20 minutes then turn onto cake plate. Sprinkle with powdered sugar. Serves 10–12.

Favorites for All Seasons

Kahlúa Cake

1 package chocolate cake mix
1 pint sour cream
6 ounces chocolate chips
1 (3-ounce) box instant vanilla
   pudding

4 eggs
¾ cup oil (Wesson or Crisco)
⅓ cup Kahlúa

Combine all ingredients and pour into a greased, floured Bundt pan. Bake at 350° 45–60 minutes or until cake springs back at touch. Sprinkle with powdered sugar when cool. Makes 8 servings.

Kingman Welcome Wagon Club Cookbook

Kahlúa-Mocha Ice Cream Cake with Fudge Sauce

1 family-size frozen Sara Lee
  pound cake, defrosted
½ cup Kahlúa
¼ cup white rum (optional)
¼ cup ground espresso, divided
1 (2-ounce) bittersweet chocolate,
  grated, divided

1 pint Haagen-Daaz coffee ice
  cream, softened
1 pint Haagen-Daaz chocolate ice
  cream, softened

Slice cake with large serrated knife horizontally into thirds (save tin). Place on cookie sheet and toast in a 350° oven until lightly browned. Remove from oven and brush each cake top with the Kahlúa and rum. Line the Sara Lee cake tin with two sheets of overlapping plastic wrap, leaving plenty of overhang. Place one cake slice, Kahlúa side up, on the bottom of the tin. Sprinkle with espresso and chocolate. Spread coffee ice cream over the cake slice, making sure to reach sides of the tin. Sprinkle ice cream with espresso and chocolate. Repeat with second cake slice, sprinkles, chocolate ice cream, sprinkles. Cover with third cake slice. The cake will exceed the tin height. Place plastic over the top and press a heavy wooden board over the cake top to compress all ingredients. Adjust the plastic to tightly contain the cake and press all sides of the tin with the board to get a nice compact brick. Cover entire plastic wrapped tin with foil and freeze at least 4 hours. To serve, remove cake from tin and slice all four sides so that the layers are clearly visible. (Save the scraps for a later treat!) Zigzag some Fudge Sauce on dessert plates, place a slice of cake over the sauce, and sprinkle with additional espresso and chocolate.

FUDGE SAUCE:
1 cup packed brown sugar
½ cup light corn syrup
1½ tablespoons instant espresso
3 ounces unsweetened chocolate,
  chopped

½ cup heavy cream
2½ tablespoons Kahlúa
Pinch of salt

In a small heavy saucepan, combine brown sugar, corn syrup, and espresso powder. Bring mixture to a boil over moderate heat, stirring, and boil until sugar is dissolved. Remove pan from heat, add chocolate, stirring until it is melted. Add cream, Kahlúa, and a pinch of salt. Serve warm or at room temperature. Makes 2 cups. Serves 8–10.

Favorite Recipes from the Foothills of Carefree, Arizona

Caramel Dumplings

This is an old scratch recipe from wood stove days.

SYRUP MIXTURE:

3 cups brown sugar
6 cups water

2 tablespoons butter
Salt to taste

Put in cast iron or heavy frying pan that can go in the oven and let boil while making cake batter. If too thin, thicken with cornstarch.

½ cup shortening
2½ cups flour
2 eggs
⅓ cup water

1 cup white Karo
1 teaspoon vanilla
3 teaspoons baking powder
¾ teaspoon salt

Mix as you would a regular cake. Pour over syrup mixture and bake until cake is done at 325°. Serve warm with cream.

Pioneer Family Recipes

Self-Filled Cupcakes

1 package chocolate cake mix
   (2-layer size)
1 (8-ounce) package cream cheese,
   softened
⅓ cup sugar

1 egg
Dash salt
1 (6-ounce) package semisweet
   chocolate pieces (1 cup)

Mix cake according to package directions. Fill paper baking cups in muffin pans ⅔ full. Cream the cheese with the sugar. Beat in egg and salt. Stir in chocolate pieces. Drop 1 rounded teaspoon cheese mixture into each cupcake. Bake as package directs. Makes 30 cupcakes. Not necessary to frost.

Dishes from the Deep

Harvey House
Chocolate Puffs

1 cup flour	**3 eggs**
1 cup water	**1 teaspoon strawberry preserves or**
1½ cups butter	**sugared fresh berries**
1 ounce chocolate, melted	**Whipped cream, sweetened**

Boil together flour, water and butter. Remove from fire and beat in melted chocolate and eggs, one at a time. Bake in a gun pan (muffin tins), lightly greased, filled half full. Bake in hot oven (400°) until done in peaks, 20–25 minutes.

Allow to cool, then cut off top of each cake and put in a teaspoon of strawberry preserves or fresh berries. Heap with sweetened whipped cream. (I have no record of what happened to the tops, but I am positive they were not thrown out.) Makes 10 puffs.

Arizona Highways Heritage Cookbook

The Santa Fe Railroad's food and lodging problems were solved by Fred Harvey. Arizona had five Harvey Houses along the main line. Harvey Girls, ages 18 to 30, added a rare touch of feminine charm to the Old West. Humorist Will Rogers once said, "Fred Harvey kept the West in food and wives."

Cockeyed Cake

1½ cups sifted flour
3 tablespoons cocoa
1 teaspoon soda
1 cup sugar
½ teaspoon salt

5 tablespoons cooking oil
1 tablespoon vinegar
1 teaspoon vanilla
1 cup cold water

Put sifted flour back into sifter and add cocoa, soda, sugar and salt. Sift directly into a greased 8-inch square cake pan. Make three grooves or holes in the dry mixture. Into one, pour oil; into next pour vinegar; into next pour vanilla. Now pour cold water over all. You'll feel like you're making mud pies now, but beat it with a spoon until it's nearly smooth and you can't see the flour. Bake at 350° for 30 minutes.

St. Francis in the Foothills 30th Anniversary Cookbook

The 47-foot opening in the sandstone matrix of Window Rock was carved over many millennia by water and wind erosion.

Painted Cookies

½ cup margarine
½ cup butter
2 cups sugar
2 eggs, beaten
½ teaspoon baking soda

2 teaspoons baking powder
6 cups flour, divided
½ cup buttermilk
1 teaspoon vanilla

Cream margarine, butter and sugar. Add beaten eggs. Combine soda, baking powder and 1 cup flour. Add dry ingredients alternately with buttermilk. Add vanilla to the butter mixture. Add enough of the remaining flour to make a soft dough. Turn out onto a floured board and knead until smooth. Chill dough if sticky. Roll out dough to ¼-inch thickness. Cut into shapes with a sharp knife (to make your own designs), or cookie cutters for the kids. Decorate before baking with paint or sprinkles. Bake at 350° until golden. Makes 80–100 cookies.

EGG YOLK PAINT:
1 egg yolk
½ teaspoon water

Food coloring

Mix egg yolk with water; blend well. Divide liquid among small glass cups. Tint with food coloring. Use small paint brushes to paint designs on cookies before baking. Thin paint, if necessary, with a few drops of water.

The Garden Patch

White Chocolate and Almond Cookies

¾ cup brown sugar, firmly packed
½ cup sugar
½ cup butter, softened
½ cup shortening
1½ teaspoons vanilla
1 egg

1¾ cups flour
1 teaspoon baking soda
½ teaspoon salt
8 ounces white chocolate, chopped
¼ cup sliced almonds

In large bowl, combine brown sugar, sugar, butter, shortening, vanilla and egg. Blend well. Stir in flour, baking soda, and salt. Blend well. Stir in white chocolate and almonds. Mix well. Drop by rounded teaspoonfuls, 2 inches apart, onto an ungreased baking sheet. Bake at 375° until light golden brown, about 8–10 minutes. Remove immediately. Makes 4 dozen.

Purple Sage and Other Pleasures

Chocolate Crinkles

2 cups flour
2 teaspoons baking powder
½ teaspoon salt
½ cup (1 stick) butter
1 teaspoon instant coffee
  (optional)

4 ounces unsweetened chocolate,
  coarsely chopped
2 cups sugar
4 eggs
1½ teaspoons vanilla extract
1 cup confectioners' sugar

Mix together flour, baking powder and salt. Combine butter, coffee granules and chocolate in a double boiler. Heat over hot, but not boiling, water until melted, stirring frequently. Beat chocolate mixture and sugar in mixing bowl at medium speed until blended. Add eggs 1 at a time, mixing well after each addition. Beat in vanilla. Beat in flour mixture at low speed just until blended. Chill for 2 hours or until firm.

Shape chilled dough by teaspoonfuls into balls. Drop into confectioners' sugar to coat. Place 2 inches apart on greased cookie sheet. Bake at 350° for 10–12 minutes or until the tops of the cookies are just set; do not overbake. Cool on cookie sheet for 1 minute. Remove to wire rack and cool completely. Yields approximately 5 dozen cookies.

Wild Thyme and Other Temptations

Crème De Menthe Cookies

No Bake!

1 cup vanilla wafer crumbs
1 cup powdered sugar
2 tablespoons corn syrup

¼ cup Crème de Menthe
¾ cup chopped nuts

Combine all ingredients. Roll into small balls and roll balls into confectioners' sugar. Store in airtight containers.

The Dog-Gone Delicious Cookbook

Tucson was named friendliest city by *Conde Nast Traveler* magazine.

Mrs. King's Cookies

2 cups all-purpose flour
1 teaspoon baking powder
1 teaspoon baking soda
¼ teaspoon salt
1 cup margarine, softened
1 cup packed brown sugar
1 cup sugar
2 large eggs
1 teaspoon vanilla extract

1 cup white chocolate chips
1 cup semisweet chocolate chips
1½ cups raisins
1 cup chopped nuts
½ cup toasted sunflower seeds
1½ cups old-fashioned oats
1½ cups granola (Raspberry
   Creme or your favorite)

Sift together flour, baking powder, baking soda and salt. Stir to combine. Set aside.

In the bowl of an electric mixer, cream together margarine and sugars. Add eggs and vanilla and beat until well-blended. Add dry ingredients and beat well.

Transfer cookie dough to a large bowl. Stir in white and semisweet chips, raisins, nuts, sunflower seeds, oats and granola by hand. You'll need a huge bowl and a strong arm for this. When well mixed, you may transfer dough to an airtight container and store in the refrigerator for up to 1 week.

Preheat oven to 375°. Use cookie scoop to shape balls, then flatten slightly. Bake on ungreased cookie sheets for 10 minutes or until barely golden. Best when slightly undercooked. Makes 8 dozen cookies.

Mountain Mornings

European Kolacky

2 cups flour
½ teaspoon baking powder
½ pound butter, softened
½ pound cream cheese

¼ cup sugar
1 egg yolk
1 cup filling of choice (preserves or
   frosting)

Sift flour and baking powder together. Cream butter, cream cheese and sugar, then add egg yolk. Add flour mixture. Pat into smooth dough. Roll out ⅛-inch thick. Cut with 2-inch round cookie cutter. Make impression with spoon in center of each cookie and place ½ teaspoon filling into center. Bake kolacky at 350° for 10–12 minutes or until light brown.

That Hungarian's in My Kitchen

Churros
(Mexican Crullers)

1 cup water
1 cup flour
¼ teaspoon salt
1 egg, lightly beaten

1 teaspoon sherry wine
1 cup cooking oil
Powdered sugar

Bring water to boiling point in a saucepan. Remove saucepan from fire and gradually add sifted flour with salt. Beat vigorously until fluffy and smooth. Add egg with wine and continue beating until batter is smooth and shiny. Heat oil in a deep pan until medium hot. Pour batter in a pastry tube and drop small amounts of batter, about 4–5 inches long, in the hot oil. Fry both sides until golden brown and remove Churros to absorbent paper to drain. Roll each one in powdered sugar while still hot. Serve with hot cocoa. Yields 12.

Vistoso Vittles II

100-Year-Old Oatmeal Cookies

½ cup butter, soft
2 eggs
1 cup white sugar
1 cup brown sugar
2½ cups white flour
1 cup oatmeal

¼ teaspoon baking soda
½ teaspoon cream of tartar
1 teaspoon vanilla
1 cup nuts and/or raisins
 (optional)

Mix together the first four ingredients. Mix together the flour, oatmeal, soda, and cream of tartar. Combine both with vanilla until well blended. Add nuts or raisins, if desired. Roll in balls and place on cookie sheets. Bake for 10 minutes at 375°. Makes 5 dozen.

Arizona Highways Heritage Cookbook

Oatmeal Carmelitas

1 (14-ounce) package caramels
½ cup heavy cream
1½ cups flour
1½ cups rolled oats
1½ cups packed light brown sugar
1 egg (optional)
½ teaspoon baking soda

½ teaspoon salt
¾ cup unsalted butter, cut into pieces
12 ounces semisweet chocolate chips
1 cup chopped pecans or walnuts

Heat the caramels and cream in a saucepan over medium heat. Cook until the caramels are melted, stirring constantly; set aside. Process the flour, oats, brown sugar, egg, baking soda and salt in a food processor until well mixed. Add the butter. Pulse on and off until the mixture begins to clump. Press ½ of the mixture into a greased 9x13-inch baking pan. Bake at 350° for 8–10 minutes. Scatter the chocolate chips and nuts over the crust. Drizzle with the caramel mixture. Sprinkle the remaining crumb mixture over the top. Bake for 20 minutes or until golden brown around the edges. Loosen the edges from the sides of the pan. Cool completely. Cut into squares. Chill until firm. Store in the refrigerator. Serves 20.

Reflections Under the Sun

Snickerdoodles

1 tablespoon fat-free margarine	2 tablespoons egg substitute
1 tablespoon Lighter Bake	1½ cups flour
8 tablespoons sugar, divided	¼ teaspoon baking soda
6 tablespoons brown sugar	½ teaspoon baking powder
1½ teaspoons vanilla	1 tablespoon cinnamon

In medium bowl, combine margarine, Lighter Bake, 6 tablespoons sugar, brown sugar, vanilla and egg substitute; mix until creamy and smooth. Add flour, baking soda and baking powder and mix until dry ingredients are moistened and blended. Lightly spray plastic wrap with nonfat cooking spray; wrap dough in plastic wrap and refrigerate 1–2 hours. In small cup, combine cinnamon and 2 tablespoons sugar and mix well.

Shape batter into 1-inch balls and roll in cinnamon-sugar mixture to coat. Place on baking tray and slightly flatten. Bake in 350° oven 10–15 minutes, until lightly browned. Centers of cookies will still be soft when removed from oven. Refrigerate or freeze unused batter 1–2 weeks. Yields 12 cookies.

Nutritional Analysis Per Serving: Cal 120; Carbo 28g; Chol 0mg; Dietary Fiber <1g; Fat <1g; Prot 2g; Sod 42mg; Exchanges ⅔ starch; 1 fruit.

The Fat Free Living Family Cookbook

Fig Pinwheels

Anyone with a fig tree will love using this recipe.

1 cup figs, put through food chopper	½ cup brown sugar
¼ cup water	1 egg
1 cup granulated sugar, divided	2 cups flour
1 cup nuts, chopped	½ teaspoon baking soda
½ cup butter or margarine, softened	¼ teaspoon salt

Combine chopped figs, water, and ½ cup sugar. Cook until thick. Cool. Fold in nuts. Cream butter, remaining granulated sugar and brown sugar. Mix in egg. Sift flour, soda, and salt and add to first mixture. Roll on floured board or cloth. Spread with fig mixture; roll up like jellyroll. Chill. Cut in slices and bake at 400° for 12 minutes.

Fruits of the Desert Cookbook

Granola Raisin Cookies

2 cups flour
3 cups fat-free granola
2 teaspoons cinnamon
1 teaspoon nutmeg
1½ tablespoons baking powder
½ cup egg substitute
¾ cup brown sugar

¼ cup sugar
1 tablespoon cinnamon applesauce
1 tablespoon corn syrup
2 tablespoons vanilla
½ cup raisins
¼ cup cinnamon-sugar blend

Preheat oven to 350°. Line cookie sheets with foil and lightly spray with nonfat cooking spray.

In large bowl, combine flour, granola, cinnamon, nutmeg and baking powder; mix well. Add egg substitute, brown sugar, sugar, applesauce, corn syrup and vanilla; mix until all ingredients are blended. Fold in raisins. Drop batter by rounded tablespoons onto cookie sheets and sprinkle with cinnamon-sugar blend; bake in preheated oven 10–12 minutes until lightly browned. Let cool 5 minutes; remove to wire rack or platter with spatula. Serves 24.

Nutritional Analysis Per Serving: Cal 114; Carbo 27g; Chol 0mg; Dietary Fiber 1g; Fat <1g; Prot 2g; Sod 73mg; Exchanges ⅔ starch; 1 fruit.

The Fat Free Living Family Cookbook

Butter Cookies
(Vajas Pogacsa)

5 cups flour
2 teaspoons baking powder
1 cup sugar or 9 packets artificial
  sweetener

Pinch salt
1 pound butter or margarine
3 eggs
1 tablespoon sour cream

Preheat oven to 350°. In a mixing bowl, mix together flour, baking powder, sugar, and salt. Cut in softened butter or margarine and mix together. Make a hole in the center and add eggs and sour cream. Mix together into a soft dough. Cut dough in two pieces. Roll out each dough piece on a floured board to about ¼-inch thickness. Cut with a small round cookie cutter. Place cookies on a greased cookie sheet and bake in a 350° oven for 20–22 minutes until light beige. Yields 12 dozen cookies.

Kosher Kettle

Chocolate Peanut Popcorn Squares

1 bag microwave popcorn, popped
  or ⅓ cup popcorn, popped
2 tablespoons butter
1 (10½-ounce) package miniature
  marshmallows

½ cup milk chocolate chips
½ cup peanuts

Remove and discard unpopped kernels. Place butter in a 4-quart microwavable bowl or casserole. Microwave on HIGH until melted, about 1–2 minutes. Stir in marshmallows and chips until coated. Microwave on HIGH just until mixture can be stirred smooth, 2–4 minutes, stirring once each minute. Carefully fold in peanuts and popcorn until coated. Press mixture into greased 9x13-inch pan with wooden spoon. Drizzle with Chocolate Glaze. Makes about 24 (2-inch) squares.

CHOCOLATE GLAZE:
½ cup milk chocolate chips   2 teaspoons butter or shortening

Place chips and butter in 1-cup microwavable measure. Microwave, uncovered, on HIGH until melted, 1–3 minutes, stirring every 30 seconds.

Heavenly Delights

Chewy Pecan Pie Bars

¼ cup butter or margarine,
  melted
2 cups packed brown sugar
⅔ cup all-purpose flour
4 eggs

2 teaspoons vanilla
¼ teaspoon baking soda
¼ teaspoon salt
2 cups pecans, chopped
Confectioners' sugar

Pour butter into 9x13x2-inch baking pan, set aside. In mixing bowl, combine brown sugar, flour, eggs, vanilla, baking soda and salt; mix well. Stir in pecans. Spread over butter. Bake at 350° for 30–35 minutes. Remove from oven, and immediately dust with confectioners' sugar. Cool before cutting. Makes 2 dozen.

Par Excellence

Desert Dream Bars

½ cup butter or margarine,
  softened
½ cup brown sugar
1 cup flour
2 eggs
1 cup brown sugar

1 cup coconut
1 cup pecans
2 tablespoons flour
¼ teaspoon salt
½ teaspoon baking powder
1 teaspoon vanilla extract

In medium bowl, mix butter, ½ cup brown sugar and flour. Press into greased 9x13-inch pan. Bake in a 350° oven for 15 minutes. In large bowl, combine remaining ingredients and spread over baked first mixture. Bake another 25–30 minutes. Cut into bars while still warm.

Sedona Cook Book

Tucson enjoys more sunshine than any other city in the United States, about 350 days each year.

Nanaimo Bars

½ cup butter
¼ cup sugar
1 square unsweetened chocolate
1 teaspoon vanilla
1 egg
2 cups graham cracker crumbs
½ cup chopped walnuts or
　　almonds
1 cup flaked coconut

½ cup butter, softened
2 tablespoons instant vanilla
　　pudding
3 tablespoons milk
2 cups powdered sugar
1 tablespoon butter
4 squares semisweet chocolate
⅔ cup chocolate chips

Melt first four ingredients together in double boiler. To this mixture, add egg. Cook 5 minutes and mix in graham cracker crumbs, nuts, and coconut. Press into 8x8-inch pan. Chill 15 minutes. Cream together butter, vanilla pudding, milk, and powdered sugar. Spread over graham cracker mixture and chill 15 minutes. In double boiler, melt last three ingredients and spread over entire mixture. Chill until easy to cut.

Red, White & Blue Favorites

Banana Bars

1½ cups sugar	2 teaspoons vanilla
½ cup soft margarine	2 cups flour
1 cup sour cream	1 teaspoon soda
2 eggs	¾ teaspoon salt
1½ cups mashed bananas	½ cup chopped nuts

Heat oven to 375°. Grease and flour jellyroll pan. Mix sugar, margarine, sour cream, and eggs for 1 minute. Beat in bananas and vanilla. Beat in flour, soda, and salt for 1 minute. Stir in nuts. Bake 20–25 minutes. Cool and frost with Butter Frosting.

BUTTER FROSTING:

¼ cup margarine	1 teaspoon vanilla
2 cups powdered sugar	3 tablespoons milk

Heat margarine over medium heat until lightly brown. Remove from heat and mix in powdered sugar. Beat in vanilla and milk until smooth.

Arizona State Fair Blue Ribbon Recipes

Blonde Brownies

2⅔ cups sifted flour
2½ teaspoons baking powder
½ teaspoon salt
⅔ cup butter or shortening
1 pound light brown sugar

3 eggs
1 cup chopped nuts
1 cup Nestle® semisweet chocolate
  morsels

Sift together flour, baking powder, and salt. Set mixture aside. Melt butter and light brown sugar in large pot; let cool. Beat in 3 eggs, 1 at a time, into brown sugar mixture. Add flour mixture, nuts, and chocolate morsels. Spread mixture into 10x15x1-inch greased pan. Bake at 350° for 25–30 minutes. Makes three dozen 2-inch squares.

Coronado's Favorite Trail Mix

Raspberry Snow Bars

¾ cup shortening
¾ cup sugar, divided
¼ teaspoon salt
¼ teaspoon almond extract
2 egg yolks

1½ cups flour
1 cup raspberry preserves
1 cup flaked coconut
2 egg whites

Cream the shortening, ¼ cup of the sugar and salt in a mixer bowl until light and fluffy. Beat in the almond extract and egg yolks. Add the flour and mix well. Pat the dough over the bottom of a 9x13-inch pan. Bake at 350° for 15 minutes. Spread the preserves over the hot crust. Top with the coconut.

Beat the egg whites in mixer bowl until foamy. Add the remaining ½ cup sugar gradually, beating constantly until the egg whites form stiff peaks. Spread over the coconut. Bake for 25 minutes. Cool in the pan on wire rack. Cut into 24 bars.

Tucson Treasures

Tessie's Baklava

NUT MIXTURE:

1½ pounds finely chopped walnuts
½ pound finely chopped pecans

1 teaspoon cinnamon
½ teaspoon ground cloves

Mix the ingredients together and set aside.

2½ cups water
3 cups sugar

2½ tablespoons lemon juice

In a saucepan, add water and sugar. Bring to a low boil for about 10 minutes, stirring continuously. Add lemon juice and boil for another 5 minutes. Set aside and let cool.

1 pound unsalted butter
1 pound filo dough

Whole cloves

Melt butter in dish in the microwave (1 stick at a time). Lay filo out on wax paper and cover with a sheet of wax paper and over that a slightly damp tea towel. Brush pan with butter and lay filo, one sheet at a time, in the pan. Brush butter on each sheet of filo. For the first 3 or 4 sheets, have the filo come up on the sides of the pan and drape over the sides. Layer about 6 sheets of filo for the bottom. Sprinkle ⅓ of the nut mixture on the filo, one sheet at a time. Don't forget to brush each sheet with butter. After about 4 sheets, sprinkle another ⅓ of the nut mixture on the filo and drip the butter again. Repeat another 4 sheets and then sprinkle the remaining ⅓ cup nut mixture on the filo and then drip butter. Layer the remaining sheets of filo. Before you layer the last 2 sheets, fold the sides of the filo onto the center. Place the last layer of filo on and then trim the edges neatly. Cut the Baklava into diamond-shaped pieces before baking. Place a whole clove in each piece. Bake for 40–50 minutes, or until the Baklava is golden brown. Immediately after taking the Baklava out of the oven, pour the cold syrup on it and let set for 5 or 6 hours before cutting and taking the pieces out of pan.

Note: In Flagstaff, you must have a humidifier on in the room or the filo will dry out too quickly.

Recipes from Our Mothers' Kitchens

Hawaiian Macadamia Rouchers

Delicious with vanilla ice cream.

Scant ½ cup sugar
1 tablespoon water
1¾ cups macadamia nuts, roasted
   and coarsely chopped

1 teaspoon butter
1¼ cups semisweet chocolate,
   chopped

In a small saucepan, cook sugar and water until mixture reaches soft ball stage (234°). Immediately pour nuts into syrup. Mix well and cook slowly until a light caramel color. Add butter and mix well. Pour out and cool on a cookie sheet. Melt chocolate in double boiler. Pour macadamia mixture into chocolate and mix well. Spoon the mixture into small paper or foil cups and let cool.

Contributed by A.J.'s, Scottsdale
Arizona Chefs: Dine-In Dine-Out Cookbook

Prickly Pear Pops

Prickly pears (enough to yield
   2 cups juice)
1 cup water

2 tablespoons lemon juice
   concentrate
½ cup sugar

Wash the pears and put in blender (stickers too) with 1 cup water. Blend then strain the juice through several thicknesses of cheesecloth.

Add lemon juice concentrate and sugar. Pour mixture into plastic ice-pop makers (or use paper cups and wooden sticks). Freeze.

Fruits of the Desert Cookbook

Pistol Packin' Mama
Pecan Cups

1 (3-ounce) package cream cheese
½ cup butter or margarine
1 cup flour
2 eggs
1 cup brown sugar

2 tablespoons butter or margarine,
  softened
1 teaspoon vanilla
Dash of salt
1 cup broken pecans

Mix cream cheese and butter. Blend into flour with fork. Chill 1 hour or longer. Shape into 1-inch balls. Press in tiny muffin tins (12 to a tin). Combine eggs, brown sugar, butter, vanilla, and salt. Beat until smooth. Divide pecans in half. Use ½ to sprinkle on bottom of each cup. Add filling and top with remaining pecans. Bake at 325° for 25 minutes. Remove quickly before filling hardens. Makes 24.

Cowboy Cookin'

Sister Kathleen's
Cocoa-Oatmeal Candy

2 cups sugar
3 tablespoons cocoa
½ teaspoon salt
½ cup margarine

½ cup milk
½ cup peanut butter
4½ cups uncooked oatmeal
1 teaspoon vanilla

Mix sugar, cocoa, salt, margarine, and milk in saucepan. Boil for 2 minutes. Remove from heat and add peanut butter, oatmeal, and vanilla. Mix thoroughly . Drop on waxed paper and let harden. Makes 4 dozen.

Padre Kino's Favorite Meatloaf

Pies & Other Desserts

A Hopi Indian shown in traditional native dress. The Hopi tribe, now living on a reservation of 4,000 square miles in northeast Arizona, is regarded as one of the best preserved Native American cultures in North America.

Margarita Pie

CRUST:

1 cup finely crushed pretzels
3 tablespoons sugar

¼ cup melted butter

Combine pretzels, 3 tablespoons sugar, and butter. Put in a 9-inch pie pan and make crust. Refrigerate.

⅔ cup sugar
1 (.25-ounce) envelope unflavored gelatin
1 cup milk
2 egg yolks, beaten
¼ cup lime juice

¼ cup tequila
2 tablespoons triple sec
1 cup whipping cream
2 egg whites
Lime slices for decoration

In saucepan, combine ⅔ cup sugar and gelatin. Gradually stir in milk and beaten egg yolks. Cover and stir over low heat until slightly thickened and mixture coats metal spoon. Cool to room temperature. Stir in lime juice, tequila, and triple sec. In a small bowl, whip cream until soft peaks form. Fold into custard mixture. Refrigerate until mixture mounds when dropped from a spoon, 30–45 minutes.

In small bowl, beat egg whites until stiff, but not dry. Fold into partially set custard mixture. Spoon evenly into chilled pie shell. Cover with foil or plastic wrap. Freeze until firm, 3–4 hours. Place in refrigerator about 15 minutes before serving. Decorate top with lime slices. Serves 6.

Favorite Recipes from the Foothills of Carefree, Arizona

My Father's Lemon Pie

As good as lemon meringue pie—but not so fragile.

4 eggs
1½ cups sugar
1 tablespoon flour
1 tablespoon white corn meal
¼ cup milk

¼ cup melted butter or margarine
⅓ cup fresh lemon juice
Rind grated from one lemon
1 unbaked pie shell

Beat eggs with sugar in medium bowl. Mix flour and corn meal; stir into egg mixture. Mix rest of ingredients into the above. Pour into pie shell. Bake at 375° for about 40 minutes. Refrigerate leftovers—if any. Pie can be frozen.

Portal's Best Little Cookbook

Lemon Pie

1¼ cups sugar	3 tablespoons butter
5⅓ tablespoons cornstarch	4 tablespoons lemon juice
1½ cups hot water	1½ tablespoons grated lemon rind
3 eggs, separated	1 Pie Crust, pre-baked

Combine sugar, cornstarch and water in large saucepan. Cook over medium-high heat until mixture begins to boil and becomes thick. Remove from heat.

In small bowl, beat egg yolks until thick and lemon colored. Gradually add 3 tablespoons of cooked mixture to egg yolks and stir well. Now add the egg yolks to the saucepan and incorporate. Cook over medium-high heat for about 1 minute, stirring constantly. Add butter, lemon juice and lemon rind. Pour into Pie Crust and top with Meringue. Bake at 375° for 10–15 minutes or until meringue becomes golden.

PIE CRUST:

2½ cups flour	1 egg
1½ teaspoons baking powder	½ teaspoon vinegar
½ teaspoon salt	Cold water
¾ cup shortening	

Combine flour, baking powder and salt in large mixing bowl. Stir to combine with wire whisk. Cut in shortening with pastry cutter and blend until the dough resembles crumbs.

Break egg into a liquid measuring cup; beat lightly. Add vinegar and enough water to measure ⅓ cup. Stir well. Add to flour and shortening mixture. Stir only enough to moisten and combine. (Over-mixing will result in a tough crust.) If it seems too wet, add a little more flour.

Divide dough in half and roll out on a floured surface. Makes 2 (9-inch) pie crusts. Reserve one for later use.

MERINGUE:

3 egg whites	1 teaspoon lemon juice
¾ cup sugar	

Beat egg whites in large bowl until soft peaks form. Gradually beat in sugar and lemon juice until stiff peaks form.

Taste of Tombstone

Arizona's Supreme Citrus Pie

Prepare and bake your favorite pie crust in 9 or 9½-inch deep dish pie plate. Cool completely.

FLUFFY FILLING:

1 (8-ounce) package cream cheese, softened
1 (14-ounce) can sweetened condensed milk
1 (6-ounce) can frozen lemonade concentrate, thawed

1 (4-serving) package lemon flavor instant pudding and pie filling mix (not sugar free)
1 cup whipping cream, whipped

Combine cream cheese and sweetened condensed milk in large bowl. Beat at low speed of electric mixer until smooth. Add lemonade concentrate. Blend well. Beat in pudding mix until smooth. Fold in whipped cream. Spoon into baked pie crust. Make a shallow depression in filling 1 inch from edge. Refrigerate.

CLEAR FILLING:

½ cup cornstarch
⅓ cup water
4 egg yolks
½ cup fresh lemon juice

1½ cups granulated sugar
1½ cups water
1 tablespoon butter or margarine

Combine cornstarch and ⅓ cup water in small bowl. Stir to blend. Combine egg yolks and lemon juice in medium bowl. Beat until smooth. Combine granulated sugar and remaining water in medium saucepan. Cook on medium heat until mixture comes to a boil. Stir in cornstarch mixture slowly. Cook and stir until thickened and clear. Remove from heat. Stir in egg yolk mixture slowly until blended. Return to heat.

Cook and stir 1–2 minutes or until mixture comes to a boil. Remove from heat. Stir in butter until blended. Cool completely. Spread gently over fluffy filling.

TOPPING:

1 cup whipping cream
2 tablespoons confectioners' sugar

¾ teaspoon vanilla

For topping, beat whipping cream in small bowl at high speed of electric mixer until stiff peaks form. Beat in confectioners' sugar and vanilla. Spread over clear filling. Refrigerate until firm.

Arizona State Fair Blue Ribbon Recipes

Peanut Butter Pie

Great to make ahead and put in freezer!

½ cup confectioners' sugar
1 (8-ounce) package cream cheese (lite)
½ cup peanut butter

1 (8-ounce) tub Cool Whip (lite)
1 banana, sliced
1 chocolate crumb crust

Mix sugar, cheese, and peanut butter until well blended. Beat in Cool Whip until smooth. Put banana slices in bottom of the pie crust and add beaten mixture. Refrigerate for 3 hours.

Dishes from the Deep

Hot Fudge Pie

½ cup (1 stick) butter
2 squares semisweet chocolate
2 eggs, beaten
1 cup sugar

¼ cup all-purpose flour
⅛ teaspoon salt
1 teaspoon vanilla extract
1 cup chopped nuts

Preheat oven to 350°. Melt butter and chocolate together in small saucepan over low heat. Combine remaining ingredients and blend with chocolate mixture. Spray 9-inch pie pan with nonstick cooking spray. Pour batter into pie pan and bake for 25 minutes. Serve warm with sweetened whipped cream or ice cream. Makes 8 servings.

What's Cooking Inn Arizona

Blue Ribbon Cafe's
Old-Fashioned Chocolate Cream Pie

CRUST:

1 cup flour	**⅓ cup shortening**
½ teaspoon salt	**2 tablespoons ice water**

In bowl, combine flour and salt. Cut in shortening until mixture is consistency of coarse meal. Add ice water, 1 tablespoon at a time, until mixture stays together when formed into a ball. Roll out on floured board until about ⅛-inch thick. Place in 9-inch pie pan and crimp around edges. Prick crust several times with fork. Bake in 350° oven for 10–12 minutes. Set aside to cool.

FILLING:

2 cups evaporated milk	**4 tablespoons cocoa**
½ cup water	**4 egg yolks, beaten**
2¼ cups sugar, divided	**1 tablespoon butter**
3 tablespoons flour	**1 teaspoon vanilla**
½ teaspoon salt	**4 egg whites**

In medium saucepan, combine milk and water. Bring to scalding (not boiling) point. In another bowl, combine 1½ cups sugar, flour, salt, and cocoa. Add egg yolks and mix into a thick batter. Add batter to milk-water mixture, stirring constantly with whisk. Cook over medium heat until thickened. Remove from heat and add butter and vanilla, stirring well to blend. Pour into baked pie shell and allow to cool.

Prepare meringue by beating egg whites at high speed in bowl until stiff. Add remaining ¾ cup sugar and beat until peaks form. Top pie with meringue. Bake in 350° oven for about 6–8 minutes until top is golden brown. Cool and serve.

Arizona's Historic Restaurants and their Recipes

Banana Split Pie

12 (2½-inch) graham cracker
  squares
4 tablespoons low-fat oleo, melted
1 tablespoon sugar
1 small package instant vanilla
  pudding

2 cups skim milk
1 banana
1 cup crushed pineapple, drained
Non-fat whipped topping
  (optional)

Crush crackers and mix with oleo and sugar to make a pie crust. Bake at 350° for 15 minutes. Make pudding according to directions with skim milk. Pour pudding into cooled pie crust. When set, top with sliced banana. Just before serving, top with well-drained pineapple and a dollop of whipped topping, if desired. Serves 8.

Bon Appétit

Soda Cracker Pie

3 egg whites
1 cup sugar
1 teaspoon vanilla

½ teaspoon baking powder
14 crumbled soda crackers
1 cup chopped nuts

Beat egg whites until foamy. Gradually add sugar, beating until stiff. Add vanilla. Fold in remaining ingredients. Pour into well-buttered 9-inch pie pan. Bake at 375° for 30 minutes. Cool and top with whipped cream. Refrigerate for 4–5 hours.

Cooking with Cops

Skillet Apple Pie à la Mode

This is a delicious "quicky" when you're in a hurry. The butter rum sauce stores well.

PIE:

1 (9-inch) apple pie (from a bakery, frozen and baked or, if you feel ambitious, made from scratch)

Butter Rum Sauce
Vanilla ice cream

BUTTER RUM SAUCE:

1 teaspoon water
2 tablespoons unsalted butter, divided
2 tablespoons sugar
2 tablespoons Karo dark corn syrup

2 tablespoons Karo light corn syrup
1 teaspoon Myer's rum
½ teaspoon rum extract
1 teaspoon vanilla extract

In a saucepan, combine water, 1 tablespoon butter and sugar. Bring to a boil. Add syrups to pan, bring to a boil again, and lower to a simmer. Simmer 10 minutes. Add rum, rum extract, vanilla extract, and remaining tablespoon of butter and turn off heat. Let cool for 1 hour. Stir again.

ASSEMBLY:

Preheat oven to 350°. Place heavy 10-inch skillet in oven and heat. Carefully remove pie from baking pan and place in hot skillet. Pour ½ cup butter rum sauce over and around pie and place in oven. Remove when heated through and sauce is bubbling. Cut pie into wedges, place on plates with scoop of ice cream on top.

Contributed by Manuel's, Phoenix
Arizona Chefs: Dine-In Dine-Out Cookbook

Fresh Pumpkin Pie

Pastry for one-crust pie
2 eggs, slightly beaten
2 cups evaporated milk
1⅓ cups fresh pumpkin purée*
¾ cup brown sugar

1 teaspoon salt
1½ teaspoons cinnamon
1½ teaspoons ginger
¼ teaspoon cloves

Line pie plate with pastry. Stir eggs and milk into pumpkin. Add sugar, salt and spices and mix well. Pour pumpkin mixture into pastry and bake at 450° for 10 minutes, then reduce heat to 350° and bake for an additional 30 minutes, or until a knife inserted in the center comes out clean.

*Pumpkin Purée: Cut pumpkin in half and remove seeds, peel and cut into 1-inch cubes. Put cubes into a saucepan and add ½–1 cup water (only enough to keep pumpkin from burning). Cover saucepan and simmer pumpkin, stirring often, until it becomes thick and mushy. Mash pumpkin or whirl in a blender to purée.

Note: Yellow squash can be substituted for pumpkin in this recipe.

Hopi Cookery

Green Grape Pie

1 baked graham cracker crust
1 quart green seedless grapes
¾ cup sugar
3 tablespoons cornstarch
¼ cup cold water

1 tablespoon lemon juice
1 cup sour cream
1 tablespoon sugar
1 teaspoon vanilla

Combine grapes and ¾ cup sugar in pan. Dissolve cornstarch in cold water and gently stir into grape mixture. Bring to a boil, stirring gently, then reduce heat and simmer about 5 minutes. Remove from heat; stir in lemon juice. Cool. Turn grape filling into pie shell. Blend sour cream with 1 table-spoon sugar and vanilla and spread evenly over top. Serves 6.

Fruits of the Desert Cookbook

Banana and Raspberry Tarts

Until recently, flavoring ingredients were never added to tortillas; but now all kinds of savory tortillas can be purchased in grocery stores. Vincent takes it one step further and adds orange juice and zest to make this unique dessert. This recipe works equally well with sheets of frozen puff pastry.

ORANGE-FLAVORED TORTILLAS:

1 cup unbleached all-purpose flour
¼ teaspoon salt
1 teaspoon baking powder
2 tablespoons unsalted butter

1 teaspoon grated orange zest
¼ cup freshly squeezed orange juice
1–2 tablespoons water

In large bowl, stir together flour, salt and baking powder. With pastry blender, a fork, or your fingertips, work in the butter and orange zest until incorporated. Gradually add orange juice and enough water to make a soft, not sticky, dough. Turn out onto a floured board and knead until smooth, about 5 minutes. Cover with a clean towel or plastic wrap and allow to rest for 30 minutes. Divide dough into balls, about ¼ cup each; flatten slightly. Cover with plastic wrap and let rest for 10 minutes. Roll out each ball between sheets of waxed paper into a flat round about 8 inches in diameter. Heat a heavy skillet over high heat; when very hot, add a tortilla and cook until small brown dots appear on underside, about 1 minute. Turn over and cook other side about 30 seconds more. Remove and repeat with remaining tortillas.

FILLING:

2 bananas, cut into ¼-inch slices
1 cup fresh raspberries
2–3 tablespoons confectioners' sugar, depending on the sweetness of the raspberries

½ cup freshly squeezed fresh orange juice
1 tablespoon sugar
2 tablespoons butter, cut into ¼-inch pieces

In bowl, mix together bananas, raspberries, confectioners' sugar and orange juice. Marinate for 15 minutes. Strain the fruit over a small saucepan, reserving the accumulated juice in the pan.

Preheat oven to 375°. Sprinkle granulated sugar evenly on top of the cooked tortillas. Place tortillas on baking sheet. Arrange strained fruit on tortillas, stopping one inch from edge, and top fruit with bits of butter. Bake tarts until lightly browned and crisp, about 15 minutes.

Heat the pan with reserved juices over medium-high heat; bring to a

(continued)

(continued)

boil, reduce heat, and simmer until the mixture is thick enough to use as a glaze, about 10 minutes. Remove tarts from oven and spread thickened juices over tops of tarts and serve. Serves 4.

Note: The tortillas can also be flavored with lime, lemon, or grapefruit.

*Recipe by Vincent Guerithault / **Savor the Southwest***

Cookie Pie

This scrumptious pie is a simple yet delightfully different treat. The entire family will love it.

1 cup (2 sticks) unsalted butter, softened
3 cups dark brown sugar
2 extra-large eggs
1½ teaspoons vanilla extract
5 cups flour

1 teaspoon baking soda
1 cup semisweet chocolate chips
⅔ cup white chocolate chips
½ cup pecan pieces
½ cup coarsely chopped walnuts

Preheat oven to 275°.

Using an electric mixer set at medium speed, in a large bowl, cream butter and sugar until fluffy, then add eggs and vanilla. Slowly add flour and baking soda and mix well. Fold in chocolate chips.

Butter and flour a 10-inch springform pan. Pour nuts into the bottom of the pan and press cookie dough over the nuts. Bake at 275° for approximately 1 hour or until a toothpick inserted in the center comes out clean. Serves 12.

Approximate values per serving: Cal 661; Fat 30g; Chol 77mg; Carbo 94g; Sod 124mg; Cal from Fat 41%.

By Request

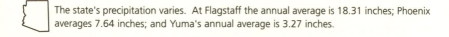

The state's precipitation varies. At Flagstaff the annual average is 18.31 inches; Phoenix averages 7.64 inches; and Yuma's annual average is 3.27 inches.

Creamy Apple Tart

TART SHELL:

1¼ cups all-purpose flour
2 tablespoons sugar
⅛ teaspoon salt
10 tablespoons margarine, cut
   into pieces

⅛ teaspoon lemon oil or
   1 teaspoon lemon zest
2–3 tablespoons ice water
1 large egg yolk mixed with
   1 tablespoon water

Measure flour, sugar, and salt into the bowl of a food processor fitted with steel blade. Process for a few seconds until dry ingredients are well mixed. Add margarine pieces and pulse on and off a few times until mixture resembles coarse sand. Sprinkle the lemon oil or zest over the mixture, then sprinkle the ice water 1 tablespoon at a time, processing after each addition. Process just until dough starts to form and ball up. Wrap dough in plastic wrap and chill 1 hour or overnight.

Roll out dough to ¼-inch thickness and gently place in center of an 11-inch tart pan. Double over sides and crimp edges. Prick bottom with a fork. Freeze 15 minutes or refrigerate for ½ an hour.

Preheat oven to 425°. Cut waxed paper to fit bottom of tart, then spread dried peas or beans evenly over the waxed paper to act as weights and bake 15 minutes. Remove weights and waxed paper, turn the oven down to 375° and finish baking until shell begins to brown, about 10 minutes. Brush bottom of crust with egg-water mixture. Return to oven for 5 minutes or just until crust hardens. Cool.

TART FILLING:

3 large Granny Smith apples,
   about 1⅓ pounds
1 large egg
1 large egg yolk
3 tablespoons sugar

⅔ cup crème fraîche or whipping
   cream
2 tablespoons dark rum or Calvados
   apple brandy
Powdered sugar

Preheat the oven to 350°. Peel, quarter, and core the apples. Cut each quarter into 4–5 thin wedges. Arrange the apple wedges in overlapping concentric circles in the pre-baked, cooled tart shell.

Break the egg and the egg yolk into a small mixing bowl. Whisk in sugar, cream, and rum or brandy. Pour this custard over the apples and bake until the filling is lightly set and the apples are cooked through, about 30 minutes. Cool to lukewarm. Sprinkle with a light dusting of powdered sugar. Serve warm or at room temperature. Serves 10.

Mountain Mornings

Lemon Tarts

1 cup all-purpose flour
½ cup sugar
Pinch salt
1 egg yolk

½ cup butter or margarine,
  softened
½ teaspoon vanilla

Sift flour, sugar and salt into a mixing bowl. Add remaining ingredients and mix with hands until dough is like pie dough and sticks together. After mixing, turn out on lightly floured surface. Make walnut-size dough balls and press into mini-muffin pan. Bake at 300° for 15 minutes (no longer). Fill shells with Lemon Filling.

LEMON FILLING:
2 eggs
2 egg yolks
½ cup butter or margarine
1 cup sugar

6 tablespoons lemon juice
  (2 lemons)
Zest from 2 lemons

Put whole eggs and egg yolks in the top of a double boiler. Beat gently until eggs are mixed well. Add remaining ingredients and stir with a wooden spoon. Cook over gently boiling water until it reaches the consistency of mayonnaise. Fill shells just before serving and top with whipped cream or Cool Whip.

Note: Filling can be stored in a covered jar and refrigerated up to 2 weeks.

Hospice Hospitality

Buttermilk-Crusted Blackberry Cobbler

FILLING:

1½ pounds blackberries
1⅓ cups sugar

3½ tablespoons flour
1⅓ tablespoons vanilla extract

In a medium bowl, combine blackberrries, sugar, flour, and vanilla. Pour into greased 8x12x2-inch pan.

CRUST:

1 tablespoon plus 2½ teaspoons
 sugar
¾ teaspoon baking powder
¼ teaspoon salt

⅓ cup shortening
½ cup buttermilk
1⅓ cups flour, divided
½ tablespoon melted butter

Preheat oven to 350°.

In a large bowl, stir together 1 tablespoon of the sugar, baking powder, salt, shortening, buttermilk and ¾ cup of the flour to form a sticky dough. Spread remaining flour on a work surface and knead dough until most of the flour is incorporated and dough is manageable. Roll dough to about ¼-inch thickness and cut with a knife into large pieces. Cover blackberry filling with dough, overlapping pieces. Drizzle melted butter over dough and sprinkle with remaining 2½ teaspoons sugar.

Bake until crust is golden brown and filling is bubbly, about 50 minutes. Serves 8–10.

Approximate values per serving (based on 8 servings): Cal 345; Fat 10g; Chol 77mg; Carbo 44g; Sod 184 mg; Cal from Fat 49%

By Request

Warm Peach Compote with Basil

⅓ cup sugar
1 cup water
2 pounds fresh peaches, peeled
   and cut into bite-sized pieces or
   thawed frozen peaches, cut into
   bite-sized pieces
1 tablespoon margarine, cut into
   small pieces

½ cup chopped basil leaves,
   loosely packed, or 1 tablespoon
   dried basil
½ teaspoon vanilla extract
Sprigs of fresh basil for garnish or
   1 teaspoon dried basil

In a large skillet, combine sugar and water. Cook, stirring, over medium heat until the sugar dissolves. Add peaches and simmer 2 minutes. Whisk in margarine a few pieces at a time, then add basil leaves. Cook until the basil wilts, about 30 seconds. Remove from heat and stir in vanilla.

Serve warm in small fruit dishes, or spoon over pancakes, shortcake, or ice cream. Garnish with a sprig of fresh basil leaves or a light sprinkling of dried basil. Makes 8 servings.

Mountain Mornings

Tortilla Apple Strudel

2 quarts cooking apples, pared
   and cut fine
4 ounces nuts, chopped
1 cup raisins
¾ cup sugar

2 teaspoons cinnamon
1 package large flour tortillas
½ cup melted butter
½ cup crushed cornflakes

Mix apples, nuts, and raisins. Stir in sugar mixed with cinnamon. Place tortilla on flat surface and spread with melted butter, using brush. Sprinkle some crushed cornflakes lightly over buttered tortilla and then spread with some of apple mixture.

Fold ⅓ of tortilla over mixture, brush with butter; fold both sides of tortilla to center, brush with melted butter and then roll. Brush entire outside with melted butter. Repeat for each tortilla. Place rolled tortillas on buttered baking pan and bake at 350° until brown and crisp. They can be frozen after baking.

Fruits of the Desert Cookbook

Cobbler

½ cup butter or margarine
1 cup flour
1 cup sugar
1 teaspoon baking powder
½ cup milk

2 cups fruit (apricots, peaches, or other)
1 cup sugar (or less)
Almond flavoring
¼–½ teaspoon cinnamon

Melt butter in 10-inch baking dish. Mix flour, sugar, and baking powder, then add milk and mix. Spoon over melted butter. Heat fresh or canned fruit with sugar, adding less sugar for canned fruit. Add a small amount of almond flavoring to apricots, if desired, or cinnamon to fruit. Bake 30 minutes until crust is brown. Crust will rise to top. Serve hot or cold.

Pioneer Family Recipes

Chocolate and Fruit Tortillas

1 pint fresh strawberries, cleaned and hulled
2 teaspoons sugar
Chocolate Sauce

2 or 3 tablespoons butter
2 (8-inch) fresh, flaky and thin flour tortillas
1 large ripe, firm banana

Prepare berries and cut in large dice, or maybe halved; add sugar and refrigerate at least an hour.

When ready to serve, warm butter in skillet large enough to hold 1 flat tortilla at a time. Heat each tortilla in butter just a few seconds on first side, then turn over and heat just until it starts to puff up on the second side. Quickly remove to serving plates. Slice banana; divide strawberries and apportion fruit over middle of each heated tortilla. Spoon hot Chocolate Sauce over fruit and berries combination and fold sides over middle to close. Present immediately. Serves 2.

CHOCOLATE SAUCE:

3 ounces (3 squares) chocolate (blended such as semisweet or bittersweet), grated or finely chopped

½ cup whipping cream
3 tablespoons butter

Chocolate Sauce should be made just before serving. Heat chocolate in small saucepan, blend in cream to heat through, then add butter. Stir over medium heat until smooth. Makes 1 cup.

Gourmet Gringo

Strawberry Trifle

CUSTARD SAUCE:

1½ tablespoons cornstarch
2¼ cups milk, divided
¼ cup sugar

1 teaspoon vanilla
3 beaten egg yolks

Mix cornstarch with ½ cup milk. In heavy saucepan or double boiler, heat 1¾ cups milk with sugar just to boiling. Remove from heat. Stir in cornstarch mixture until smooth. Cook, stirring constantly, until thickened. Simmer 3 minutes. Remove from heat and stir in vanilla extract and 3 beaten egg yolks. Cover and chill.

TRIFLE:

1 (10-ounce) angel loaf cake
⅓ cup strawberry jam or jelly
⅓ cup cream sherry or orange
   juice
3 cups strawberries
Custard Sauce

¾ cup whipping cream
2 tablespoons powdered sugar
1 teaspoon vanilla extract
2 tablespoons sliced almonds
   (toasting optional)

Split cake into 3 layers. Spread jam in between the layers and reassemble the layers. Cut into 2-inch cubes. Arrange cubes in 2-quart bowl. Sprinkle with sherry. Wash strawberries. Pick 8–12 berries for garnish. Remove hulls from the remaining strawberries, slice, and spoon over cake. Pour chilled custard over berries. Cover and refrigerate for 1 hour or more. Meanwhile, whip cream to soft peaks. Add sugar and vanilla and whip until stiff. Spread cream over the custard. Garnish with whole strawberries and sprinkle with almonds. Chill; serve within a few hours.

Kids in the Kitchen

Charlotte Des Pommes

This dessert can be served hot or cold.

4 quarts apples, sliced ⅛ inch thick	**¼ cup dark rum**
½ cup apricot preserves	**2 teaspoons vanilla extract**
⅔ cup sugar	**¾ cup melted butter**
3 tablespoons butter, divided	**12 slices bread, ¼ inch thick**

Place peeled, sliced apples in large skillet and cover. Cook over low heat for 20 minutes; stirring occasionally. (Apples should be tender when done.) When tender, add preserves, sugar, 2 tablespoons butter and rum. Cook over high heat, stirring constantly, until mixture begins to thicken. Add vanilla; remove from heat.

Remove crusts from bread. Cut some of the bread into pieces to fit the bottom and sides of your mold. Brown these in 1 tablespoon butter and put in mold. Cut remaining bread into ½-inch wide strips. Heavily brush the strips with melted butter and line the mold with them. Make sure that each strip overlaps the other so there are no spaces in between.

Pour apples into mold and press down lightly. The apples should be mounded on top as they will settle when cooking. Trim off any uneven bread. Cover top with additional buttered bread strips. Thoroughly brush top again with melted butter. Place mold on a baking sheet and bake at 425° for 30 minutes. Cool in mold for 15 minutes. Turn out onto serving platter by slowly lifting mold off the charlotte. If the charlotte starts to collapse, set mold down, and try again in 5 minutes. Brush charlotte with Glaze.

GLAZE:

½ cup strained apricot jam	**2 tablespoons sugar**
3 tablespoons dark rum	

Boil ingredients until thick. Brush Charlotte.

Taste of Tombstone

Tombstone, "the town too tough to die," is most famous for the Gunfight at the OK Corral.

Pavlova

3 egg whites	1 teaspoon vinegar
3 tablespoons cold water	4–6 drops vanilla
3 teaspoons cornstarch	Cool Whip
1 cup sugar	Sliced fruits of various colors

Beat egg whites until stiff, gradually adding water, cornstarch, sugar, and vinegar and vanilla. When as stiff as possible, turn onto a cookie sheet that has wax paper on it which has been sprayed. Heap it up in a mound and shape the egg whites like a cake. (Could use a sprayed springform pan to get the shape.) Put it in an oven at 300° for 10 minutes, then reduce the heat to 250° and bake 30 minutes. Then turn off the oven leaving the Pavlova in the oven until is COOLED OFF (hours). Take it out of the oven and frost it with Cool Whip, then place sliced various colored fruit in some kind of design across the top. Serves 8–10.

Bon Appétit

Historic Saxon House's Chocolate Amaretto Mousse

2 tablespoons water	½ cup butter
½ ounce (½ square) unsweetened chocolate	4 eggs, separated
	1 cup heavy cream
6 ounces semisweet chocolate morsels	½ cup sugar
	1 tablespoon amaretto liqueur

Heat water in saucepan and add chocolate. Stir and cook chocolate until blended. Add butter, cook, and stir until blended. Remove from heat but keep warm. In separate bowl, beat egg yolks and gradually add to hot mixture. Allow to cool. Whip heavy cream and add sugar. In separate bowl, beat egg whites until stiff but not dry. Fold cream, egg whites and amaretto liqueur into chocolate mixture. Divide mousse into 4 dessert dishes and serve. Serves 4.

Arizona's Historic Restaurants and their Recipes

Chocolate Tacos Filled with Hazelnut-Chocolate Mousse

That Donna Nordin is a chocolate artist as well as a fine cook is amply demonstrated with this whimsical dessert. The tacos are easily formed out of rounds of melted chocolate draped over dowels until they harden. The shells make an eye-catching presentation, even simply filled with a flavored whipped cream or soft ice cream.

MOUSSE:

8 ounces bittersweet chocolate, coarsely chopped
½ cup heavy cream
3 tablespoons confectioners' sugar

2 tablespoons hazelnut liqueur (Frangelico)
½ cup toasted, ground hazelnuts

Place chocolate in top of a double boiler over hot, not boiling, water. Melt completely, stirring occasionally, about 5 minutes. Place cream in bowl and, with a whisk or electric mixer, whip until soft peaks form. Add sugar and liqueur and whisk until completely incorporated (do not overbeat or it will be difficult to fold in the chocolate). Fold in the nuts. Remove chocolate from heat and gently fold into whipped cream. Refrigerate mousse until firm enough to pipe, about 1 hour or up to 1 day ahead.

CHOCOLATE TACOS:

1 pound bittersweet chocolate, coarsely chopped

¼ cup toasted, coarsely chopped hazelnuts

On parchment paper draw 12 rounds, each 4½ inches in diameter. Cut out the rounds with scissors and arrange them on a work surface. Place chocolate in top of a double boiler over hot, not boiling, water. Melt completely, stirring occasionally, about 10 minutes. Remove from heat. Using the back of a spoon, spread a thin layer of chocolate smoothly over each circle. Sprinkle half of each circle with 1 teaspoon chopped hazelnuts. Let sit until chocolate begins to set but is still pliable, about 30 minutes. Drape the pliable parchment-chocolate discs over 2 wooden dowels, 1 inch thick and 20 inches long, and balance over a roasting pan. Place the roasting pan in the refrigerator and chill tacos until hard. Remove the tacos from the dowels and carefully peel off parchment paper.

RASPBERRY SAUCE:

1 cup frozen raspberries, thawed   **1 cup seedless raspberry jam**

In food processor or blender, purée raspberries; strain into a bowl. Stir in jam and mix well. Refrigerate, covered, until ready to serve.

(continued)

(continued)

PAPAYA-KIWI SALSA:

**1 papaya, peeled, seeded, and
finely diced**

**3 kiwis, peeled and finely diced
1 tablespoon confectioners' sugar**

Mix all ingredients in a bowl. Let flavors marry for at least 30 minutes. Refrigerate, covered, until ready to serve.

Place mousse in a pastry bag fitted with a star tip. If mousse has been chilled until it's too firm to pipe, let it come to room temperature and then fill pastry bag. Pipe mousse into chocolate taco shells. Refrigerate until ready to serve. Place about 1 tablespoon raspberry sauce on the bottom of each of 12 plates; top with mousse-filled taco. Spoon a tablespoon of papaya-kiwi salsa on the side of the taco. Serve immediately.

Recipe by Donna Nordin / ***Savor the Southwest***

Chocolate Mousse

**½ cup boiling water
1 (¼-ounce) package unflavored
gelatin
½ cup cold water
3 tablespoons skim evaporated
milk**

**1 teaspoon vanilla extract
3 tablespoons sugar
¼ cup powdered nonfat milk
2 tablespoons unsweetened cocoa
powder
1 cup plain nonfat yogurt**

Beat hot water and gelatin with an electric mixer for 1 minute. Add cold water and beat for 1 minute. Add evaporated milk and vanilla and beat until frothy. Chill for 45 minutes. Beat in sugar, powdered milk, and cocoa until thick, about 2 minutes. Gently fold in yogurt until color is uniform. Refrigerate for at least 1 hour before serving. Serves 4.

Variations: Artificial sweetener to taste may be substituted for the sugar. Instant coffee powder, almond extract, grated orange rind, or puréed raspberries may be added with the sugar and cocoa during the final mixing.

Cal 107; %Fat 4; Fat 1g; Sat Fat 0.3g; Chol 2mg; Sod 86mg; Carbo 19g; Prot 8g; Fiber 1g. Exchanges: Starch ½, Dairy 1

Arizona Heart Institute Foundation Cookbook

Peaches 'N' Cream Cheese Bread Pudding with Raspberry Sauce

The entertainer Melba Moore was eating dinner at a famous restaurant in New York City. The chef created a special dessert for her, peaches topped with a raspberry sauce. Ever since, the combination of peaches and raspberries has been referred to as "Peach Melba."

6 cups ½-inch bread cubes
2 (8-ounce) packages lowfat cream
   cheese, softened
¾ cup sugar
8 large eggs
2 cups skim milk
2 teaspoons vanilla extract
1 teaspoon almond extract
¼ teaspoon lemon oil or
   2 teaspoons lemon zest

4 teaspoons sugar
1 teaspoon ground cinnamon
¼ cup sliced almonds
33 fresh or frozen peach slices
   (if using frozen peaches, thaw
   and drain)
Raspberry Sauce

THE NIGHT BEFORE:

Spray a 9x13-inch pan with nonstick cooking spray. Spread bread cubes evenly in the pan. Set aside.

In the bowl of an electric mixer, beat cream cheese and ¾ cup sugar until smooth. Beat in eggs. Scrape down sides and continue to beat until well blended. On low speed, mix in milk, vanilla, and almond extracts and lemon oil. Mix for 5 minutes or longer. (The longer you mix, the fluffier the bread pudding.)

Pour egg-milk mixture evenly over the bread cubes in the pan. Make sure the bread pieces are submerged in the liquid. With the back of a large spoon, gently press down any bread cubes that are floating on top.

In a small bowl, mix together 4 teaspoons sugar and the cinnamon. Sprinkle over the top of the bread-eggs-milk, then sprinkle the sliced almonds over the top. Finally, place peach slices in rows on top, 3 rows wide, about 11 slices in each row. Cover with foil and refrigerate overnight.

IN THE MORNING:

Preheat oven to 350°. Uncover casserole and bake for 1 hour or until set. Remove from oven and let sit 5 minutes before cutting. Serve hot with Raspberry Sauce. Serves 12.

(continued)

(continued)

RASPBERRY SAUCE:

1½ cups fresh raspberries or 1 (10-ounce) bag frozen raspberries

2 tablespoons sugar
1 tablespoon cornstarch

In a small saucepan, heat berries and sugar over medium heat until hot and juicy. Measure cornstarch into a small bowl. Spoon a small amount of hot berry liquid into the bowl and mix thoroughly with the cornstarch to create a thin paste. Pour cornstarch paste back into the hot berries and stir to mix. (This method will prevent lumps in the sauce.) Continue heating until thick and bubbly.

Spoon sauce over Peaches 'N' Cream Cheese Bread Pudding to create "Peach Melba."

Mountain Mornings

Crêpes–Hungarian Style

4 cups flour
4 eggs
4 cups milk
½ cup sugar

4 tablespoons melted butter
2 tablespoons vanilla
Filling of your choice

Put all ingredients, except filling, in large bowl in an electric mixer. Beat well. The batter should be thin. Pour mixture from measuring cup into buttered fry pan, about 2 ounces at a time. Make thin pancakes. Brown and turn over to do the other side. Cool and fill with favorite filling, such as cheese, cherry, or apple. Serves 12.

That Hungarian's in My Kitchen

The sun shines in southern Arizona 85% of the time, which is considerably more sunshine than Florida or Hawaii. Arizona also frequently has the nation's hottest and coldest temperatures on the same day. The mean temperature is 75° average in the desert to 45° in the high country, but it usually gets a lot meaner in the summer!

Éclair Supreme Pudding

PUDDING:

3 cups nonfat milk
2 (3-ounce) packages Fat-Free
  Instant Vanilla Pudding mix

1 (8-ounce) carton Lite Cool
  Whip
Graham crackers

Beat the milk and pudding mix until thick. Add the Cool Whip and set aside. Line a 9x13-inch baking dish with whole graham crackers. Pour ½ pudding mixture over crackers. Add another layer of crackers, then the remaining pudding. Set aside.

TOPPING:

3 tablespoons cocoa powder
3 tablespoons nonfat milk
1 teaspoon vanilla

5 tablespoons low fat margarine (or
  butter)
⅛ teaspoon salt

Mix these ingredients in a small pan. Bring to a boil, stirring constantly. Beat a few times. Let cool. Pour over pudding. Refrigerate until serving. Serves 10.

Note: By using fat-free ingredients, this dessert is so low in calories, the cook probably ends up ahead of the game. It possibly takes more calories to make this dish than are consumed in the eating.

Portal's Best Little Cookbook

Strawberry Almond Crème

To make this great dip for fluffy pieces of angel food cake nonfat, use nonfat sour cream and yogurt.

½ cup puréed strawberries
  (process about 12-15 small berries
  in a blender or food processor)
½ cup sour cream

½ cup plain yogurt
¼ teaspoon almond extract
2 tablespoons confectioners' sugar

In a small bowl, fold strawberries into sour cream. Fold in yogurt. Gently stir in almond extract and sugar. Chill in the freezer for 20 minutes (set a timer!) then move to the refrigerator for 1 hour. Serve with cake or mixed berries. Makes ¾ cups.

Chips, Dips, & Salsas

Chocolate Custard

2 cups heavy cream
**½ vanilla bean (or substitute 1½
   teaspoons vanilla extract)**
½ cup sugar

8 egg yolks
**6 ounces fine quality chocolate,
   (Couverture, if possible)**

Preheat oven to 300°. Combine cream and vanilla bean and heat mixture to boil. Remove from heat.

   In separate bowl, blend sugar with egg yolks until smooth. Temper this mixture by adding heated cream a little at a time to prevent curdling. Add chocolate. Let sit 5 minutes. Mix well and force sauce through fine sieve. Pour mixture into custard cups and bake in large pan of boiling water (bain-marie). Bake until custards are set (about 50 minutes). Serves 8.

Recipe from Barrio Restaurant / **Tucson Cooks!**

Lemon Dessert

1 (3-ounce) package lemon Jell-O
1¼ cups hot water
1 cup sugar
¼ cup lemon juice
**1 medium to large can crushed
   pineapple (or other fruit), drained**

**1 (12-ounce) can evaporated milk,
   chilled**
20 vanilla wafers

Dissolve Jell-O in hot water; add sugar and lemon juice. Chill until partially set. Add fruit. Whip milk and add to Jell-O mixture.

   Crush vanilla wafers, reserving some for top, and place in the bottom of a large dish. Add Jell-O mixture and sprinkle top with crumbs.

Pioneer Family Recipes

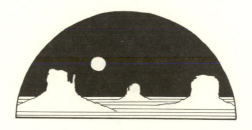

Pears de Noel

2 cups dry red wine	1 tablespoon vanilla
1 cup water	6 large firm pears
¾ cup sugar	Chocolate syrup (1½ cups)
6 whole cloves	1 tablespoon orange-flavored
1 cinnamon stick, broken in half	liqueur
1 tablespoon grated orange peel	Mint leaves

Cook wine, water, sugar, cloves, cinnamon stick, orange peel and vanilla over medium-high heat for 10 minutes in a large saucepan. While this is cooking, peel the pears, leaving stem on. Place pears in wine mixture, reduce heat to simmer and poach pears for 10 minutes. Remove pan from heat and let pears cool to room temperature in syrup. Remove pears from syrup and chill in refrigerator at least an hour.

Mix chocolate syrup with orange liqueur and spoon onto dessert plates. Place a pear on top of chocolate, garnish with mint leaves. Serves 6.

Christmas in Arizona Cook Book

Baked Bananas

6 bananas, peeled	1 teaspoon cinnamon
⅓ cup butter, melted	1 cup coconut, grated
3 tablespoons lemon juice	1 cup walnuts, chopped
⅓ cup brown sugar	

Place bananas in large baking dish. Combine butter, lemon juice, sugar, cinnamon, coconut and walnuts. Distribute evenly over the bananas, turning them to thoroughly coat each banana. Bake in 375° oven for 20 minutes, turning once after 10 minutes. Serve warm. Serves 6.

Sedona Cook Book

Banana Split Float

2 ripe medium-sized bananas
3 cups cold milk
1 (10-ounce) package frozen
   strawberries, sliced, sweetened,
   and thawed

1½ pints chocolate ice cream,
   divided

In a mixer or blender, mash bananas. Add milk, strawberries, and ½ pint chocolate ice cream; beat until just blended. Pour into tall chilled glasses and top each with a scoop of chocolate ice cream.

Variation: Use 1¼ cups sliced, sweetened fresh strawberries for the frozen ones.

Arizona Cook Book

The Jerome Grille's Deep-Fried Ice Cream

½ pound cornflakes
1½ quarts French vanilla
   soft-serve ice cream
4 cups vegetable oil
6 pre-formed tortilla bowls
   (optional, available in specialty
   stores)

⅔ cup honey
1 tablespoon ground cinnamon
6 tablespoons sugar
1 cup whipped cream
6 sweet, fresh cherries, for
   garnish

Crush cornflakes with rolling pin or mash flakes into small pieces in large bowl. Use ice cream scoop and hand to form ice cream into 6 round balls. Roll ice cream balls in crushed flakes, covering completely. Freeze overnight until hard.

In 2-quart pan, heat oil to boiling. Drop frozen ice cream balls, one at a time, into oil for 5 seconds only. Remove with slotted spoon or tongs. Place each ball in a tortilla bowl or ice cream sundae dish. Pour an equal amount of honey over each ice cream ball. Mix cinnamon and sugar together and sprinkle over each serving. Top each serving with dollop of whipped cream and a cherry. Serves 6.

Arizona's Historic Restaurants and their Recipes

Lemon Ice

1 teaspoon unflavored gelatin	¼ teaspoon salt
1 tablespoon cold water	1 cup lemon juice
4 cups boiling water	4 egg whites
4 cups sugar	

Soften gelatin in cold water in a bowl for 5 minutes. Combine boiling water and sugar in mixing bowl and stir until sugar dissolves. Add salt, lemon juice and gelatin mixture, stirring until gelatin dissolves. Place in freezer until partially frozen. Beat at medium speed until smooth. Return to freezer. Freeze until partially frozen. Beat at medium speed until smooth. Beat egg whites in a separate bowl until stiff peaks form. Fold into lemon mixture. Freeze, covered, until ready to serve, stirring occasionally. Serves 8.

Wild Thyme and Other Temptations

Mango & Lime Sorbet

This makes a light finale or use between courses of a large holiday meal to "refresh the palate."

1 cup water	Juice of 2 limes
½ cup sugar	½ teaspoon grated orange peel
1½ cups peeled and chopped mangoes	Lime peel

Stir water and sugar together in a saucepan and cook over medium heat for 5 minutes, stirring occasionally. Let cool to room temperature. Purée the mangoes and lime juice in a blender until smooth. Stir mango mixture into sugar water. Stir in grated orange peel and freeze until set. Garnish with twisted lime peel. Serves 4.

Note: Best bet for fresh mangoes is the refrigerated section of your produce department.

Christmas in Arizona Cook Book

Contributing Cookbooks

The Wigwam Village Motel, on historic Route 66 near Holbrook, is a one-of-a-kind attraction. The motel, originally built in 1950, consists of captivating concrete Tee Pee-shaped motel rooms.

Catalog of Contributing Cookbooks

All recipes in this book have been selected from the cookbooks shown on the following pages. Individuals who wish to obtain a copy of any particular book may do so by sending a check or money order to the address listed by each cookbook. Please note the postage and handling charges that are required. State residents add tax only when requested. Prices and addresses are subject to change, and the books may sell out and become unavailable. Retailers are invited to call or write to same address for discount information.

THE ARIZONA CELEBRITY COOKBOOK

by Eileen Bailey
Northland Publishing   800-346-3257
P. O. Box 1389   Fax 800-257-9082
Flagstaff, AZ 86002   E-mail jandrews@northlandpub.com

Based on the popular *Arizona Republic* column "Eating With," this cookbook reveals the secrets of the stars through personal interviews and a favorite recipe from each. A must for fans of the Grand Canyon State.

$16.95   Retail price
  .98   Tax for Arizona residents
 5.00   Postage and handling

Make check payable to Northland Publishing. Visa/MC accepted.
ISBN 0-87358-692-1

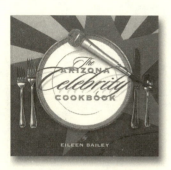

ARIZONA CHEFS: COOKING AT HOME WITH 36 ARIZONA CHEFS

by Elin Jeffords   602-248-8323
4710 N. 16th Street/Ste 102   Fax 602-248-8308
Phoenix, AZ 85016   E-mail jjophoto@uschefs.com

Enjoy 144 recipes from 36 of Arizona's leading chefs. Full-color photos of all the dishes along with cooking and beverage tips. Also included are gift certificates from participating restaurants.

$17.95   Retail price
 1.27   Tax for Arizona residents
 2.00   Postage and handling

Make check payable to Arizona Chefs. Visa/MC accepted.
ISBN 0-9659883-1-7

ARIZONA CHEFS: DINE-IN DINE-OUT COOKBOOK

by Elin Jeffords   602-248-8323
4710 N. 16th Street, Ste 102   Fax 602-248-8308
Phoenix, AZ 85016   E-mail jjophoto@uswest.net

Thirty-five of Arizona's leading chefs share 140 of their recipes. Full-color photos of all dishes along with cooking and beverage tips.

$14.95   Retail price
 1.05   Tax for Arizona residents
 2.00   Postage and handling

Make check payable to Arizona Chefs. Visa/MC accepted.
ISBN 0-9659883-0-9

ARIZONA COOK BOOK

by Al and Mildred Fischer
Golden West Publishers   800-658-5830
4113 N. Longview Avenue   Fax 602-279-6901
Phoenix, AZ 85014   E-mail goldwest@goodnet.com

A taste of the Old Southwest! Includes recipes for sizzling Indian fry bread, prickly pear marmalade, cactus candy, beef jerky, sourdough biscuits, and refried beans.

  $5.95   Retail price
   3.00   Postage and handling

Make check payable to Golden West Publishers.
ISBN 0-914846-00-0

ARIZONA HEART INSTITUTE FOUNDATION COOKBOOK

Arizona Heart Institute Foundation   602-266-2200 ext 4619
2632 N. 20th Street   Fax 602-650-1531
Phoenix, AZ 85006   E-mail foundation@azheart.com

More than 400 recipes, including 120 from 40 professional chefs. Easy recipes for beginners. Challenging and unusual recipes for amateur chefs. Complete descriptions of nearly 50 herbs and spices. Glossary of culinary terms, techniques and ingredients.

 $19.95   Retail price
   5.00   Postage and handling

Make check payable to Arizona Heart Institute Foundation.
ISBN 0-9635767-1-2

ARIZONA HIGHWAYS HERITAGE COOKBOOK

Arizona Highways Magazine
Arizona Department of Transportation   800-543-5432
2039 West Lewis Avenue   Fax 602-254-4505
Phoenix, AZ 85009   E-mail arizonahighways.com

From frontier to Mexican, Spanish to Indian, this cookbook showcases Arizona's diverse cultural heritage. Author Louise DeWald combines intriguing history and regional flavor in 200 tempting recipes. Historical photographs, anecdotes, and a culinary glossary add to the fun. 176 pages. Hardcover.

  $7.95   Retail price
   3.95   Postage and handling

Make check payable to Arizona Highways Magazine. Visa/MC/AmEx/DC accepted. ISBN 0-916179-16-8

ARIZONA SMALL GAME & FISH RECIPES

by Evelyn Bates
Golden West Publishers   800-658-5830
4113 N. Longview   Fax 602-279-6901
Phoenix, AZ 85014-4949   E-mail goldwest@goodnet.com

For avid outdoorswoman Evelyn Bates the challenge of hunting and fishing and the gratification of being able to provide food for the family table naturally evolved into the challenge of creating new recipes and recording old favorites. The finest of these recipes are now presented to you.

  $5.95   Retail price
   3.00   Postage and handling

Make check payable to Golden West Publishers.
ISBN 0-914846-74-4

ARIZONA STATE FAIR BLUE RIBBON RECIPES

Golden West Publishers   800-658-5830
4113 N. Longview Avenue   Fax 602-279-6901
Phoenix, AZ 85014   E-mail goldwest@goodnet.com

A collection of blue ribbon-winning recipes donated by dozens of recent Arizona State Fair Blue Ribbon winners. 5½ x 8½, 144 pages.

  $10.00   Retail price
    3.00   Postage and handling

Make check payable to Golden West Publishers.
ISBN 1-885590-19-9

ARIZONA TERRITORY COOK BOOK

by Daphne Overstreet
Golden West Publishers   800-658-5830
4113 N. Longview Avenue   Fax 602-279-6901
Phoenix, AZ 85014   E-mail goldwest@goodnet.com

Arizona Territory pioneers prepared their food the hard way! Dutch ovens, open fires, barbecues . . . they used many methods to overcome the difficulties of cooking on the trail. Authentic recipes from Indians, Cowboys, The Military, Mexicans, Miners, and Mormons.

  $6.95   Retail price
   3.00   Postage and handling

Make check payable to Golden West Publishers.
ISBN 0-914846-75-2

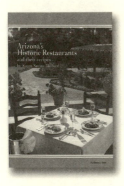

ARIZONA'S HISTORIC RESTAURANTS & THEIR RECIPES

by Karen Surina Mulford
John F. Blair, Publisher   800-222-9796
1406 Plaza Drive   Fax 366-768-1374
Winston-Salem, NC 27103   E-mail blairpub@aol.com

Chefs from 50 restaurants housed in buildings 50 or more years old share their favorite recipes. From the urban sprawl of Phoenix to the natural splendor of the Grand Canyon, from dusty ranch houses to lavish hotels, Arizona's historic restaurants mirror the wide range of tastes throughout the state.

  $16.95   Retail price
    5.00   Postage and handling

Make check payable to John F. Blair, Publisher. Visa/MC accepted.
ISBN 0-89587-132-7

BON APPÉTIT: HEALTHY RECIPES

Diane Holloway, Ph. D., Editor
20402 N. 150th Drive   623-546-8026
Sun City West, AZ 85375   E-mail dianepsych@aol.com

Three-hundred recipes from 82 Sun City West residents were donated and adapted to make them as healthy as possible, using medical research about diseases that can be delayed or prevented by diet. The recipes are now distributed with an emphasis on a retirement population.

  $9.95   Retail price
    .55   Tax for Arizona residents
   2.00   Postage and handling

Make check payable to Dr. Diane Holloway.

BY REQUEST

by Betsy Mann
Northland Publishing   800-346-3257
P. O. Box 1389   Fax 800-257-9082
Flagstaff, AZ 86002   E-mail jandrews@northlandpub.com

Betsy Mann has compiled the best of the *Arizona Republic*'s column "By Request." *By Request* takes the irresistible flavors of the Southwest out of the state's most popular restaurants and delivers them into your home.

$9.95   Retail price
  .68   Tax for Arizona residents
4.00   Postage and handling

Make check payable to Northland Publishing. Visa/MC accepted.
ISBN 0-87358-730-8

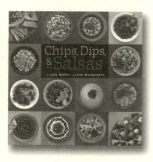

CHIPS, DIPS & SALSAS

by Judy Walker and Kim MacEachern
Northland Publishing   800-346-3257
P. O. Box 1389   Fax 800-257-9082
Flagstaff, AZ 86002   E-mail customerservice@northlandpub.com

Looking for salsa with spunk, dip with zang, or chips with lots of pizzazz? *Chips, Dips, & Salsas* offers easy ways to make scrumptious variations of America's number-one condiment. A must-have for salsa lovers and anyone who entertains.

$9.95   Retail price
  .58   Tax for Arizona residents
4.00   Postage and handling

Make check payable to Northland Publishing. ISBN 0-87358-737-5

CHRISTMAS IN ARIZONA COOK BOOK

by Lynn Nusom
Golden West Publishers   800-658-5830
4113 N. Longview Avenue   Fax 602-279-6901
Phoenix, AZ 85014-4949   E-mail goldwest@goodnet.com

Christmas in Arizona is the desert, decorated with cactus strung with twinkling colored lights, snow-covered pine forests and bright luminarias lighting holiday paths. It is also festive foods steeped in tradition—Mexican, Spanish, Indian, Western Pioneers—Southwestern recipes sure to celebrate your holiday spirit!

$9.95   Retail price
3.00   Postage and handling

Make check payable to Golden West Publishers.
ISBN 0-914846-65-5

CHUCK WAGON COOKIN'

by Stella Hughes
University of Arizona Press   800-426-3797
1230 North Park Avenue, Ste. 102   Fax 520-621-8899
Tucson, AZ 85719   E-mail www.uapress.arizona.edu

The mysteries of chuck-wagon cooking are served up in this tantalizing collection of roundup lore, cowboy humor and old-time recipes. Stella Hughes has cooked over countless campfires stirring up stew and conversation.

$15.95   Retail price
  .80   Tax for Arizona residents
3.00   Postage and handling

Make check payable to University of Arizona Press. Visa/MC accepted.
ISBN 0-8165-0432-6

COOKING WITH COPS

Kingman Police Department
2730 E. Andy Devine Avenue   520-753-2191
Kingman, AZ 86401   Fax 520-753-2542

A collection of recipes by employees of the Kingman Police Department, family, and friends. There are 217 recipes, 105 pages with a Mother Goose on the cover and nursery rhymes on the recipe dividers. The proceeds go to help members of the community who are in need of clothing, food, medications, minor home repairs, etc.

$7.50   Retail price
 1.00   Postage and handling

Make check payable to Kingman Police Department.

CORAZÓN CONTENTO
SONORAN RECIPES AND STORIES FROM THE HEART

by Madeline Gallego Thorpe and Mary Tate Engels
Texas Tech University Press   800-832-4042
Box 41037   Fax 806-742-2979
Lubbock, TX 79409-1037   E-mail ttup@ttu.edu

Distinctive regional recipes, family stories and sayings, plus herbal remedies from Gallego Thorpe's grandmother.

$24.95   Retail price
 4.00   Postage and handling (.75 each additional)

Make check payable to Texas Tech University Press. Visa/MC/Disc accepted.
ISBN 0-89672-417-4

CORONADO'S FAVORITE TRAIL MIX

Community Food Bank, Inc.   520-622-0525
P. O. Box 26727   Fax 520-624-6349
Tucson, AZ 85726-6727   E-mail foodtuc@flash.net

Monies raised from this cookbook will be used to help fulfill the vision that no child, woman or man in our community shall ever be hungry because food is not available. There are 102 recipes, including seven restaurants that helped underwrite printing costs.

$9.95   Retail price
 3.00   Postage and handling

Make check payable to Community Food Bank.
ISBN 9648339-1-3

COWBOY COOKIN'

by Sharon Wilson Walton
Outlaw Books
40088 Old Stage Road
Cave Creek, AZ 85331   480-575-8991

A must for everyone who loves the West and Western cooking. Its 51 pages are filled with recipes that cover four generations of Western cooks. From the famous Bar W Ranch to a Montana sheriff and stage driver in the 1890s. Mouth watering and unique. A true original.

$9.98   Retail price
 2.00   Postage and handling

Make check payable to Sharon Walton.

DISHES FROM THE DEEP

by Arizona Perch Base Submarine Veterans
Roger Cousin
13754 Via Montoya
Sun City West, AZ 85375-2053   623-546-9980

The Submarine Veterans of Arizona, USS Perch Base, have come up with this unique, 140-page cookbook. Most of the recipes come directly from the submarine veterans who have been preparing them for years (including the famous "SOS"). The majority of the recipes are quick and easy. We believe that all those who purchase it will find it most interesting and delicious.

   $7.00   Retail price
    3.00   Postage and handling

Make check payable to Arizona Perch Base

THE DOG-GONE DELICIOUS COOKBOOK

Humane Society of the White Mountains
P. O. Box 1070   520-368-5295
Pinetop, AZ 85935   Fax 520-368-4216

The *Dog-Gone Delicious Cookbook* is a special book put together by the love and compassion of the White Mountain Humane Society friends and families, for the benefit of homeless animals. The cookbook has 123 recipes and pages with a special section for our wonderful beloved pets.

   $8.00   Retail price

Make check payable to White Mountain Humane Society.

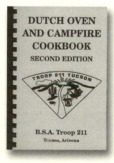

DUTCH OVEN AND CAMPFIRE COOKBOOK

Boy Scouts of America / Troop 211   520-544-8635
PMB #235, 7925-A North Oracle Road   Fax 520-544-0609
Tucson, AZ 85704   E-mail rreeves496@aol.com

The Boy Scouts of America Troup 211, Tucson, AZ and their families are thrilled to share over 250 recipes for great Dutch oven and campfire cooked outdoor meals. This book includes recipes for breakfast, bread, meat, poultry, fish and vegetable dishes that make outdoor cooking fun.

  $10.00   Retail price
    2.00   Postage and handling

Make check payable to BSA Troop 211.

THE FAT FREE LIVING FAMILY COOKBOOK

by Jyl Steinback   602-996-6300
Fat Free Living, Inc.   Toll free 1-866-FitCoach (866-348-2622)
15202 N. 50th Place   Fax 602-996-9897
Scottsdale, AZ 85254   E-mail jyl@AmericasHealthiestMom.com
                                website: AmericasHealthiestMom.com

All new fat free recipes from Jyl Steinback. Nine new cookbooks in one; plus a bonus in the back of the book "Roll Yourself Thin" the 12 minute Exercise Book.

  $16.95   Retail price
    4.00   Postage and handling

Make check payable to Fat Free Living, Inc.
ISBN 0-9636876-9-7

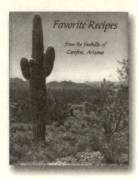

FAVORITE RECIPES FROM THE FOOTHILLS OF CAREFREE, ARIZONA

Our Lady of Joy Catholic Church
P. O. Box 1359
Carefree, AZ 85377   480-488-2229

Colorful hard cover with scenic picture of beautiful Carefree, Arizona desert landscaping. Some of the 500 recipes included are treasured family keepsakes, some are from favorite cookbooks or magazines, and some are originals; however, they all reflect the love of good cooking.

$12.95   Retail price
  4.00   Postage and handling

Make check payable to Our Lady of Joy Church.

FAVORITES FOR ALL SEASONS

Desert Foothills Library
P. O. Box 4070   480-488-2286
Cave Creek, AZ 85327   Fax 480-595-8353

Favorites for All Seasons is a collection of favorite recipes contributed by the library staff, volunteers, board members and Friends of the Library members. It includes everything from appetizers to desserts and has become an important part of kitchens throughout our community.

$6.50   Retail price
 1.95   Postage and handling

Make check payable to Friends of Desert Foothills Library.

FIRST BAPTIST FAVORITES...CAN I HAVE THAT RECIPE?

by First Baptist Church   520-432-3904
P. O. Box 4490   Fax 520-432-4647
Bisbee, AZ 85603   E-mail Fbcbisbee@juno.com

The First Baptist cooks offer a wide variety of family and potluck favorites in this diversified cookbook of over 330 recipes. It includes cooking tips, helpful household hints and humorous quips compiled in an easy to find, concise, indexed format. A delightful, delicious addition to any cookbook collection.

$10.00   Retail price
   .75   Tax for Arizona residents
  1.50   Postage and handling

Make check payable to First Baptist Church

FLAVORS OF THE SOUTHWEST

by Robert Oser
The Book Publishing Co.   800-695-2241
P. O. Box 99   Fax 931-964-2291
Summertown, TN 38483   E-mail bookpubl@usit.net

Here are 192 pages of delicious vegetarian recipes that represent the fusion of traditional southwestern ingredients with new flavors, foods and spices that reflect the lifestyle changes of the '90s. Included is an interesting introduction and glossary of ingredients as well as nutritional analysis for each recipe.

$12.95   Retail price
  3.50   Postage and handling

Make check payable to The Book Publishing Co. Visa/MC accepted.
ISBN 1-57067-049-8

FRUITS OF THE DESERT

by Sandal English
The Arizona Daily Star   520-323-2857
129 S. Irving   Fax 520-795-3413
Tucson, AZ 85711   E-mail tres@starnet.com

This cookbook suggests 350 ways to use southern Arizona's native and culti-
vated fruits: prickly pear, citrus, dates, olives, nuts, etc. Published by Tucson's
Arizona Daily Star, the book is now in its fifth printing. Sandal English, former
Star food editor, is a national award winner for food writing.

$15.95   Retail price
  1.50   Postage and handling

Make check payable to Sandal English.
ISBN 0-9607758-0-3

THE GARDEN PATCH

by Kay Hauser   520-337-4545
Box 397   Fax 520-337-2263
St. Johns, AZ 85936   E-mail khauser@co.apache.az.us

The Garden Patch has a split-back binder, is self-standing. It has a newly print-
ed, 24 page supplement with an additional 200 recipes. There are 600 original
recipes in 212 pages.

$20.00   Retail price
  2.50   Postage and handling

Make check payable to Kay Hauser.

GOURMET GRINGO

by Mari Meyers
Golden West Publishers
4113 N. Longview   800-658-5830
Phoenix, AZ 85014-4949   Fax 602-279-6901

Presenting tempting appetizers, festive dips and salads, one-dish meals and dinner casseroles, spicy entrées, and sweet desserts. Celebrates the Mexican influ-
ence on American kitchens.

$14.95   Retail price
  3.00   Postage and handling

Make check payable to Golden West Publishers.
ISBN 1-885590-16-4

HEARD IN THE KITCHEN

The Heard Museum Guild
2301 North Central Avenue
Phoenix, AZ 85004   480-946-1073

Heard in the Kitchen, a unique cookbook, includes 436 recipes of diverse
cuisines as well as a special section featuring traditional Southwest recipes.
Historical information on the internationally acclaimed Heard Museum appears
in the introductory pages and fascinating facts on Native American foods of the
"New World" are interspersed throughout the various sections.

$18.95   Retail price
  3.00   Postage and handling

Make check payable to The Heard Museum Guild Cookbook.
ISBN 0-934351-43-0

HEAVENLY DELIGHTS

United Methodist Women
P. O. Box 1345   520-645-2881
Page, AZ 86040   E-mail pcumc@page.az.net

You know how Methodists love to eat! This is a collection of some of the favorite recipes of our members—everything from Elephant Stew to Death by Chocolate.

$5.00   Retail price
1.25   Postage and handling

Make check payable to United Methodist Women.

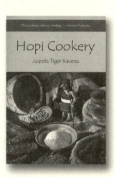

HOPI COOKERY

by Juanita Tiger Kavena
University of Arizona Press   800-426-3797
1230 North Park Avenue, Ste 102   Fax 520-621-8899
Tucson, AZ 85719   E-mail www.uapress.arizona.edu

Hopi Cookery preserves more than 100 authentic recipes along with historical and cultural tidbits about the Hopi people. Enjoy such dishes as Blue Cornmeal Hotcakes, Fresh Corn Chile Fritters, and Native Greens with Cornmeal Dumplings.

$14.95   Retail price
.75   Tax for Arizona residents
3.00   Postage and handling

Make check payable to The University of Arizona Press. Visa/MC accepted.
ISBN 0-8165-0618-3

HOSPICE HOSPITALITY

Sharon J. Chessum & Karen Griffin
Hospice of Yuma
1824 South Eighth Avenue   520-343-2222
Yuma, AZ 85364   Fax 520-343-0688

Hospice Hospitality contains 145 pages of recipes from Hospice of Yuma volunteers and staff, plus 40 pages of household hints. The cover is a photo of a hand-stitched quilt depicting Yuma, Arizona entitled "Yuma—Then & Now." It contains recipes from hors d'oeuvres through desserts, including local cultural favorites.

$10.00   Retail price
3.20   Postage and handling

Make check payable to Hospice of Yuma.

JANOS: RECIPES AND TALES FROM A SOUTHWEST RESTAURANT

by Janos Wilder   800-841-2665
Ten Speed Press, P. O. Box 7123, Attn: Order Dept.   Fax 510-559-1629
Berkeley, CA 94707   E-mail order@tenspeed.com

Reviews and awards have been lavished on Janos Wilder since he brought together his European culinary training, the taste of the American Southwest, and a remarkable 19th century adobe building to create a truly great restaurant. Chef Wilder brings four-star recipes within the reach of any home kitchen.

$16.95   Retail price
5.50   Postage and handling ($1.00 each additional)

Make check payable to Ten Speed Press. Visa/MC/AmEx accepted.
ISBN 0-89815-655-6

KIDS IN THE KITCHEN

Parents Who Care,
New Beginnings Child Development Center   520-533-5209
P. O. Box 12100   Fax 520-533-3680
Ft. Huachuca, AZ 85670   E-mail kidsfirst_pwc@yahoo.com

Parents Who Care is an unofficial group whose children attend programs operated by the Army Child / Youth Services, Ft. Huachuca, Arizona. *Kids in the
Kitchen* is a fundraiser and recipes were contributed by parents and staff. The
cookbook has 100 pages and 300+ recipes.

$7.25   Retail price
  1.25   Postage and handling

Make check payable to Parents Who Care.

KINGMAN WELCOME WAGON CLUB COOKBOOK

Welcome Wagon Club of Kingman   520-757-2879
5122 E. Camelback Loop   Fax 520-757-7934
Kingman, AZ 86401   E-mail bhilby@ctaz.com

Among the many pleasures of sampling each others' recipes at Welcome
Wagon social functions is having them in print. These 131 recipes are all in one
book for convenience and to relive the good times we've enjoyed in Kingman
. . . our home in the high desert of northwest Arizona.

$6.25   Retail price
  2.00   Postage and handling

Make check payable to Welcome Wagon Club of Kingman.

KOSHER KETTLE

Edited by Sybil Ruth Kaplan
Five Star Publications, Inc.   800-545-STAR
P. O. Box 6698   Fax 480-940-8787
Chandler, AZ 85246-6698   E-mail info@fivestarsupport.com

You can travel the world collecting hundreds of kosher recipes, or you can let
acclaimed cook and author Sybil Ruth Kaplan do it for you. This comprehen-
sive compilation of recipes is a must-have for any kosher kitchen. 496 pages.

$18.00   Retail price
  1.35   Tax for Arizona residents
  4.50   Postage and handling

Make check payable to Five Star Publications, Inc. Visa/MC/AmEx/DC accepted.
ISBN 1-877749-19-2

LICENSE TO COOK ARIZONA STYLE

Penfield Press   800-728-9998
215 Brown Street   Fax 319-351-6846
Iowa City, IA 52245-5842   E-mail penfield@penfield-press.com

The essence of the Grand Canyon state is captured in this delightful little book.
Recipes, facts, illustrations and much more packed into 158 pages. A must for
those seeking Arizona cuisine.

$6.95   Retail price
  2.00   Postage and handling

Make check payable to Penfield Press.
ISBN 1-57216-069-1

LION'S CLUB OF GLOBE, ARIZONA COOKBOOK

Globe Lion's Club
1118 Granite Street   520-473-3676 or 425-4669
Miami, AZ 85539-1026   Fax 520-425-9508

When the Lion's Club of Globe decided to produce a cookbook for their fundraiser, the members came forward with their favorite recipes. You can bet that within these 68 pages you'll find foods that will put a smile on the faces of all who taste them. We hope you will enjoy our efforts.

$7.00   Retail price
  1.50   Postage and handling

Make check payable to Globe Lion's Club.

MOUNTAIN MORNINGS

Sally Krueger   520-774-0088
410 N. Leroux Street   Fax 520-774-6354
Flagstaff, AZ , 86001   E-mail info@inn410.com

Within these 128 pages, you'll find the ingredients for creating memorable breakfasts and brunches. Ninety-two delicious recipes include Breakfast Favorites, Southwest Specialties, and Brunch Menus. Innkeeper Sally Krueger notes low-fat options, altitude adjustments and tips to ensure satisfying results.

$10.95   Retail price
   .80   Tax for Arizona residents
  2.00   Postage and handling

Make check payable to The Inn at 410. Visa/MC accepted.
ISBN 0-883651-02-6

THE NATIONAL FIREFIGHTERS RECIPE BOOK

by Candice M. DeBarr and Louis A. DePasquale
Eakin Press   800-880-8642
P. O. Drawer 90159   Fax 512-288-1813
Austin, TX 78709-0159   E-mail eakinpub@sig.net

More than a cookbook, *The National Firefighters Recipe Book* includes 245 pages of 177 tested recipes submitted by firefighters from all 50 states and the District of Columbia; helpful comments on every recipe; illustrated home fire safety tips; and a glossary of firefighting terminology.

$16.95   Retail price

Make check payable to Eakin Press. Visa/MC/Amex accepted
ISBN 1-57168-408-5

OUTDOOR COOKING: FROM BACKYARD TO BACKPACK

Arizona Highways Magazine
Arizona Department of Transportation   800-543-5432
2039 West Lewis Avenue   Fax 602-254-4505
Phoenix, AZ 85009   E-mail arizonahighways.com

Food always seems to taste better outdoors. Whether it's mesquite-grilled chicken and veggies for weekend guests, a quick snack along the bike trail, a hearty tailgate picnic, or a campfire cookout, you'll find more than 200 recipes to go along with you

$7.95   Retail price
  3.95   Postage and handling

Make check payable to *Arizona Highways Magazine*. Visa/MC/AmEx/DC accepted. ISBN 0-916179-32-X

PADRE KINO'S FAVORITE MEATLOAF

Community Food Bank, Inc.
Tucson, AZ

Monies raised from this cookbook were used to help fulfill the vision that no child, woman or man in our community shall ever be hungry because food is not available. Although this book is no longer available, some of the 117 recipes are preserved here. For information on the new book, see *Coronado's Favorite Trail Mix*.

PAR EXCELLENCE

Pinetop Lakes Golf & Country Club   520-369-4184
P. O. Box 1643   Fax 520-369-1217
Pinetop, AZ 85935   E-mail plcca@whitemtns.com

Because of our monthly potluck suppers, we were inspired to compile this cookbook. These recipes are some of the favorites of our members. The book contains 128 pages and 374 recipes. We hope you enjoy the result of our endeavors. Bon appétit!

$7.50   Retail price
  .41   Tax for Arizona residents
 2.00   Postage and handling

Make check payable to Pinetop Lakes Country Club / Cookbooks. Visa/MC/DC accepted.

PIONEER FAMILY RECIPES

by Danielle Stephens
HC 30 Box 362   520-753-1020
Kingman, AZ 86401-9508   Fax 520-753-7171

Pioneer Family Recipes was written for the Centennial 1882-1982 celebration in Kingman. The recipes came from pioneers and their families of the area with the goal of preserving our heritage.

$8.95   Retail price
  .65   Tax for Arizona residents
 2.97   Postage and handling

Make check payable to Danielle Stephens.

PLEASURES FROM THE GOOD EARTH

Rock of Ages LWML
390 Dry Creek Road   520-282-4091
Sedona, AZ 86336   E-mail jsacher@serendipsys.com

This is an eclectic collection of 300 recipes representing not only Arizona and the Southwest but also recipes from around the world . . . a true melting pot. Some are quick and easy and others are a little more complex but all are worth the effort.

$10.00   Retail price
 3.00   Postage and handling

Make check payable to Rock of Ages LWML.

PORTAL'S BEST LITTLE COOKBOOK

Portal Rescue
Portal, AZ

Each year community members sponsor a three-day soup kitchen to raise money for the local volunteer fire and rescue organization. *Portal's Best Little Cookbook* is a result of requests for the home-cooking recipes. There are a total of 81 recipes on 52 pages for soups, breads and desserts. Currently out of print.

PURPLE SAGE AND OTHER PLEASURES

Junior League of Tucson, Inc.
2099 E. River Road   520-299-5753
Tucson, AZ 85718   Fax 520-299-5774

This vibrant cookbook captures the flavor and lifestyle of Tucson and appeals to good cooks everywhere. The League selected and tested over 300 recipes that are easy to read and prepare. Take pleasure in the ten chapters separated by beautiful full-color pastel chalk illustrations by Arizona artist Angela Simon.

$24.95   Retail price
  3.80   Postage and handling

Make check payable to Junior League of Tucson. Visa/MC accepted.
ISBN 0-9616403-0-8

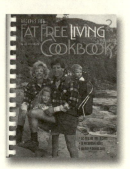

RECIPES FOR FAT FREE LIVING COOKBOOK 2

by Jyl Steinback   602-996-6300
Fat Free Living, Inc.   Toll free 1-866-FitCoach (866-348-2622)
15202 N. 50th Place   Fax 602-996-9897
Scottsdale, AZ 85254   E-mail jyl@AmericasHealthiestMom.com
                              website: AmericasHealthiestMom.com

Jyl Steinback has done it again. 275 Gourmet fat free recipes; 50 microwave recipes and a holiday menu planner all in one book.

$15.95   Retail price
  4.00   Postage and handling

Make check payable to Fat Free Living, Inc.
ISBN 0-9636876-8-9

RECIPES FROM ARIZONA WITH LOVE

by Ferol Golden and Lisa Golden
Strawberry Point, Inc.
16163 Fillmore Avenue SE   800-999-5858
Prior Lake, MN 55372   Fax 612-447-5901

The cuisine of Arizona, influenced by a passing parade of people and the ever presence of Mexico, is a blend of rich, varied, and often spicy delights. This book brings you a taste of the sun-drenched Sonora Desert, as well as a glimpse of the lesser known mountainous and agricultural regions of the state.

$13.95   Retail price
  1.50   Postage and handling

Make check payable to Strawberry Point, Inc. Visa/MC accepted.
ISBN 0-913703-10-9

RECIPES FROM OUR MOTHERS' KITCHENS

Greek Orthodox Mission of Northern Arizona
P. O. Box 2164
Flagstaff, AZ 86003-2164

520-773-9507
Fax 520-773-4705

Some of the most long-revered and memorable meals of our lives came from the kitchens of our mothers who gave so unselfishly from their hearts. We dedicate this cookbook to all of our mothers and, yes, to their kitchens, too.

$10.00   Retail price
   2.00   Postage and handling

Make check payable to Greek Orthodox Mission of Northern Arizona.

RED, WHITE & BLUE FAVORITES

American Legion Auxiliary Unit 81
181 Paseo del Sol
Lake Havasu City, AZ 86403

520-453-9486
Fax 520-854-2337
E-mail havamom@ctaz.com

Recipes collected from members, friends and relatives of Unit 81, American Legion Auxiliary, Lake Havasu City, Arizona. 188 pages, over 450 recipes.

$8.00   Retail price
  .58   Tax for Arizona residents
 2.00   Postage and handling

Make check payable to American Legion Auxiliary Unit 81

REFLECTIONS UNDER THE SUN

Junior League of Phoenix
P. O. Box 10223
Phoenix, AZ 85064

602-230-9573
Fax 602-241-9155

Reflections Under the Sun is a collection of the best and brightest recipes from the Junior League of Phoenix, featuring favorites from past books. It includes more than 100 exciting new recipes, including contributions from famous area chefs. *Reflections* is a hardcover book with 190 pages.

$19.95   Retail price
  4.00   Postage and handling ($1.00 each additional)

Make check payable to Junior League of Phoenix. Visa/MC accepted.
ISBN 0-9613174-2-6

SAVOR THE SOUTHWEST

Barbara Pool Fenzl
Bay Books, an imprint of Bay Books & Tapes, Inc.
555 De Haro Street #220
San Francisco, CA 94107

800-647-3600

In *Savor the Southwest,* companion book to the public television series of the same name, Barbara Pool Fenzl introduces readers not only to her region's remarkable cuisine and foodway, but also to its finest chefs. She has gathered fourteen preeminent Southwestern chefs and asked them for their opinions, recipes and tips. Barbara's own recipes and well-seasoned advice complete this definitive collection containing over 140 recipes.

$19.95   Retail price
ISBN 0-912333-70-7

SAVORY SOUTHWEST

by Judy Hille Walker
Northland Publishing   800-346-3257
P. O. Box 1389   Fax 800-257-9082
Flagstaff, AZ 86002   E-mail jandrews@@northlandpub.com

Guaranteed to be full of flavor, not fire, these recipes were gathered from cooking contests sponsored by the *Arizona Republic*. Simple to sophisticated, mild to spicy, the award-winning recipes in this book offer something for every menu.

$12.95   Retail price
  .75   Tax for Arizona residents
5.00   Postage and handling

Make check payable to Northland Publishing. Visa/MC accepted.
ISBN 0-87358-501-1

SEDONA COOK BOOK

by Susan K. Bollin
Golden West Publishers   800-658-5830
4113 N. Longview   Fax 602-279-6901
Phoenix, AZ 85014-4949   E-mail goldwest@goodnet.com

Mouth-watering recipes inspired by the beauty of Sedona guarantee an extraordinary culinary experience. Includes fascinating Sedona trivia and original art. Available in comb or perfect binding.

$7.95   Retail price
3.00   Postage and handling

Make check payable to Golden West Publishers.
ISBN 0-914846-98-1

ST. FRANCIS IN THE FOOTHILLS 30TH ANNIVERSARY COOKBOOK

St. Francis in the Foothills UMC
4625 E. River Road
Tucson, AZ 85718   520-299-9063

A collection of favorite recipes from members and friends has grown into 80 pages of fine dining suggestions. These recipes have been shared at our gatherings and are sure to please your palate. Proceeds from the sale of the cookbook will support youth programs.

$10.00   Retail price
2.00   Postage and handling

Make check payable to St. Francis in the Foothills UMC.

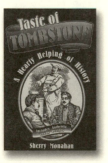

TASTE OF TOMBSTONE: A Hearty Helping of History

by Sherry A. Monahan
Royal Spectrum Publishing / Sierra Coyote Publications   919-773-1995
P. O. Box 212   E-mail monahan@lynxus.com
Garner, NC 27529-0212   www.wildwestinfo.com

Tombstone, Arizona's 1880s restaurant fare varied from simple old-fashioned recipes to exotic French cooking. Imagine Wyatt Earp ordering Salmon Baked à la Richelieu or Charlotte des Pommes. Enjoy recipes from a bygone era that shaped Arizona's famous town. 230 pages.

$16.95   Retail price
3.00   Postage and handling

Make check payable to Sierra Coyote Publications.
ISBN 1-880473--97-9

THAT HUNGARIAN'S IN MY KITCHEN!

by Linda F. Radke
Five Star Publications, Inc.   800-545-STAR
P. O. Box 6698   Fax 480-940-8787
Chandler, AZ 85246-6698   E-mail info@fivestarsupport.com

A compilation of 135 authentic Hungarian / American / Kosher recipes from one family's heritage of cooking. Bring the taste of Hungary to your table by choosing among the easy-to-follow recipes from stuffed cabbage to chicken paprikas.

$14.95   Retail price
  1.21   Tax for Arizona residents
  4.50   Postage and handling

Make check payable to Five Star Publications, Inc.
ISBN 1-877749-28-1

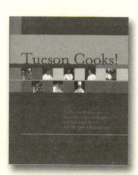

TOSTITOS FIESTA BOWL COOKBOOK

Fiesta Bowl   480-350-0900
120 S. Ash Avenue   Fax 480-736-4181
Tempe, AZ 85281   E-mail ggilmartin@fiestabowl.org

The combined efforts of the Fiesta Bowl Women's Committee have made this cookbook possible. This unique group of recipes was put together to commemorate the Silver Anniversary of the Fiesta Bowl as well as the 1995-1996 Championship Season.

$10.00   Retail price

Make check payable to Fiesta Bowl.

TUCSON COOKS!

Primavera Foundation
702 S. 6th Avenue   520-623-5111
Tucson, AZ 85701   E-mail info@primavera.org

Sixty Tucson restaurants share their favorite recipes and stories to benefit the Primavera Foundation. Paperback, 216 pages.

$22.00   Retail price
  3.00   Postage and handling

Make check payable to The Primavera Foundation.
ISBN 0-9643613-4-5

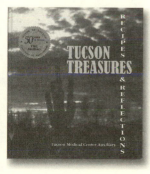

TUCSON TREASURES: RECIPES AND REFLECTIONS

Tucson Medical Center Auxiliary   800-526-5353, ext. 45359
5301 E. Grant Road   Fax 520-324-5360
Tucson, AZ 85712   E-mail www.tmcaz.com

Tucson has many treasures and this book is a wonderful selection of unique recipes from the auxiliary and from great chefs and culinary artists of some of Tucson's famous restaurants. More than a cookbook, it boasts many photographs, line art, and information about the community and its treasures.

$21.95   Retail price
  3.05   Postage and handling

Make check payable to Tucson Medical Center Auxiliary. Visa/MC accepted.
ISBN 0-9670247-0-6

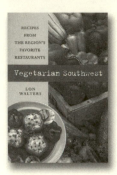

VEGETARIAN SOUTHWEST

by Lon Walters
Northland Publishing   800-346-3257
P. O. Box 1389   Fax 800-257-9082
Flagstaff, AZ 86002   E-mail jandrews@northlandpub.com

Flavorful and colorful combinations like Black Bean and Roasted Corn Soup, Jalapeño Cheese Bread, and Poblano Chiles Stuffed with Pasta, Olives, and Sun-Dried Tomatoes unlock the incredible flavors of the region.

$14.95 Retail price
   .86 Tax for Arizona residents
 5.00 Postage and handling

Make check payable to Northland Publishing. Visa/MC accepted.
ISBN 0-87358-710-3

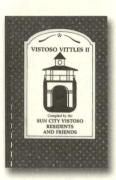

VISTOSO VITTLES II

Sun City Vistoso   520-825-3711
1495 E Rancho Vistoso Blvd.   Fax 520-825-0432
Tucson, AZ 85737   E-mail m/o@primenet.com

Book has "tried and true" recipes, longtime favorites of Sun City residents, their family and friends. It contains 250 pages, over 500 recipes of appetizers, beverages, soups, salads, vegetables, main dishes, breads, rolls, and desserts.

$9.00 Retail price
  .63 Tax for Arizona residents
4.95 Postage and handling

Make check payable to Sun City Vistoso Community Association, Inc.

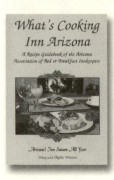

WHAT'S COOKING INN ARIZONA

Tracy and Phyllis Winters
Winters Publishing   800-457-3230
P. O. Box 501   Fax 812-663-4948
Greensburg, IN 47240   E-mail tmwinters@juno.com

An outstanding cookbook featuring 126 recipes from 21 inns throughout the state of Arizona. Tempting recipes from Breakfast Chimichangas to Hot Fudge Pie—favorite dishes from the finest Bed & Breakfasts in the state. Also includes complete information about participating inns.

$12.95 Retail price
  2.00 Postage and handling

Make check payable to Winters Publishing. MC accepted.
ISBN 1-883651-03-4

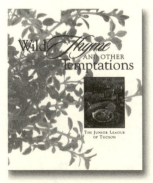

WILD THYME AND OTHER TEMPTATIONS

Junior League of Tucson, Inc.
2099 E. River Road   520-299-5753
Tucson, AZ 85718   Fax 520-299-5774

Within each of the 10 chapters, you will find recipes collected from the Junior League of Tucson membership, a menu idea, a color photograph of a prepared recipe, a color photograph and history of a location in Tucson, and a collection of sidebars that range from beverage sips to Tucson tips.

$26.95 Retail price
  4.00 Postage and handling (1.00 each additional)

Make check payable to Junior League of Tucson. Visa/MC accepted.
ISBN 0-9616403-1-6

Perfectly preserved tracks of numerous species of dinosaurs can be viewed on a rocky plain west of Tuba City.

Preserving America's Food Heritage

BEST OF THE BEST STATE COOKBOOK SERIES

Cookbooks listed below have been completed as of September 31, 2001.
Note: All cookbooks are ringbound except California, which is paperbound.

Best of the Best from
ALABAMA
288 pages, $16.95

Best of the Best from
ARIZONA
288 pages, $16.95

Best of the Best from
ARKANSAS
288 pages, $16.95

Best of the Best from
CALIFORNIA
384 pages, $16.95

Best of the Best from
COLORADO
288 pages, $16.95

Best of the Best from
FLORIDA
288 pages, $16.95

Best of the Best from
GEORGIA
336 pages, $16.95

Best of the Best from the
GREAT PLAINS
288 pages, $16.95

Best of the Best from
ILLINOIS
288 pages, $16.95

Best of the Best from
INDIANA
288 pages, $16.95

Best of the Best from
IOWA
288 pages, $16.95

Best of the Best from
KENTUCKY
288 pages, $16.95

Best of the Best from
LOUISIANA
288 pages, $16.95

Best of the Best from
LOUISIANA II
288 pages, $16.95

Best of the Best from
MICHIGAN
288 pages, $16.95

Best of the Best from the
MID-ATLANTIC
288 pages, $16.95

Best of the Best from
MINNESOTA
288 pages, $16.95

Best of the Best from
MISSISSIPPI
288 pages, $16.95

Best of the Best from
MISSOURI
304 pages, $16.95

Best of the Best from
NEW ENGLAND
368 pages, $16.95

Best of the Best from
NEW MEXICO
288 pages, $16.95

Best of the Best from
NEW YORK
288 pages, $16.95

Best of the Best from
NO. CAROLINA
288 pages, $16.95

Best of the Best from
OHIO
352 pages, $16.95

Best of the Best from
OKLAHOMA
288 pages, $16.95

Best of the Best from
PENNSYLVANIA
320 pages, $16.95

Best of the Best from
SO. CAROLINA
288 pages, $16.95

Best of the Best from
TENNESSEE
288 pages, $16.95

Best of the Best from
TEXAS
352 pages, $16.95

Best of the Best from
TEXAS II
352 pages, $16.95

Best of the Best from
VIRGINIA
320 pages, $16.95

Best of the Best from
WISCONSIN
288 pages, $16.95

Special discount offers available!
(See previous page for details.)

To order by credit card, call toll-free **1-800-343-1583** or send check or money order to:
QUAIL RIDGE PRESS • P. O. Box 123 • Brandon, MS 39043
Visit our website at **www.quailridge.com** to order online!

- -

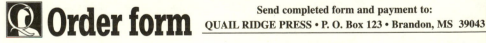

Order form

Send completed form and payment to:
QUAIL RIDGE PRESS • P. O. Box 123 • Brandon, MS 39043

❏ Check enclosed

Charge to: ❏ Visa ❏ MasterCard
❏ Discover ❏ American Express

Card #_____

Expiration Date _____

Signature _____

Name _____

Address _____

City/State/Zip_____

Phone # _____

Qty.	Title of Book (State)	Total

Subtotal _____

7% Tax for MS residents _____

Postage ($3.00 any number of books) **+ 3.00**

Total _____